Balboa Press books may be ordered through booksellers or by contacting:

Balboa Press
A Division of Hay House
1663 Liberty Drive
Bloomington, IN 47403
www.balboapress.com
844-682-1282

Print information available on the last page.

Scripture quotations marked RSV are taken from the Revised Standard Version of the Bible, copyright © 1946, 1952, 1971 by the Division of Christian Education of the National Council of the Churches of Christ in the USA. Used by permission.

ISBN: 978-1-9822-7850-2 (sc)
ISBN: 978-1-9822-7851-9 (e)

Balboa Press rev. date: 11/22/2022

Love and Loss

A Journey through Fear to Peace

Volume Two

Soul of Darkness

June 2011 to April 2014

Betty Hibod

BALBOA.PRESS

A DIVISION OF HAY HOUSE

Why am I not made of stone like you?

– Quasimodo to a cathedral gargoyle, *The Hunchback of Notre Dame*

Contents

Foreword

Our task is not to leave a record of what happened on this date for those who will inherit the Earth; history will take care of that. Therefore, we will speak about our daily lives, about the difficulties we have had to face. That is all the future will be interested in, because I do not believe very much will change in the next thousand years. – Paul Coelho, *Manuscript Found in Accra*[1]

Many books have been written as histories recounting events that shaped the life of a group, society, nation, or civilization, or as biographies recounting events and achievements relating to one person's life and work. Many books have been written putting forth ideas, philosophies, and words of wisdom to live by. Some of these we call holy books, or scripture.

Fewer books have been written like this one, which go behind the scenes of history, lay bare the feelings behind the philosophies, and document the painful and joyful inner path along which historical events and philosophical ideas emerge. This book is intensely, even shockingly, personal, not clinical or abstract or detached. It is an intimate, detailed, sensual, and sometimes disturbing account of a life lived on the cusp that bridges time and eternity. Its focus is narrow; it does not reveal much at all about anyone's visible public life or accomplishments, but it explores in great depth the invisible contents of minds, hearts, and souls.

The books of history, biography, religion, and philosophy transmit the end results of the spiritual process, the visible outward effects of invisible inner struggles. This book goes inward, looks directly at the inner struggles and makes visible the invisible forces that shape the end result. It is not a recitation of historical or biographical facts. It speaks "about our daily lives, about the difficulties we have had to face," and in so doing traces the line drawn by the finger of God from darkness to light.

The scriptures and scriptural commentaries of most religions describe a path to salvation or inner peace, and provide instructions or guideposts for moving along the path, but they are still only theoretical, hypothetical, mythical, or metaphorical accounts. This book seeks to show how theories and hypotheses play out in real time and space, how myths come alive in the flesh, how metaphors become the very things they symbolize. How does daily life look from inside someone in the throes of awakening? How does she know who or what she is? How is her destiny revealed? How do seemingly ordinary mundane events become miracles?

Joseph Campbell said: "Words can act as barriers…. There's a saying that appears both in Lao-tzu's work and in the Upanishads: 'Those who know do not speak. And those who speak do not know.' That's hard for one giving a lecture." [2] It's also hard for one writing a book. Can indescribable occurrences and perceptions, sensory and extrasensory, nevertheless be described somehow in thoughts and words? This book is an attempt to find out.

A Reader's Guide

The journal from which this book is excerpted spans over thirty years and in its unabridged form occupies thousands of pages. It is a true story, and all the characters in this drama are real people. To protect the privacy of these people and their families, most names, locations, and dates are fictitious. Some characters may be composites of more than one real person.

There are many words used throughout the book that can be defined in various ways, words like "God," "spiritual," "consciousness," "miracle," "time," "love," "heaven," and "hell." These words are intentionally left amorphous. As you progress through this story, the meanings of words will change, come into sharper focus, or you will see that precise definitions really don't matter and can even be counterproductive, having a limiting effect if applied to the mind-expanding metaphors in which they are often used.

This book begins with two concurrent threads. One is a chronological account of powerful events and sensory perceptions that propelled the author's mystical journey. The other is the author's intellectual analysis of those events and perceptions, and of the art, science, religion, and philosophy that informed and gave meaning to her experience. Eventually a third stream joins the other two, which represents the emergence into consciousness of a hidden force beyond the sensory body and analytical mind which we discover has been directing this process all along.

The basis of this book is a very personal diary which, like most diaries, was not meant for public consumption. This is the author's view not into the world, but into herself, a voyage of discovery in which no social proprieties were observed and no dark backwaters were left unexplored. Many of the statements herein would be considered audacious, boastful, embarrassing, or offensive in polite company and would never have been uttered in public. These private utterances are now made public in this book because the author's spiritual call demands it.

This book is not intended to teach or preach, but simply to describe in great detail one person's journey to awakening. If you question some of the opinions and conclusions expressed in the beginning of the book, just wait – the author's views often changed with new experiences and new insights. This story evolves through many amazing twists and turns, and as with all journeys worth taking, this one is not so much about the point of arrival, if there is one, as about the process of getting there.

Prologue

I was twenty-one years old when I graduated from college and embarked on a great adventure. Armed with only my diploma and one steamer trunk of belongings, I set out to begin a new job in a strange, distant land. I was exhilarated, anxious to see and learn and experience new things.

I loved my new home, but expected to stay only a couple years and then move on. I also expected to remain single and independent. I had such high standards and expectations for a life partner that I figured I would never marry, never find a man who could live up to my impossibly high standards. Maybe I would have a boyfriend from time to time, but no commitments.

Within weeks of my arrival in my new home, I met the man I would marry, the love of my life, Louis. There were many obstacles to our love, many social and cultural differences, but our glorious connection as star-crossed lovers was undeniable, and all the obstacles were finally overcome. Our shining path of destiny was clear. After a seven-year courtship, we were married.

Then, after a seven-year marriage, Lou died. My grief was devastating, sending me into a dark abyss. With Lou's death I came to know that my marvelous adventure with him was not just a finite earthly journey, but also an infinite spiritual one. In an effort to heal my broken spirit, I began to spew my thoughts, feelings, and revelations into a journal – a spiritual journal, a cathartic chronology of my quest for healing and restoration. This book is taken from that journal, my travelogue through life, love, loss, and eternity.

PART 17

Opening

June 2011 – August 2011

~ 388 ~

NEW LOVE REAWAKENS

I wrote:

I think perhaps we did begin to see the blessed oneness today? You brought me great joy. Thank you so much.

Then you wrote:

It was my joy too, and I am grateful. Thank you, thank you, thank you.

Five thousand volts if we plug in to our love. That's what you said. Powerful and dangerous. Now I know that you feel it, too. A joyful look, not a terrified one, when I raised the idea of living together. I asked that question to see which emotion would rise up in you, the love or the fear, and the love won! I think I saw, for the first time, a smile of pure joy on your face, with no tinge of sadness behind it. Is this the breakthrough I've been waiting for? Let's see where it goes. But regardless, this stunning moment of karmic union, however fleeting, is like the sun finally coming out from behind a huge dark cloud.

~ 389 ~

As my euphoria from yesterday started to wind down, I began to see forewarnings of dangers ahead – the 5,000 volts we might unleash by accepting and expressing our love. Your electric description of our kinetic earthly state was brilliant, because that's exactly what it is.

I see danger, but I also see this supremely powerful electric force being harnessed and used for good, if we are careful and walk the Middle Way.

Right now you don't know how we supremely busy people can make more time for each other. But have faith; once you have made the decision to walk the path, the path will appear. Opportunities for blossoming will happen without our forcing, as soon as we cast aside the obstacles to them.

Love at the highest level is a passive process, not an active one. It is not something to be grasped, but to be released from within. You switched on the light and opened the door to our love. Just let love happen. As we surrender to its power, the light of the spirit will show us the way.

> Your task is not to seek for love, but merely to seek and find all the
> barriers within yourself that you have built against it.
>
> – Rumi

~ 390 ~

My brother-in-law John's Celebration of Life was this evening. I delivered the eulogy. It is amazing to me that in a large family with several living siblings, children, grandchildren, cousins, nieces and nephews, a distant in-law – me – was chosen to speak for the family.

A lady from the old market next to John's office said to me, "I met you only once, back when you used to come down to the market, but I still remember you!" She said that Elaine, John's wife, always had nice things to say about me, that I was kind and loyal, a good wife to Lou, a "good spirit." Many people thanked me for my eulogy; one man told me I should go into public speaking, and both sides of the warring factions of Lou's family treated me warmly and appreciatively. Lou was right when he told me to stay out of his family's squabbles: "If you aren't involved they will all be nice to you after I am gone." That's what happened.

~ 391 ~

Tonight at the Buddhist temple there was a discussion about Zen. In attendance were laypeople and several priests from various Buddhist temples in the area. The conversation started with introductions, went into a talk about Buddha-Dharma-Sangha, then a five-minute *zazen* (sitting meditation), and concluded with general discussion.

He then sat down under another tree, and his first thought was, "This cannot be taught." Indra and Brahma said, "Please teach, for the salvation of mankind and the gods and all the world." And the Buddha said, "I will teach. But what I teach is not Buddhism; it is the way to Buddhism." [2]

I understand why the Buddha had to be cajoled into becoming a teacher. He did not want to teach, knowing that enlightenment cannot be taught. One can point the way with *koan* and sutras, but enlightenment does not come from learning; it comes from suffering, surrender, and the grace of God.

As the meeting went on, I had the feeling I sometimes get with Ignacio's discussion group, of being like the boy Jesus teaching among the elders at the temple. Even as a child, Jesus had an understanding of scripture greater than that of ordained priests, an understanding that came not from study and effort, but from deep intrinsic and experiential knowledge. Jesus knew, as did the Buddha, that the words of the dharma cannot be fully understood except in the context of revelatory experience. As the Zen proverb says, "The path cannot be taught; it can only be taken."

I was bothered by both the Zen teacher and the Hongwanji minister, for the same reasons. Both seemed prideful and authoritarian in their Buddhist practice. They seemed to be working from a preset script and were unable to adjust to questions and comments that didn't fit into their script. I kept pulling them off point. When the Zen teacher was showing us his suggested hand position, or mudra, for meditation, left hand over right, I asked, "What happens if you reverse the hands?"

He seemed annoyed by my question and shrugged it off, saying, "Different temples do it different ways." Strangely, he did not recognize my question as a *koan*, like "What is the sound of one hand clapping?" What is the answer to my *koan*? The same as to the "one-hand-clapping" one.

It was painful to listen to ministers and laypeople alike talk about the Four Noble Truths, the Eightfold Path, the dharma, the sangha, nirvana, meditation, and enlightenment from a strictly theoretical, intellectual perspective, glossing over the essential mystical elements that must be present for deep understanding.

I cannot recite the Eightfold Path, but I can demonstrate a life that lives it – not by conscious intention, but through the effortless unobstructed expression of the buddha-nature. This is what Zen and all of Buddhism is about. I still have a ways to go; I slip off the path from time to time; I am not perfect in my practice. But this I know: The path to enlightenment is not about moralizing, teaching, meditating, following rules, or setting goals and guidelines. It is about being quiet, opening the mind and perception, stripping away the masks, listening, observing, letting go, and getting out of the way. Not about adding on thoughts, forms, and constructs of mind, but taking them away.

Beware of words. Scripture, commentary, and analysis are dangerous. There are no words or even thoughts that can completely and accurately describe eternity, *agape*, or emptiness, because every descriptive word you use rules out its opposite. This is the mysterious paradox of the *Heart Sutra*: In eternity there are neither opposites nor no opposites. Words and concepts are limited and limiting and can be misunderstood, misinterpreted, misapplied, and manipulated, intentionally or unintentionally. This is why Jesus, the Buddha, and other mystics spoke in riddles, parables, and metaphors that were meant to take us beyond the literal meaning of words.

All of this is a reminder to me to take my own good advice. Listen, don't preach. Be humble in the face of eternity, not proud of my unearned progress toward knowledge of it.

~ 392 ~

Why did you play your sexy song for me? Why did you suggest I move to your town? What is the basis of your love? You could be thinking that it isn't polite for me to love you and you not love me back. Or to accept my gifts without giving me something of what you think I want in return. Or needing my money or my skills to the point that you would feign love to gain access to them.

I also wonder if your wife really means it when she says she loves me. Perhaps she is simply resigned to me, thinking that you love me and I love you and there is nothing she can do about it so she might as well accept it and go along – if you can't fight 'em, join 'em.

I have never lied or withheld sensitive information from either you or your wife, because I want to lay myself bare, leaving nothing to the imagination, so you will know that I am completely genuine, without guile, secrets, or hidden motivations, and you will trust the meaning and purpose of all that I do. I still harbor concerns, though, that neither of you quite grasp the true nature of my love.

From the beginning I have done my best to thwart any negative or unhealthy feelings arising from our love, being that such feelings come from the incomplete perception in this world of a perfection that can only be fully visualized from a perspective beyond this world. I have tried to describe our love from that eternal vantage point, but if I have failed, if there is to be jealousy, suspicion, distrust, or fear among us, then so be it; I cannot do anything more to prevent it.

There are so many ways in which our love can be misinterpreted. There are those who wonder about our three-way relationship. There is no way to explain us to them, and I don't really care what they think, but I do care deeply what we three think. We are not the ordinary clandestine affair, nor are we the typical *ménage á trois*, nor are we in a Mormon-like polygamy where wives share a husband. Our love straddles time and eternity; one love does not take away from another; we all have each other 100%.

If our love is true and pure, it cannot be based on lust or greed or gratitude or obligation or dependency of any kind. My love for you arose out of the ether of eternity, not motivated by wants or needs or earthly concerns. Yours must come from the same place and be driven by the same independent unsupported thought (~356~) if our journey together is to be righteous.

~ 393 ~

At the time of my deepest suffering after Lou's death, I was furious with people who said I would be stronger for this experience, that it would build character. I didn't feel my character being built; all I felt was my sanity being torn down. Now I see the larger eternal purpose for my painful odyssey. I don't think that when bad things happen it necessarily means that bad karma from past lives is coming back to haunt us. The future has already happened; we are now living the past.

Perhaps experiences of extreme suffering are given to us as tools to heal the future. They are not punishments for the past, but preparations and perhaps reparations for the future. I dread the thought of living through such terrible experiences again, and I wouldn't wish them on anyone, but I learned things through suffering that I couldn't have learned any other way, and forged a connection with the eternal that could not have happened otherwise. We who suffer so deeply have been selected for a special kind of spiritual training, like the Navy Seals who endure an especially grueling boot camp. We are damaged goods, but we are elevated by the same forces that brought us down.

~ 394 ~

I watch the gentle waves reflecting off the pier. It makes me dizzy. Little waves inside bigger waves inside even bigger waves, bouncing against each other in infinite phases, at infinite oblique angles, creating an undulation both chaotic and ordered.

No more separation anxiety. Now that you have opened the door to our love, I feel a connection that does not break every time we part company. It is the slenderest of threads, but eternally strong.

~ 395 ~

The *Ch'uan Teng Lu* records a fascinating encounter between Tao-hsin and the sage Fa-yung, who lived in a lonely temple on Mount Niu-t'ou, and was so holy that the birds used to bring him offerings of flowers. As the two men were talking, a wild animal roared close by, and Tao-hsin jumped. Fa-yung commented, "I see it is still with you!" referring, of course, to the instinctive passion (*klesa*) of fright. Shortly afterwards, while he was for a moment unobserved, Tao-hsin wrote the Chinese character for "Buddha" on the rock where Fa-yung was accustomed to sit. When Fa-yung returned to sit down again, he saw the sacred Name and hesitated to sit. "I see," said Tao-hsin, "it is still with you!" At this remark Fa-yung was fully awakened … and the birds never brought any more flowers. – Alan Watts, *The Way Of Zen*[7]

I always wondered about the reference to the birds bringing flowers in this passage. What did awakening have to do with birds bringing flowers? I now understand the metaphor. In my pilgrimages this week there were no miracles. My incantations to the gods did not evoke marvels of nature; no turtle sighting at the beach – the birds have stopped bringing me flowers. The myriad miracles of the last three years were sent to direct me, to motivate me to take action in regard to my spiritual development. They were flowers being brought to me. In retrospect, I see the pattern: at each juncture in my journey, as each phase of my awakening is completed, the miracles stop. When it is time for the next round of dharma to arise, the miracles will resume.

I recently saw a picture of St. Frances of Assisi surrounded by a flock of birds, which reminded me of the day I was sitting on my favorite stone wall by the ocean eating lunch. Several doves came by to join in my feast, then a few more, and more. By the time the birds and I were finished eating, at least a dozen birds had congregated around me, one sitting on my leg, others on the wall beside me or on the ground at my feet. They sat with me for a long while after all the food was gone, peaceful and safe in my company.

A great teacher of shamanism says that the farther along the path, the more elevated, you are, and the older your soul is, the less present your spirit guides are. You are expected to learn and act on your own, receiving guidance from your own inner buddha-nature/God-self/oversoul. A doctoral student gets less help from the professor than a freshman. At some point old souls become guides themselves, like graduate students teaching introductory courses. Indeed, I feel

I am on a post-graduate mystic course, serving others who are at the beginning of the path as I complete my own lonely journey.

Miyamoto Musashi (1584-1645), a great samurai warrior and master of the sword, said, "The teacher is as a needle, the disciple is as thread." The teacher guides the disciple through many layers of fabric, but when the stitching is finished, only the disciple remains. The teacher is gone.

> He [Gampopa] suddenly remembered on the twenty-fifth day that he was to go and see Milarepa on the fifteenth, so he decided to set out. He rushed, but halfway there some travelers came to him with the message that Milarepa was dead. He had sent a piece of his robe and a message for Gampopa.
>
> Situations like that take place all the time. They are a kind of encouragement, showing us that we are able to work with ourselves and that we will achieve the goal – but we will not receive the congratulations of the guru anymore. Again you are alone: you are a lonely student or you are a lonely teacher. You are continuously becoming alone again. With such independence, relating with spiritual scenes or other such situations is not so important. But relating with ourselves is very important and more necessary.
>
> Nobody is going to be initiated as a fully enlightened person decorated by the guru. So any external reliance does not work. It is the individual, personal intuition, working on oneself, which is important. – Chögyam Trungpa[36]

~ 396 ~

SEX, Part 14

I have had three spirit-in-space-time sexual encounters with you. The first was in 2009, when I shared a bed with your wife and felt your conjugal sorrow. (~250~) The second was two months later, when Shiva and Shakti visited me in the pre-dawn fog of the ancient forest. (~269~)

I cannot remember exactly when the third one happened. It was a dream that taught me about the sacrifice of the bodhisattva in this world and showed me the line of demarcation between the physical and the spiritual, the line my body may not cross with you.

If you knew about this dream, you would understand why I say that you and I talking sex would not betray your wife. But I don't think you will ever let me tell you this dream, so I am relating it here, now, so that you will know of it if you ever find your way to this tome.

I am asleep in the guest room at your house. You come into my room and lay down with me in bed. I feel your arms and legs around me. I hear you gasp, and then choke with tears. Your hardness is pressing against me. "You have brought me back to life," you whisper joyously into my ear. "I want you so much."

And I want you, too, with an ardor that reaches to the depths of the Dao. Loving you in the flesh is the one and only aspect missing from our otherwise complete divine love. Sex with you would be perfect, the ultimate union, the sacred connection between flesh and spirit as I knew it with Lou. But now tears fill my eyes as I say to you, "Your body belongs to your wife. Take your reborn manhood back to the other room and share your joy with her."

I sleep little and poorly at your house. I do not like to remember this dream.

~ 397 ~

When I first sensed the bodhisattva arising in me, I began to puff up, feeling specially chosen and privileged above other people. Now I am humbled. I have discovered that the life of the bodhisattva is far from privileged, far from the limelight, far from comfort, far from any reward in the earthly sense. It is characterized by the five S's – Suffering, Surrender, Service, Solitude, and Sacrifice.

Suffering comes first. A catastrophe of some kind is usually required to compel us to look beyond this world for rescue. C.S. Lewis said, "We will not turn to [God] as long as He leaves us anything else to turn to." I had no choice but to turn to God when the spiritual devastation I suffered after Lou's death brought me to my knees. Suffering was the catapult that threw me onto the bodhisattva path.

Surrender comes next, and with it, the subjugation of the ego, leading to unsupported thought, vulnerability, poverty, chastity, and obedience. This ultimate surrender is not an act of volition or conscious decision, not a calculated negotiation with God, but a lightning bolt of spiritual transformation. Serendipities and synchronicities naturally follow once the barriers to the indwelling God-self/buddha-nature have been removed.

I have money and possessions, life and health, but they hold no value to me except as they are useful in my sacred mission of **Service**. As I surrender all that I have to God, my money, possessions, and my life itself become God's tools for effecting the world's healing, comfort, and awakening.

A bodhisattva lives in deep **Solitude**, because few can understand the bodhisattva's total preoccupation with the deepest aspects of dharma and engage with him/her at that level. Dualism is experienced at its farthest extremes, creating an intense and unremitting tension between the pairs of opposites that few can appreciate. Every attempt to discuss matters of such spiritual intensity risks serious misunderstanding, so the bodhisattva turns inward, seeking solace from his/her own buddha-nature. I have many friends, but even my deepest loves cannot help me with the psychic pain that is my destiny as I let go of worldly support and replace it with the worldly suffering of others. There is no getting around the fact that the final steps to awakening must be taken alone.

It is a life of **Sacrifice** where money, home, possessions, time, energy, skills, and all manner of physical and emotional support are freely and joyously given away and given up. Such sacrifice, while indeed joyous, is not easy or painless; ridicule, rejection, persecution, and loss of reputation, honor, trust, respect, and liberty are often part of the package. Ultimately life itself is sacrificed.

~ 398 ~

Sometimes in my frustration with the roadblocks that impede our spiritual progress, my mind explodes and in protective reflex tries to back up and back out, to extract itself from your life and not be involved with you at all. But then the pain of contemplating that crushing loss becomes too much to bear and I crawl back into my dualistic torture chamber and re-engage with you in the world. So here I am, jumping endlessly from the frying pan into the fire and back again.

When I am strong, I am like the Tibetan monk who immolates himself but has trained his mind to accept pain. Or like Jesus, in agony on his cross but still able to direct his mind to forgive his tormentors. Like Jesus and the burning monk, I am spiritually afire, suffering in solitude, being sacrificed and purified in the fire of Achala. I withstand the suffering, solitude, and sacrifice by training my mind to focus on nirvana – no suffering – and letting go of my worldly strife. But sometimes I lose my grip on nirvana; anguish rises to the surface, overwhelms the endorphins, and I feel the fiery pain. I want you to throw a bucket of water on me to douse the flames, but Achala will not be denied.

~ 399 ~

The source of your inner conflict is also the source of your relief from it. You have your wife, someone to distract you from thoughts of me, to share your daily life, to love, to comfort and be comforted by, to hold at night when you are lonely or fearful – and someone who can serve as a surrogate to accept the open expression of your love that is meant for me.

I have no one – no one to comfort me, to hold me or be held by me, no one to stand in for you in your absence. No one to break the silence of my profound solitude. All I have to keep me company is my blurry vision of bliss in another realm where I share my karmic love with a dead man and with you. I am starving for the tender affection that you divert to another. And yet, in those fleeting moments when my wisdom rises above my despair, I know that this is how it must be.

I think of death a lot these days, yours and mine, wondering how long I can hold off my death wish.

> Get busy livin' or get busy dyin'.
> – *The Shawshank Redemption*

~ 400 ~

When I ever so gently nudge the spinning gyroscopes of people's lives, they are apt to career off in unpredictable and chaotic directions. This is happening ever more frequently and dramatically, and sometimes I don't even know I am doing it. Hence the reason I am so frightened by my increasing spiritual power. Since my teenage years I have known it to be my destiny to delve into the spirit realm, to open Pandora's Box, to unearth buried secrets, to be a "truth-teller in the native tradition," as a musician friend dubbed me. Now my reach into the spirit is so deep that I am touching lives at their emotional and psychic core. I pray that whatever force gave me this power will show me how to use it, to move forward from the uncovering of deep psychic pain to the relieving of it.

My efforts to provide comfort and support sometimes seem to have the opposite effect. My vision of the future grows dark. The shining light at the far end of my path that had been drawing me forward for the last three years is now dim. Old chapters of my life are closing, and the ones I thought were opening now seem stalled, perhaps evaporating, in silent, murky shadows.

Near the end of *A Christmas Carol*, Ebenezer Scrooge asks the Ghost of Christmas Yet To Come, "Assure me that I yet may change these shadows you have shown me, with an altered life? … Oh, tell me I may sponge away the writing on this stone!" I wonder if Dickens was also a sojourner in spirit realms with shadowy visions of future potentialities. In the story, Scrooge was indeed able to change the outcome of his life. I hope that the dark writing on my stone may be expunged, my shining light will return, unarisen phenomena will arise, and I will not die from exhaustion fighting terminal existential anguish.

~ 401 ~

Our restorative dinner and breakfast have largely healed my troubled soul. Thank you.

You ask why I cannot leave our relationship alone and just let it be. If I seem too intent on asking probing questions and seeking answers, it is because our relationship in its current state is still awkward, impeded by tensions that demand resolution. You seem content to ride in a car with one flat tire, intentionally left that way, perhaps because you are afraid of the lightning speed that our perfected vehicle might attain – the 5,000 volts of our love, as you described it – and what damage might be done if it crashes into other sacred vehicles on the road of life.

I am not afraid to put air in the flat tire because I have ridden in the perfect vehicle before, and I welcome the surge of 5,000 volts, knowing that this energy propels us to heavenly realms of spirits, magic, miracles, and grace. I know that this car does not crash, but rather flies at the speed of light above and ahead of all other life forces and pulls all others along with it, drawing them into its loving sphere.

After dinner, a little spotting.

~ 402 ~

Another discussion from our dinner lingers in my mind. You expressed frustration that your wife continues to fall short of your expectations in completing routine household and office tasks. I asked if there was some way I could help her with them. You said no.

I want to help your wife with these tasks that she isn't good at (but I am), not only because I want to relieve her distress and yours, but also because I see that her inadequacy in these areas and your frustration over it causes tension between you. I want to help your wife, but even more importantly, I want to help you both find harmony and peace in your marriage.

This is what I meant when I said that our relationship turns the concept of "the other woman" on its head; in our miraculous *ménage á trois* I am not sent to come between you and cause tension, I am sent to remove obstructions and relieve tension. When you understand our spiritual togetherness, you will understand this as well.

~ 403 ~

THE FOUR SOULS

I am seeing that ideas like Einstein's Relativity, the Christian Trinity, Jungian psychology, and many Eastern and Western philosophies ultimately arrive at the same spiritual understanding. Here are four souls, or aspects of being, as described in various ways by various disciplines, and how they relate to each other:

1) **Self** = M = **Jesus** = **unconscious mind (physical, in space-time)**
2) **Ego** = M = **Jesus** = **conscious mind (ephemeral, in space-time)**
3) **Soul** = E = **Holy Spirit** = **subconscious mind (spiritual, bridging space-time and eternity)**
4) **Spirit** = c^2 = **God** = **no mind (spiritual, in eternity)**

1) **Self.** The first soul sends and receives sensory signals – sight, sound, taste, smell, touch – and is the seat of instinct and intuition, thought and feeling. It is the biological body-mind that houses the other souls in space-time and takes orders from them. This is the soul that literally brings the spirit to life and makes latent potentialities kinetic.

Its vehicle through space-time, from life to life, is the transmission of a genetic code, DNA, from one generation to the next. It is the spirit made flesh.

The *unconscious mind* is the aspect of the Self that runs the backstage part of the show. It breathes for us, pumps blood, regulates hormonal balances, sends nerve impulses, and digests our food without our having to think about it; it controls the daemonic systems of the body. It does our technical thinking – "To walk, I must move these muscles this way," or "I'm hungry, get food."

2) **Ego.** The second soul is a space-time manifestation like the first, but it is removed from direct association with the physical Self, standing aloof from the body and observing, analyzing, and directing the thoughts, feelings, sensations, and actions of the body-mind. It holds our memory and is the seat of creativity, intellect, reasoning, rationality, and synthesis. It analyzes,

interprets, translates, organizes, filters, and communicates messages from the other souls, like a grand switchboard or control center.

Its vehicle through space-time, from life to life, is the fruit of the creative and intellectual impulse, made tangible in works of art, science, culture, philosophy, and religion.

The *conscious mind* is the thinking, analyzing, probing mind, the mind that is writing these words right now. This analytical mind is perhaps the greatest achievement in human evolution, but when fear and desire take over the Ego, it can become an obstruction to the Spirit. It stands apart not only from its own body, but also from God, deftly manipulating sensations, thoughts, and emotions to defend against challenges to its autonomy. Those who teach "no self" or "annihilation of the ego" are encouraging us to push aside this alienating aspect of Ego and clear a path so that the buddha-nature/God-self – the Spirit – can come through.

3) **Soul.** The third soul, the one that lives after we die, is the part of us created in the image of God. It is the part that we can recognize and identify after death in voices and visions of ancestors, angels, and saints.

Its vehicle through space-time, from life to life, is reincarnation, carrying our karma through countless cycles of birth, death, and rebirth in bodily forms. When the body dies, the Soul dissolves into the eternal ether as the salt doll dissolves in the ocean (~612~), ready to re-precipitate, reemerge, in the next incarnation. This is the soul that is tracked for all time in the Akashic Records.

Hindus call this soul the *atman*. Buddhists generally do not subscribe to the Hindu *atman*, but rather to *anatman* – no-self – holding that nothing recognizable survives death to be reincarnated. They do, however, acknowledge that some indefinable thing, like a stream of consciousness, connects one life to the next. They describe that "something" not with a noun, but with a verb – *punabbhava* – which means "again becoming."

The *subconscious mind* is my favorite place, the home of the Soul. I see it as the place described by Carl Jung as the "collective unconscious," or by Wayne Dyer as the "universal subconscious." It is a subterranean wonderland that accesses both life and eternity. It is the place we go when we sleep, where dreams occur, where our physical self and our eternal spirit join with all other spirits living and dead in the vast ocean of eternal realms, a portal through which space-time connects to eternity. Going there is like dipping into the communal well in the center of the village where all go to be refreshed. The subconscious is like a placenta connecting our space-time body-minds directly to the eternal source. The many powerful dreams I have received in that place have given me confidence that the spirits are indeed guiding me and have been largely responsible for my spiritual survival in this life of suffering.

4) **Spirit.** The fourth soul is the God-self, the buddha-nature, the Kingdom of God that Jesus said is within us. It does not think or act or even exist, as we know that term in our minds. It is the nothingness from which all form and substance emanates. Space-time/the world/the universe – life – is the emergence of matter and energy from this eternal emptiness. Life is a lens that gives us a specially enhanced but limited view of eternity from one angle, that of the Soul, which blossoms out of the unlimited Spirit at birth, as a flower blossoms out of a tree.

It has no vehicle through space-time, from life to life, because it is itself all space and all time. When a bodhisattva comes to the end of his last incarnation and is ready for unexcelled complete awakening and the end of karma, his Soul dissolves into the Spirit upon his death and is no more. The iceberg melts into the vast ocean.

No mind is a Zen concept that means removing the analyzing, judging, fearing, hoping Ego and just experiencing life directly as it is in the moment, without thinking or separate awareness. "No mind" takes us out of this world even while we are in it.

Some ancient cultures recognize three points through which different souls enter or leave the body: the Soul or Spirit (the eternal, ever-present Now) through the top of the head, the Ego (the temporal past) through the umbilicus, and the Self (the temporal future) through the genitals.

Many religious and philosophical traditions combine the Soul and the Spirit. The words "subconscious" and "unconscious" are sometimes used interchangeably. Psychologists, including Freud and Jung, often use terms like "self," "ego," "id," and "mind" in different ways or in combination. This is perfectly okay. We all know what we mean.

PART 18
Love in the Four Souls
September 2011 – January 2012

~ 404 ~

Earlier I described the four souls as I understand them in terms of religion, science, and philosophy. How is love expressed in each of the four souls? Love can manifest anywhere, as physical sensations, thoughts, and feelings in the Self, as artistic or intellectual creativity in the Ego, and as visions of God in the Soul. The fourth soul, what I call the Spirit, is nothing but love; it is love *itself*. Here is how I understand love in the four souls, how I have experienced it.

– Physical Love –

Our temporal body-mind, which I call the Self, experiences love initially as gratitude for whatever fulfills our needs and desires, protects us from pain, and generates pleasant thoughts and emotions. Physical love arises in response to instinct, usually involves physical or emotional dependency, and includes parental love, filial love, and marital love. These loves usually involve some kind of comforting sensory stimuli – tender touch, soothing voice, beautiful appearance, sweet aroma, kindness, sympathy, or similar mental/emotional images – feelings of pleasure, safety, comradery, support, affection, belonging.

Physical love often fades (but does not disappear) when sensory delights fade or mutual dependency becomes unbalanced or unnecessary, when one party no longer fulfills the desires of the other for sex, comfort, food, shelter, money, or protection. When sexual gratification, emotional comfort, or financial support is no longer being provided by a marriage, people often get divorced. When children grow up and begin to provide for themselves, they usually leave their parents' home and allow other worldly loves, like marital love or intellectual love, to come to the fore.

– Intellectual Love –

Intellectual love, manifested through the Ego, depends on connections made at a higher level of human awareness than physicality, in the realms of art, science, and philosophy. This is the collegial love between and among people who work closely together in creative or intellectual pursuits, like artists, scientists, teachers, and close teammates or coworkers in any field. It is the deepest kind of friendship, in which the connection that began in the thoughtful mind moves to the feeling heart. When the intense collegial relationship that spawned intellectual love is over, that love may become dormant, but like all forms of true love, never ends.

– *Spiritual Love* –

All love that arises in this world – love that springs from the Self or the Ego – is dependent on something. Spiritual love, on the other hand, is beyond all worldly conditions and dependencies. It is not a response to the instinctive drives of the body or to the analytical or creative exercise of the intellect. Its eternal force flows through countless incarnations, one continuous stream from before birth to after death, unchanging and immovable through infinite permutations, binding the web of Indra's Net together. It has nothing to attain, no goal to reach, no needs to satisfy, but seeks only the fulfillment and elevation of the lovers, in selfless service and sacrifice to each other. There are no decisions to be made, no actions to be taken, and no thoughts, only unquestioning surrender to the eternal power that has taken possession of the Self/Ego and made it a vehicle for spiritual awakening.

Spiritual lovers lose their separate identities and disappear into each other, dissolving into each other, becoming indistinguishable from each other, invisible except as reflected in the mirror of the other. They give everything and take nothing, becoming empty vessels, one soul flowing into the empty vessel of the other, freely and joyously living in unsupported thought in the emptiness and fullness of the Dao. Individual identities blur into each other and manifest the eternal oneness in this temporal world.

– *Love from Soul to Soul* –

All kinds of love, whether arising in the body, mind, or spirit, can flow into and find expression in any or all of the other souls. The worldly loves, relational loves experienced in the body-mind/Self-Ego, arise in duality from the spiritual love eternally present in the Soul/Spirit. All forms of true love are interconnected.

The Self is usually deemed to be the lowest soul because it is most closely attached to the physical body, and the Spirit the highest because it is liberated from the body. Yet, love at all levels is sacred. The temporal world is contained in eternity, inseparable from it. The body is a sacred portal through which the eternal is visible in space-time, and thus the worldly loves that nurture, enable, and protect the body are as precious as any other.

– *Love in the Body* –

Physical love, which we have all experienced in some form with somebody, starting with our mothers, can open the door to something more, can include intellectual love and even awaken spiritual love. An attraction that began as lust or familial connection can open the door to the discovery of deeper connections at higher levels. The constancy of true love in the body, intellect, or spirit keeps married couples together after sex, children, and financial dependency have left the marriage, and keeps parents close to their children even after they have left home to live independent lives.

The physical expression of intellectually based love adds a physical/emotional union to the mental/intellectual union, binding people even more tightly in their higher artistic and intellectual pursuits. Intellectual love often finds physical expression in sex – a meeting of minds demands a meeting of bodies. In his book *Organizing Genius*, Warren Bennis writes, "Great Groups are not only fun, they are sexy. There is often an erotic element to working together so closely and intensely. In the charged atmosphere of these groups, people sometimes look across a crowded lab or cubicle and see more than a colleague."

Love that originates in the body feels the same as love that originates in the intellect or spirit that *finds expression* in the body-mind. The sensations experienced in the body are the same – physical and emotional attraction, the desire for intimacy – regardless of which soul the love comes from. This can cause confusion as to the nature of the love being expressed and confuse true love with bodily sensations that are not love at all, but merely lust, desire, or relief.

[This explains your discomfort with our physical attraction; you can't distinguish between the bodily sensations of our spiritual love and the simple lust that you have known with other women. My physical attraction to you reflects my reverence for the holy vessel of the Spirit that is your body. You think I just want sex.]

– *Love in the Mind* –

Most of us have experienced intellectual love, perhaps with a favorite teacher or close coworker. As I described my love with my office colleague James (~110~/~134~), intellectual love, like physical love, can awaken or reflect the eternal connection of buddha-natures in the Spirit.

The intellectual expression of physical or spiritual love brings lovers together in their minds and thoughts, into creative or philosophical union, melding their love into their daily social and vocational lives.

[Spiritual love as I knew it with Lou and now with you, in both cases was introduced through the artistic Ego.]

– Spiritual Love in the Body and Mind –

While love in the Self or Ego may or may not rise to the Spirit, spiritual love, because it washes over everything, always seeks expression in the other souls. At the juncture of temporal and eternal love, spiritual love manifests the complete physical and metaphysical union that is the oneness of the Dao. Every kind of physical/emotional expression in the body-mind is without taint or flaw, in total acceptance of and surrender to the eternal source manifesting in this world in the present moment. This realization of eternity in the physical body usually includes the sacred ritual of tantric sex – Shiva and Shakti in the flesh.

It matters not what sex the two lovers are. The masculine and feminine sides of both lovers are recognized and reconciled, balanced and unified. Many literary and pictorial images of enlightened beings are sexually ambiguous, by artistic intention or because in eternity gender is irrelevant. The buddha-nature is both male and female, equally masculine and feminine, and neither. When the buddha-nature is fully expressed in spiritual love, all potentialities can be realized.

Physical love begins in the body-mind as gratitude for those who serve us, who satisfy our needs, bring us comfort, and protect us as we respond to our own instincts and natural dependencies. As our ever-present spiritual love arises in us and manifests in the body-mind, gratitude morphs into true love, in service to the other, satisfying the needs and bringing comfort and protection to the other, not ourselves. We are free of all clinging and dependency, even unto the total sacrifice of one's life for the other. Jesus said, "I have told you this so that my joy may be in you and that your joy may be complete. My command is this: Love each other as I have loved you. Greater love has no one than this, that he lay down his life for his friends." (John 15:11-13) And of course, Jesus did exactly that.

[I revere your physical body as the vessel holding your buddha-nature, as Buddhists revere the Dao in the human form of Gautama Buddha, as Christians revere God incarnated in the man Jesus Christ – all exemplifying and actualizing the connection of life with eternity.]

Loves that originate in the Self and Ego are worldly loves, satisfying worldly dependencies, needs, and desires, and thus imply expectations, demands, and obligations. As we mature, dependency moves from the Self (dependence on others) to the Ego (independence, providing for ourselves) and then to the Soul and Spirit, where all dependency disappears ("unsupported thought," no dependence on anyone or anything, no longer wanting or needing those things upon which we were once dependent).

A baby is totally dependent on his mother, and by instinct a mother naturally wants to provide food and protection for her child. Our biology hardwires behaviors into our genetic code that make the baby's demand and the mother's acceptance of parental obligation to satisfy that demand almost automatic. This is the unconscious daemonic action of the Self.

Marital love, arising in the Self and mediated by the Ego, is likewise a worldly connection of mutual dependency rooted in duality, the union of separate individuals, responsive to biological instincts and emotions, and limited to this life: Jesus said, "For in the resurrection they neither marry, nor are given in marriage, but are like angels in heaven." (Matthew 22:29-30) It is an *exclusive* love, cutting out all others from its sphere, as per the marriage ceremony: "forsaking all others as long as we both shall live."

Love that originates in the Spirit is different. Because this eternal love is not dependent on anything, there are no expectations or demands, no right or wrong, no beginning or end. It is an *inclusive* love expanding infinitely to embrace all within its sphere, casting its light upon everything in its path, even beyond this space and time, extending to past and future generations as well as to all beings in the present circle of love.

[Look at how far my spiritual love for you has spread – from you at the hub, back in time to your mother, uncles, grandparents, all the way to your ancestors hundreds of years ago; forward in time to your nephew, his wife and daughter and their yet unborn children; to your wife and her mother, sister, brother, nieces and nephews. My love even extends to your family with whom you are out of touch, embracing your estranged brother and even your father who abandoned you when you were a baby. Because you are unconditionally beloved, so are all those who are connected to you.]

~ 405 ~

I went to visit my sister-in-law Elaine at the nursing home where she now lives. She is about the same, physically weak, mentally foggy. She mostly mumbled things I couldn't understand, but she had a lucid moment and revealed a startling thing: "For years I worried all the time about John and my family. I cooked and cleaned the house. John never appreciated that. I was tense all the time. Now I am only concerned for myself. I know what a vacation is. I don't worry about anything, just relax."

I didn't realize how deeply she resented her long life as the dutiful wife and mother. She actually prefers being an invalid in a nursing home to her past able-bodied life in service – or as she saw it, servitude – to her family. Although she is now trapped inside a dysfunctional body that cannot respond to her commands, her spirit is strangely free.

A reason Elaine is still alive is to teach me the art of letting go; how to accept the loss of physical control, the death of the body, while gaining life in other ways. I do feel sorrow, though, that Elaine spent her years of youth and strength in a virtual prison that the rigid rules of her society a generation ago would not allow her to escape. The most amazing irony is that my life with Lou was the exact opposite, totally without defined domestic expectations or responsibilities, yet John and Lou were both raised in the same home at the same time by the same parents, in the same strict culture with the same social expectations.

Our divine love made all the difference. It flew free, rising above culture, rules, ceremony, dependency, work, money, all worldly things. It came from a place of miracles – miracles that transform and transcend all.

~ 406 ~

You called. You said you missed your bodhisattva. You sounded sincere, like you were really happy to talk with me.

In your unawakened ignorance of my love, you are like a newborn baby, absentmindedly self-absorbed, going about sleeping, crying, eating, pooping, all the while oblivious to his mother standing over him keeping watch, seeing all, tending, caring, loving, the whole time.

I am paying a heavy price, risking everything, for this role I play in your life. How long before this conscript into the Bodhisattva Army starts to see some sign that I am winning the battle, see some fruits of my labor, and how will I know when I am seeing them?

I wish I could be ignorant of all this. Is ignorance bliss? No, it is *faux* bliss, the third poison. I am not granted blissful ignorance; the spirits lead me down the path to true bliss instead. I must stay on course, and endure.

~ 407 ~

At the time of the economic collapse in 2008, I heard a series of vignettes on the radio about how people were coping with their unexpected financial difficulties. One story that stuck in my mind was about a man whose wife, afflicted with Alzheimer's, was being cared for in a nursing facility that the man was paying for. In the years after his wife's institutionalization the man had found another woman to share his love, and they were living happily together. When the man lost his money in the crash, he could no longer afford to keep up with the cost of his wife's institutional care. The man's new loving and compassionate companion said, "Let's bring her home with us. We'll care for her together."

You and your wife cannot allow me into the exclusive love of your marriage; I understand that, as I have explained. But you and I *can* allow your wife into the infinitely inclusive eternal love that we share. Indeed, she is with us there already, and has been all along. We'll care for her together.

~ 408 ~

The deep spiritual love that Lou and I shared is the rarest of treasures. There is only one other couple that I have ever known whom I am sure also shared it, a former teacher of mine and his wife. I have been thinking about them lately.

It was obvious, watching them together, that they were karmic lovers. They were not ostentatious with displays of affection – no hand-holding, kissing, or hugging in front of people. But the smiles, the impishness, the glances that passed between them, the easy way they connected with each other, broadcast the deep and unbreakable bond that joined them. They saw that same bond between Lou and me.

Several years ago my teacher fell seriously ill and was taken to the hospital. After weeks in the hospital, his wife brought him home and over many months nursed him back to health. Then, just as things seemed to be getting back to normal, she was diagnosed with terminal cancer and died soon thereafter, in the same hospital room where her husband had recuperated.

When I visited my teacher the following year, I could see that he would never recover from his wife's death. He died a couple years later.

~ 409 ~

SEX, Part 15

Your loss of sexual function was perfectly timed. Our inevitable sexual attraction in divine love was sure to be trouble. God knew that if your marriage in this life was to be protected, it would help us to have an insurance policy. In case our spirits succumbed to temptation, our bodies wouldn't be able to follow through.

God and Shiva/Shakti gave me a vision of our eternal sexual union to relieve the space-time tension – testament to the depth of my spiritual awareness. But my memory of tantric sex with Lou, fulfilled in this life in the flesh, refuses to be overwritten. I know what we are missing.

~ 410 ~

LOVE, Part 2

Is it really love? Or only greed? How can I tell?

Greed and fear lead to possessiveness and its flip side, dependency. Both poles of this dichotomy reflect a perceived incompleteness, striving to fill an empty hole. The dependent man is limited by that upon which he depends. His happiness, self-image, and definition of success revolve around fulfilling the needs of those upon whom he depends.

The possessive man is limited by his possessions. His happiness, self-image, and definition of success revolve around fulfilling his own needs by corralling those who want him to fill their empty hole and conscripting them into his service. The possessed and the possessor, the needy one and the one who provides what is needed, both measure their wealth and happiness in terms of what they have. Both are also constrained by the demands made upon them by those who provide what they have.

We claim ownership and exercise power by controlling the things our dependents want and need, most especially their food supply. We domesticate animals by feeding them; even when we take off the leash and let the animals run free, they return home for food. This same theory extends to the ultimate human indignity – slavery – even to willing slaves: "In the end they will lay their freedom at our feet, and say to us, 'Make us your slaves, but feed us.'" (Fyodor Dostoyevsky, *The Brothers Karamazov*)

Anything we desire – food, money, sex, material things, and emotional support – can become tools for controlling. Husbands control wives with the carrot of money; wives control husbands with the carrot of sex; parents control children with food, shelter, and toys. And everyone controls everyone else with emotional carrots of affection, flattery, validation, affirmation, and comfort.

With control comes responsibility. Possessions can be turned to the service of their owner, but at the same time they demand attention to their needs. Slaves must be fed. Things as well as people make demands; your house shelters you but needs repair from time to time. The need to control is itself a kind of dependency; the controller is also controlled, limited by that which he controls and for which he bears responsibility. In every case, from the most benevolent to the most malevolent, both the controlled and the controller are locked in a limited existence defined by satisfying needs and desires. That is greed.

In the end, nothing can be depended upon or possessed. Both dependency and possessiveness grasp at illusions and cannot but lead to disappointment and frustration. Unsupported thought is the ultimate strength and freedom, wanting nothing, needing nothing, being independent and uncontrollable. "It's anxiety that sets limits," said Ingmar Bergman. If one has no dependency on anything, no need to control or submit to control, nothing to lose and thus nothing to be anxious about, then there are no limits. That is love.

~ 411 ~

I don't think I will ever be able to recite for you the chant I composed in memory of your mother. I want it to be a spontaneous unobstructed message from the Spirit, not a performance, but I am always self-conscious – my Ego gets in the way.

The Ego acts as a valve or filter between the Spirit and the Self, analyzing and synthesizing, translating and interpreting, focusing and regulating the flow of energy, which most of the time is a good thing. The action of the Ego enables teaching and learning, passing down knowledge and wisdom across boundaries of time, space, and culture. That's what my Ego does in my music and my writing. This entire journal is my intellectual translation of my spiritual soul, telling the story of its fabulous journey through space-time and its intersection with eternity, told in metaphorical mosaics meant to elicit a sideways glance at that which cannot be seen directly.

But the Ego can sometimes impede as well as a facilitate communication. Most of the Spirit's essence gets through the Ego filter, but the transmission necessarily loses something in the translation. This is why even the most skilled teaching can never quite impart as much information as direct pointing or direct experience, which is why the Buddha did not at first want to teach, and why Zen masters use *koan* as well as sutras. As Ignacio said, "Our thoughts are more than our words, and our experience is more than our thoughts."

When I chant by myself, my Ego relaxes, the scrim comes down, and I can feel the presence of Spirit without hindrances, the spiritual message flowing unimpeded to and through my body-mind. In that state, I can feel your mother's presence directly and powerfully. That's the only way I want to present my chant to you – uninhibited, without thought – like speaking in tongues, which is what it is.

~ 412 ~

LOVE, Part 3
Love in the Spirit

How can you tell if it is spiritual love or physical love? It's spiritual love if you love the totality of someone, just the way he is, embracing the weaknesses as well as the strengths, drawn as much to his suffering as to his joy. Worldly loves fill us with dependent and addictive pleasure; the fullness of spiritual love fills us with bittersweet pain to balance the pleasure and awakens us to the perfection of the whole. To love in the Spirit is to gratefully accept the beautiful, happy side, but not to crave it, knowing the impermanence of it, and to equally embrace the ugly, unhappy side, kissing the suppurating sores as well as the alluring lips.

In dependent relationships, tending a sick or troubled loved one is a choice, often done out of obligation. Sometimes the choice to tend is as much a desire to assuage one's guilt over resisting the burden of obligation as to relieve the suffering of the other. But in truly loving relationships, caretaking is automatic and spontaneous, never a matter of choice. No thought of escape, no running away when things get hard, but literally running toward the hardship, getting fully into the game, no matter the outcome, knowing that it cannot be won or lost, only played. Spiritual love plays the game well, with heart and soul fully engaged.

Let go of the craving that is the first poison, let go of the aversion that is the second poison, and let go of the fear of involvement that is the third poison. This is love in the Spirit.

~ 413 ~

Last night I watched a science program on TV about string theory and quantum mechanics, about the chaotic yet ordered movements of matter and energy in subatomic particles. This is the mechanism of creation, the fusion of physics and philosophy, the intersection of time and eternity, the evolution from dualistic separation to the unified theory that was Einstein's unfulfilled dream. This is what I saw in my great epiphany (~232~) – the timeless dancing molecules.

~ 414 ~

I am rereading *Siddhartha* by Hermann Hesse. I think Hesse must have been enlightened. He gets it. He describes all the elements of Buddhist philosophy – karma; dualism; timelessness; the Three Poisons; the illusion of life and matter; unsupported thought; the inadequacy of words and teaching relative to direct experience; the bodhisattva's solitude; the singularity of past, present, and future; finding something only after you stop seeking it; the role of pain, meditation, and sex in revealing aspects of the eternal; the oneness of all things.

Hesse was at one time a student in a seminary and at another time a patient in a sanatorium. He studied Freud, Jung, psychoanalysis and religion. He was an enlightened lunatic – crazy, like me.

~ 415 ~

A rainbow followed me home from the museum where I had been doing research for our upcoming film project. As I left the museum, the rainbow was clearly arched over the hills behind the museum, but as I drove home, it seemed to rotate 90 to 180 degrees, traveling in synch with my car, coming to rest over my house several miles away. The rainbow was in my sight the whole time I was driving, and the right side of the arc was in my field of vision as I pulled into my driveway.

A rainbow is the invisible light of God made visible to us on earth. Like most of the miracles in my recent life, this rainbow happened in full view of other people, but it was nothing out of the ordinary to them. To them the rainbow and its movement through the sky was just a random everyday application of the laws of physics. To me it was a message from heaven.

~ 416 ~

Unsupported thought: choosing poverty in the midst of wealth. My money and possessions mean nothing to me, except as they are useful in service to others. My body needs only protection from the weather and enough food to keep me alive and functional. I don't need a car or a dishwasher. Like the monks in Thailand or Tibet who come down from the monastery into the town to beg for their one meal of the day and then return to contemplation, I arise to my humble coffee and bagel and then return to writing my dharma. The monks greet the gift of deprivation with the same gratitude and equanimity as the gift of a bowl of rice. Both priceless.

~ 417 ~

The idea of freedom presents an interesting paradox – it represents both the far left and the far right, like extreme opposite poles meeting on the far side of an orb, connecting in another dimension. The words "liberal" and "libertarian" come from the same Latin root, *liberare*, to be free.

To the libertarian right, freedom is for the powerful – deregulation, *liaise faire*, the free market, and individual autonomy. To the liberal left, freedom is for the powerless – liberation from authoritarian, often tyrannical, plutocracy, fostering political equality and socio-economic control by society at large. Both of these approaches, if taken to extreme, can lead to disorder or chaos akin to anarchy.[i]

The price to be paid for anarchy is lonely isolation, no social system to lean on for support, no organized division of labor to enable a network of relationships or teamwork. No safety net or protection for the weak and vulnerable. Also no law and order to protect lives and property. Ultimately walls must be built to keep property in and danger out.

Schoenberg's 12-tone system is the most rigid pitch structure in music, but yet within it, each note is equal, liberated, freed from primary and secondary roles relative to the others. It seems there is a tipping point in every system, whether musical or political, where the rules are strung so tight that they snap, and then it seems there are no rules. This is disorienting,

---

[i] The blurry left-right overlap of these differing views of freedom can be seen in the political philosophy of libertarian socialism, or anarchist socialism, which paradoxically combines both extremes. "Libertarian socialism generally rejects the concept of a state and asserts that a society based on freedom and justice can only be achieved with the abolition of authoritarian institutions that control certain means of production and subordinate the majority to an owning class or political and economic elite, advocating for decentralized structures of political organization. This is done within a general call for liberty and free association." – *Wikipedia*

like the untethered feeling I described at the beginning of this journal, or the *Star Wars* jump to light speed, or the quantum leap from an infinitely sided polygon to a circle. But in that metamorphosis, one discovers that the strange new world is not without rules; they are just different from the old ones, and you haven't learned them yet.

~ 418 ~

Your wife described your marriage to me: "We made the choice to consciously feed the goodness and love, appreciate the beauty and potential happiness we might enjoy in our time together."

The corollary to consciously feeding the goodness is unconsciously starving the badness. But in the end, dualism will have its way with us and force an equal balance. Now I see another aspect to my role with you. While you make the choice to look only at the happy side of life, I am here to absorb the other side, take on your pain and fear, receive the blows, and see the ugliness that you blot out.

This is why the great love that embraces us has been revealed to me. Only the most powerful of eternal forces could draw me to you, against all odds, and keep me with you through all this, accepting the huge weight of this task and being willing to crumble under it.

I am forced to learn about you obliquely, indirectly, through cryptic statements like your wife's above, and from body language, provocative songs, and spiritual messages. I wish I had Mr. Spock's Vulcan mind-meld. (In a way, I do.) You won't tell me what you really think and feel, so I must build a case for our love from circumstantial evidence.

~ 419 ~

The life of Christ is a temporal metaphor for the eternal bodhisattva condition. Jesus' fear of his tragic fate was not limited to just a few moments of fervent prayer in Gethsemane. Nor was his sacrificial torment limited to the few hours from his arrest to his death on the cross.

I am continuously in grief over the loss of you even while you live, in fear of my future suffering even as I twist in the midst of it, hanging now on my cross of sacrifice. Yet even in my travail I know the peace of eternal oneness. Past, present, and future are all one. Time and eternity dwell within each other. Every moment is now. Every moment is suffering … and peace.

~ 420 ~

It was an interesting conversation about love and relationships that we had with our producer after our recording session. I was mostly silent during that discussion, but make no mistake; I have definite thoughts on the subject, which I kept to myself because they differ quite markedly from those expressed by others in the room.

Your wife said there is no such a thing as Prince Charming. Yet I stumbled upon two – Lou and *you*. She also said that we make choices in love. I never did; the great loves of my life – including *you* – were never a matter of choice. You asked if I had ever "had coitus" with anyone after Lou. The answer is no – until I had it with *you*, in that fabulous spiritual realm that you don't want to talk about. You asked when or how I knew that Lou was the man for me. The answer is that something clicked into place almost immediately, like a magnet finding its polar opposite, within days of our first meeting – as it did with *you*.

~ 421 ~

Just got word that my Aunt Minnie passed away. She was the last surviving relative of my parent's generation – mother, father, aunts, uncles – now all gone.

All my aunts were dear to me, all caring, loving, and nurturing. I treasure the values that they brought to my young life – teaching me how to cook Thanksgiving turkey, how to play bridge and euchre; listening to my troubles that I couldn't share with my parents; knitting together the strong threads of family that supported us through good times and bad. Aunt Minnie was special in her patience and simple kindness, quietly enduring everyone's surface turmoil while drawing out the love underneath.

A couple months ago I got the urge to contact Minnie. I looked through my records to see if I still had her phone number. I found it, but as my life usually goes, I got sidetracked and never did call. I was just thinking of her again a few days ago, wondering how she was. Her spirit was reaching to me from another realm. And my spirit reaches back, with deep gratitude.

~ 422 ~

I had a dream last night: *I was discovering new bedrooms in a strange house. One was the room I had just slept in; the others were rooms I didn't know were there. All the rooms were bright and clean but a little unkempt. The beds were neat but mostly unmade. One room was almost empty.*

This reminded me of another dream I had years ago: *I was exploring a new property I had just bought. I was walking downhill along the property, discovering new rooms and buildings, amazed that all these were now mine. The rooms varied widely in color, size, shape, and state of repair. As I walked farther downhill the rooms seemed to get bigger, darker, and emptier.*

From dreammoods.com:

Room – To dream that you are in a room represents a particular aspect of yourself or a specific relationship. Dreams about various rooms often relate to hidden areas of the conscious mind and different aspects of your personality. If the room is welcoming or comfortable, then it signifies opulence and satisfaction in life. If you see a dark or confined room, then it denotes that you feel trapped or repressed in a situation. To dream that you find or discover a new room suggests that you are developing new strengths and taking on new roles. You may be growing emotionally. To dream that you are in an empty white room indicates a fresh start. It is like a blank canvas where you want to start life anew.

Bed – To see your bed in your dream represents your intimate self and discovery of your sexuality. If you are sleeping in your own bed, then it denotes security and restoration of your mind. If the bed is made, then it symbolizes security. If the bed is unmade, then it indicates that certain secrets will soon be exposed or revealed.

House – To see a house in your dream represents your own soul and self. Specific rooms in the house indicate a specific aspect of your psyche. In general, the attic represents your intellect, the basement represents the unconscious. If the house is empty, then it indicates feelings of insecurity. To see a new house in your dream indicates that you are entering into a new phase or new area in your life. You are becoming more emotionally mature.

PART 19
Contradictions
January 2012 – August 2012

~ 423 ~

Last night I unwrapped another layer of our onion. How can two karmic lovers find themselves in so many misunderstandings, inadvertently hurting each other while trying so hard not to? I have part of the answer.

The "hurt" that passes between us is not the same as the normal kind of hurt that we experience in other aspects of life. We are deeply imbedded in each other. We poke each other in places that hurt because we have access to each other's deepest and tenderest parts.

Hurt happens not as a result of what people say or do, but as a result of our reaction to what people say or do. Hurt comes from within. I am totally vulnerable to you because you trigger a response from the deepest core of me where I have no defenses. You can hurt me in a way that no one else can. But it is a good hurt. I learn from it, and grow from it. It is part of my purification.

I think it is the same for you. In our recent experience with hurt, you sent me a reassuring text and sought to heal the wound by enlightening me to your view of it. You didn't just run away.

The hurt that arises between us is different from most other kinds because it leads to understanding and awakening. It does not drive us apart in resentment and distrust; it brings us closer in search of meaning and resolution. It is cathartic pain that brings new life, like the pain of childbirth. We dig into dark festering corners and bring into the light our hidden fears, liberate ourselves from invisible bonds, cleanse ourselves of the detritus of the past, peel back masks of ignorance and denial to reveal another facet of truth. We make quantum leaps into new awareness, new paradigms, new ways of thinking. We are reborn in the spirit, new and clean. Only lovers with absolute trust in their love can do this.

Everything that transpires between us in this world is just a distant echo, a reflection many times removed from its spiritual source, a tiny part of what we are in eternity. It is like looking at each other in a house of mirrors, infinitely reflecting in all directions, images distorted by the shapes of the mirrors. It is impossible to discern which image is the original, our true nature.

But karmic lovers can feel the power of their true natures emanating through all the layers of existence – it is what brought them together in the first place. They are undaunted in their quest to reach the Source, no matter how much sludge they must wade through. In karmic love all emotions, even negative ones, are harnessed in service to that true nature. Every time we get past the hurt into the deeper meaning of the experience, we remove one of the mirrors that deflect and distort our divine essence, one of the barriers between our buddha-natures.

I know you love me, but in a way that you may not understand. When our spiritual rebirth is accomplished and we are both awake in that highest spiritual plane, nothing will change, but the hurting will stop.

~ 424 ~

My writing is getting more picturesque and pointed as my soul seeks to resonate with yours at a deeper level. I write to you in metaphors because what I have to say cannot be conveyed by the literal meaning of words, only in word-pictures, poetry of sorts, words used as art, that reach beyond words, beyond thought. I am not trying to impress you with my intellect or artfulness. I am not trying to impress you at all. I am trying to reach your soul.

I see that my travails in samsara at this time are the flip side of the miracles and beatific visions that I experienced earlier. I knew all that joy would inevitably be balanced by its equal and opposite evil twin.

~ 425 ~

Love as most people know it in this world of the Self and the Ego is a creature of dependency, a clinging love. It is born of duality, drawing the incomplete self toward that which it lacks. It is a structure built by leaning one element upon another, like a house of cards. As long as the dependency is satisfied, the love remains. But when needs, desires, expectations, and demands are no longer being met, the house of cards collapses and love fades. The rainbow lasts only as long as there is rain.

My love in the Spirit is not of this world and thus is not dependent on anything. Despite all my angst over the distance between us, I have never been angry or disappointed with you, and never can be. There is no standard you must meet, nothing upon which our love depends. The buddha-nature shines through all like a beautiful white light, with or without rain.

The measures of progress along the path to enlightenment are 1) the degree of tension that one feels between the pairs of opposites, between samsara and nirvana, which is greatest in the middle between them, on the Middle Way (when one leans far in one direction or the other, the tug from the opposite side is weak, and thus one feels comfortable in one's delusion); and 2) the degree of spontaneity in practicing the Six Perfections in response to that tension, avoiding pendulum swings from one extreme to the other. There is a seismic shift between engaging one's anger and dispelling it. Similarly, between enjoying happiness and recognizing that happiness is a poison.

Although living the life of Christ takes place in discrete events over time, and the enlightenment of the bodhisattva is a progression from the first to the tenth bhūmi, I realize that time is an illusion. These events and stages can happen out of sequence in space-time and instantaneously in eternity. I have already experienced some of the horror of the final passion of Christ even though my "ministry" is only just beginning, and I haven't completed my development in the first bhūmi yet, even though I already exhibit characteristics of the eighth and ninth bhūmi. Past, present, future, all jumbled.

Time can be a cruel thing. The past is gone before you know what happened, and the future sneaks up on you before you can prepare for it. All that matters is Now.

~ 426 ~

Baby Maggie, your mother's granddaughter. Eye contact at dinner. For a long time. Seeing into each other's soul. No one hears me softly chanting to her.

Baby Maggie. During the show, while performers work on stage, I lightly touch the soft pad of her tiny finger as she looks at me over her mother's shoulder. Her finger reaches out to mine. Our fingers gently interlock, first one, then another, then all our fingertips in tender embrace. For a long time. All the while we look into each other's eyes, into each other's soul. No one notices.

The spirits of a thousand generations flow between us through fingers and eyes.

These signs mean nothing to anyone but me. It is as if they happen on another plane of existence, contained within, yet removed from, this world of thoughts and senses. They happen when I am alone, or in a crowd of people who are oblivious to the miracle in their midst. Like the time I was swimming in the ocean and a turtle, my guardian spirit, surfaced and winked at me. A swimmer and a group of children playing just a few feet away did not see the turtle.

While holding Maggie's hand I looked to her mother and aunt sitting nearby, hoping they might see our beautiful communion, but they were absorbed in the show, unaware that a miracle was occurring just inches away.

~ 427 ~

Being a bodhisattva is nothing to brag about – it is not something that comes from virtue, only through grace, and it is as much a curse as a blessing. But when the Pharisees asked Jesus if he was the son of God he said, "You have said it," and "I am." It wasn't a secret.

Our mutual friend Susan said, "You seem to be a person who came into the world to help others." She had seen my bodhisattva nature, and so I confirmed it to her. I also shared with her the story of the sin eater (~12~), and she responded:

Wow, I feel honored that you would share all of this with me. I hope I am worthy of your trust. I know that getting to know you has been a wonderful gift.

[about the sin eater:] This is so dark, and yet you seem such an upbeat and cheerful, life-loving person. Are there really two of you? Or are you just a supremely accomplished actor? I hope you have some people in your life who take care of YOU.

I told her that yes, there are two of me, and yes, there are people who take care of me, and she is one of them.

~ 428 ~

You say you understand me, but do you? You have barely scratched the surface of my nature. You avoid the conversations and experiences with me that would give you a full and true understanding.

You say you love me, but do you? Not in the way that I love you. But what is worse, I have failed to get you to understand how I love you – you don't see the jewel. If you did, you couldn't be so successful in resisting it. But how can I expect you to understand something you do not viscerally feel? How can I hope to succeed in making the invisible visible?

~ 429 ~

It followed from the special theory of relativity that mass and energy are both but different manifestations of the same thing—a somewhat unfamiliar conception for the average mind. – Albert Einstein, in the 1948 film *Atomic Physics*

String Theory – is it physics or philosophy? It cannot be proved, given the ultra-small dimensions of quantum physics.

Multi-dimensional strings form loops like the two-dimensional concentric contour lines on a topographical map representing three-dimensional topography. Quantum mechanics depicts atomic energy as chaotic eruptions, bumps and valleys in Einstein's curved gravitational plane of particulate matter. This is an apt description of what I saw in my 1/1/09 epiphany (~232~), what I called the "dancing molecules."

Each atom has a vibration, frequency, and rhythm: A cesium atom "ticks" once per second with virtually no tolerance for error. Each person has a personal sense of time and moves at a personal rate, but all is just a matter of perception. Einstein showed that motion through space affects passage through time. I remember as a child the euphoria of running at full speed – time seemed to stand still, and my feet barely touched the ground. The matter that composed my body seemed to float upward as if converted to pure energy. I soared above the earth and gazed down upon it.

~ 430 ~

The movie *Amadeus* was on TV tonight. It reminded me that the spirit of God is often contained in a crude vessel, and that beauty is often born through ugliness. Mozart was a common, earthy man, yet art of sublime beauty came through his muck and mire into this world from a place beyond it, clean and pure, as a newborn baby comes through his mother's blood and slime to emerge in this world clean and pure. Like a beautiful flower growing out of mud.

My friend Heinrich was a carpenter who made beautiful wooden artifacts – jewel boxes, picture frames, cabinets, cutting boards, and coasters. He was an old German artisan whose skill produced objects of great beauty. He was also a lover of music; he would attend every concert he could and made special trips to New York and Dresden to hear concerts there. But he was a coarse, guttural man. His hands were permanently stained by the varnishes and oils he used in his work. Two fingers were partly missing from accidents with his saw. He always smelled of turpentine, glue, and perspiration.

My house is now in such disarray that I don't think there is any hope for it. My carpet is so deeply stained that, like Heinrich's hands, no amount of vacuuming or shampooing can clean it. There are piles of paper everywhere – unfinished projects, research, history, evidence of a life lived at full speed, demands being made on me faster than I can satisfy them.

Yet the fruits that fall from my tree, the creations that emerge from my life of clutter and goo, are the clean and pure messages from another world issuing from and through the mess. My music, my writing, my communion with souls – my spiritual work – are the purification and distillation of everything that my messy life is. My creative issue, like Mozart's music and Heinrich's woodwork, arise out of the complexity of life to reveal the simplicity of the spirit. The two sides of dualism. Separation out of unity. Eternity in and out of time.

~ 431 ~

My compassionate breakthrough came a dozen years ago with my friend James. (~110~/~134~) My joy with him came from my realization that I understood him. His behavior was often rude, crude, offensive, and obnoxious, but I understood why, and was not hurt by it. I saw through his façade, I saw behind his shield of intentional grotesqueness to the buddha-nature inside.

You express your fear and hurt in the opposite way, with excessive niceness and showy, superficial kindness, but the egocentric self-protective drive behind your façade is the same.

~ 432 ~

Last night I dreamed that a turtle, caught in the curl of a wave, was washed up onto my torso as I was lying on the beach near the shore break. I wrapped my arms around him. For a while there we were, my guardian spirit and I, eye to eye, cheek to jowl, in close embrace. It felt good.

From dreammoods.com:

> **Turtle** – To see a turtle in your dream symbolizes wisdom, faithfulness, longevity, and loyalty. It also suggests that you need to take it slow in some situation or relationship in your life. With time and patience, you will make steady progress.

I have three animal guardian spirits: the turtle in the sea, the bird in the sky, and the lizard on the land. All three guardians are air breathers, spend at least some of their time walking on the land, and are of ancient reptilian lineage, like the serpents of the kundalini, the Garden of

Eden, Moses' fiery snake on a stick (~561~), the Rod of Asclepius, Hermes' caduceus, and the asp of Egyptian mythology.

~ 433 ~

I am constantly beset by people looking for my help, looking to me to fix things, solve their problems. Yet every little misstep I take, real or imagined, is held up to me. I am expected to set the missteps of others right, but I must not take any missteps of my own. When I do, I get knocked down, and there is rarely anyone to stand me up, dust me off, or offer solace.

In their single-minded worship of the divine Christ, many Christians forget that Jesus was human, too. He was overwhelmed by the entreaties of the throngs who wanted miracles to cure them. In a fit of anger he overturned the tables of the moneychangers at the temple. He was a man of peace, but he was not always peaceful.

Jesus grew weary of the weight he carried, as do I. He begged that it be lifted from him, as do I. He cried out in the pain of isolation and separation from God, as do I. Yet he felt only compassion for those who betrayed, denied, and tortured him, as do I. When will my sacrifice be enough? When will it be time for me to say, "It is finished"?

~ 434 ~

Lou told me about his days in Army boot camp, how he and his buddies learned to scale a six-foot wall on the obstacle course. He was so proud to have accomplished that. I replied, perhaps insensitively, "When you are running for your life and you need that skill the most, it'll be a seven-foot wall."

You tell me, "You really write so beautifully." Yes, I do. I love metaphors and verbal imagery. I know their power to reach beyond the simple meanings of words and touch the soul. I know I have skill with them. I can scale a six-foot wall with them. But they fail me when I need them most, to scale the seven-foot wall around you.

~ 435 ~

THE HOUSE OF ETERNITY, Part 1

The passage of time is like walking through an immense dark house with a candle. We are living the past, which becomes the present as we walk from room to room in the house, illuminating new spaces as we go. The whole house with all its rooms is there all the time; but parts of it are invisible to us until we reach the rooms of the future with our light.

The corollary to this progressive illumination of the future is the progressive darkening of the past. As our light moves into the future, it leaves the past in darkness, as if it had never been. The past recedes into the darkness, into the fullness and emptiness of the Dao, the Eternal Now, the silent invisible foundation of all things, where it joins the silent invisible future that is yet to unfold. Only the present is visible in the light, but past and future are all around.

A bodhisattva carries not just a candle as she moves through the house, but also a brilliant lightning bolt that illuminates the entire house in brief flashes. Flashes of light illuminating eternity. En*light*enment.

~ 436 ~

I dreamt last night: *I was wandering through a forest searching for things. It was a somewhat civilized forest, perhaps a park, as I came upon a conveyor belt with a huge stalk of broccoli on it, big as a log. I picked up the broccoli and began chopping it into pieces. As I chopped, it shrank down to normal size. I looked for a container to put my broccoli pieces in, but none was the right size. I started wandering again, looking for a bag to hold all my stuff. Didn't find any. The dream ended as I walked up a grassy hill out of the woods.*

From dreammoods.com:

Search – To dream that you are searching for something signifies the need to find something that is missing or needed in your life. The dream may be analogous to your search for love, spiritual enlightenment, peace or a solution to a problem.

Conveyer Belt – To see a conveyer belt in your dream suggests that you are stuck in a rut. Your daily routine has become predictable and unchallenging.

Chopping – To dream that you are chopping something indicates that you are trying to cut your problems into smaller, more manageable sizes. You need to break up the issues and attack them piece by piece. Consider also the significance of the object that you are chopping.

Broccoli – To see or eat broccoli in your dream suggests that you are in need of spiritual nourishment.

Forest – To dream that you are in or walking through the forest signifies a transitional phase. Follow your instincts.

Woods – To dream that you are walking through the woods signifies your return to an aspect of yourself that is innocent and spiritual. If you are walking out of the woods, then the dream may be a literal depiction of being "out of the woods" or being in the clear of some situation.

~ 437 ~

THE HOUSE OF ETERNITY, Part 2

As we walk through the House of Eternity with our candle, we discover that most rooms have multiple doorways in and out, like a giant maze. Which way do we turn in our journey from past to future?

Everything that will ever be, already is. The future has already happened in eternity. But as we wander through space-time we can make choices as to which direction we will take, which doorways we will walk through in our House of Eternity. The future can be arrived at by different routes. Some routes are longer or more treacherous or more picturesque than others. How we get to the future in space-time is the exercise of free will. The ultimate goal – our reunion, atonement with God – is predestined, but not every choice we make. But every possible choice we could make is already there for us, real now, in the House of Eternity.

This phenomenon is mirrored in how we get to God, or the Truth. Sometimes it is quick, through revelation or epiphany or direct pointing, a straight line from darkness to light. Other times it is a long arduous journey through religious dogma and years of prayer or meditation, going down blind alleys and dead ends until a path with meaning emerges, something resonates, and the light shines through. Or experiencing pain so great that all logic, reason, and analysis – all thoughts and sensory processes – are blotted out, overridden by elemental life-and-death forces. And sometimes, as in my case, it is all of the above.

What is the grace of God? Why do some people see the light and others not? Is it good karma, a reward for living a good life? Is there an element of quality to the choices we make as we wander through the House? Are some choices better than others? Do we really know what we are doing when we make decisions, or are our choices just freak accidents or semi-conscious knee-jerk reactions?

For myself, I know only that I follow my bliss, riding the wave of spiritual forces, going where their gravity pulls me. In the House of Eternity, I do not choose a doorway; I am swept through it. I know that I have done nothing to earn spiritual elevation. I am not a better person than anyone else. Why then, have I been graced to see eternity and cursed to bear the weight of that enlightened knowledge in a dark world of ignorance?

~ 438 ~

In the later stages of *dhyana* (meditation), it is said that the meditator can go without food and water for days without ill effect, and that breathing and pulse may stop for a while. My pulse is slower than sixty beats per minute, and I often stop breathing in meditation. My metabolism is so slow that I cannot eat even one full meal a day without gaining weight. I have mentioned this phenomenon before; it began years ago, and it is getting worse (or better, depending on how you look at it). My body seems to be in hibernation or in a cocoon, conserving its resources, remaking itself, as if preparing a grand metamorphosis.

~ 439 ~

I am staying at a luxury hotel. It's a fabulous place – too fabulous. Too much opulence, over-manicured lawn, overproduced ambience, manufactured comfort. Beauty becomes ordinary and invisible when there is no contrast. Serenity is not created by intention; it is the unintentional byproduct of natural harmony. Wildflowers are as beautiful as cultured orchids. A stream that finds its own path is as peaceful as one that flows along a course of human design. Bird feathers and grass make as soft and warm a bed as velvet and silk. A lavishly decorated chair does no better than a rough-hewn one at providing a place to sit.

~ 440 ~

As always, you give me much to think about when we talk. Although four years or so of our working and loving together seems like a short time, to me it is both a blink of an eye and forever.

You are a strange combination of self-love and self-loathing. You need to be glorified, so that you will feel worthy. You need to be seen doing good works, so that people will assuage your guilt with their praise. No matter how many hugs you give and receive, it is never enough.

Nevertheless, I do not seek to change you. You are perfect as is. There is no wrong between us. Even things that hurt are right, jerking us back onto the karmic path. There is nothing you can do or not do to change my eternally abiding love for you – that, too, is perfect.

~ 441 ~

THE HOUSE OF ETERNITY, Part 3

The razor's edge, the knife-edge ridge, the Middle Way. Veer off the ridge to one side, seeking pleasure, and you take the first poison. Veer off to the other side, avoiding pain, and you take the second poison. Choosing to not walk the ridgeline at all, to get off the wheel of life and avoid situations that present poisonous temptations, is taking the third poison.

Another insight into the House of Eternity: The future is the past. The future meets the past on the back porch of the House, which we discover is also the front porch, connecting the opposite ends of the thread, and we and our candle find ourselves traversing the same rooms again. We relive the past, reinvent the wheel, relearn the lessons of history, repeatedly retrace our steps. We keep going forward but never get anywhere. That's why history repeats itself; why art, religion, and philosophy change in style from one century to the next but are never improved. Time is a straight line, and also a closed circle.

Civilizations rise and fall, ever greater feats of technology are achieved, but human nature never changes. Many roads are traveled, but they don't go anywhere. The choices we make in life can change our route to the future, making our karma better or worse, taking us more or less time to get to the end of existence, but by any route we get to the same place in the end, which is the same place we started. The Dao is the beginning and the end, the Alpha and the Omega.

I have lived long enough now to have seen several complete cycles of birth, innocence, growth, learning, light, success, fatigue, decay, corruption, darkness, atrophy, death – and then sometimes a new burst of energy leading to another round of rising and falling. With each generation comes a rebirth, a reset, a new beginning to the cycle.

~ 442 ~

Bringing love to people in pain is very difficult. The sufferer's defenses against further hurt are obstacles to love. Like the salmon's epic swim upstream, hurdling dams and rapids and fighting against an unremitting current, the journey into the heart of a sufferer is arduous, requiring strength, persistence, and a willingness to endure many wounds along the way. As the sufferer becomes invulnerable inside an impenetrable defensive fortress, the messenger of love must become ever more vulnerable and defenseless, even unto death.

When the salmon's swim is over, his last act is to reproduce, to make new life in his dying moments. When our love swims against the current of fear, breaks through the barriers and finds its object in another's soul, we make life anew. We are living the life of Christ, all the way from the mouth of the river to the source, the place of new life, eternal life.

My life is crumbling around me, my old life dissolving, peeling off like the shedding of old skin. I am standing outside myself, watching the process. But where is my new life, my new skin? Like a skinless snake or a butterfly freshly released from its cocoon, like a salmon at the end of a long swim, I am weak and vulnerable.

I was having a down day, running into roadblocks on every path I trod. I decided to go out to my sacred place by the ocean and watch the waves. It was good, reminded me that my problems are not large, that my old life was meant to go away, and that whatever my new life is, it will be right.

~ 443 ~

Had a lovely evening with our friend and business partner Joe and his girlfriend. We went to a concert and had an in-depth conversation over dinner. I described the phases of my life to them – I'm entering the fourth phase now. I described the phases as: 1) *Scientist* - birth through high school; 2) *Artist* - college to Lou's death; 3) *Philosopher* - Lou's death to now; and 4) … Joe's girlfriend interjected "*Teacher!*" I might have said *Servant* (that's what a bodhisattva is), but perhaps she was right. A bodhisattva is a kind of teacher, too. What I am trying to do now with my music, my money, my writing, and my spirit is to teach others, reach others, with the lessons my life has taught me.

> A true spiritual teacher does not have anything to teach in the conventional sense of the word, does not have anything to give or add to you, such as new information, beliefs, or rules of conduct. The only function of such a teacher is to help you remove that which separates you from the truth … The words are no more than signposts. – Eckhart Tolle, *Stillness Speaks*

This journal is full of signposts pointing to … what? … where? To the Way that is indefinable and unnamable, to the Truth that is always paradoxical, to the Life which is ephemeral, untouchable, eternal.

~ 444 ~

SEX, Part 16

Spiritual love overrides every rule, every law of God and Man, of body and mind. It rewrites the Bible, the sutras, all dogma and doctrine, every book of Holy Scripture. It replaces all the words and symbols in these books with the very thing that those words and symbols represent.

When Lou and I first met he thought he was impotent. Sex with his first wife had become so corrupted that his life energy had left him. But as we became close, he found his energy returning. We gradually increased our level of physical intimacy, but we resisted having sex, because of his marriage. After a while I asked him if he had been having sex with his wife, and he said yes, once, "to relieve the tension." But he was ashamed to admit this; it seemed to him and to me that it was somehow wrong for him to have sex with someone other than me, even though she was his wife. I said, "If you are going to have sex, shouldn't it be with me?" At that point we let down the barrier and opened the door to our sex life, which fulfilled every bit of its promise – glorious, spiritually symbolic – eternal love expressed in worldly flesh.

To the outside world it looked like just a typical extramarital affair, but in truth it was the exact opposite. Divine love turns sex into a sacrament. The awakening of our eternal union physically in this world was righteous, ordained by God.

The divine love you and I share is the same as mine with Lou, but adapted to include, not replace, your earthly wife. Both of these conditions – the end of Lou's first marriage and the continuation of yours – reflect the purity and chastity that are absolutes in every spiritual love, but manifesting very differently from one love to another.

~ 445 ~

Thank you so much for calling and texting and spending time with me last week. I am beginning to feel more peaceful about us.

The best part was the warm smile you gave me from the side of the house when I came back from the car. I am trying not to read too much into anything, but I sense that somewhere inside, you want your love to come out. You still don't quite know how to be with me, you are not totally comfortable, but last week I think we made great strides. Our morning coffee, our business discussions, our evening dinners under the stars are beautiful memories that will be with me always.

~ 446 ~

My heart is heavy, my spirit is weak, my mind is filled with fear, my body is weary from fending off panic. Cannot sleep. Is it this time of year, Lou's death day approaching? Or is the Grim Reaper moving ever closer over my shoulder?

When my soul is at peace, my tinnitus, the ringing in my ears, is only a minor annoyance, easily ignored. But when my soul is lost, wandering in the desert, it becomes an incessant screaming in my head from which there is no escape. Panic and madness rush in. I wonder who I am, where I am, why I am, and why I cannot find peace.

The limits of my earthly life will never go away, but what about my psychic suffering? Why can't I find peace within the limits, within my life as it is? I try to remember all that I can still do, the joys that are still available to me, the miracles that brought me here and still guide me. When I find my tether and am able to focus my mind on useful work, I can deflect the sensory stimuli that frighten me and find some relief. But finding that tether and focus is so hard when my claustrophobic psyche is crashing against the walls of its space-time prison.

Unsupported thought is the ultimate liberation. When I am no longer dependent on distractions and deflections, when I no longer need to escape my fears and can be at peace in the midst of them, dropping all defenses, looking unflinchingly at unvarnished reality, I will be free inside my prison, staring down the Grim Reaper.

~ 447 ~

Had lunch today with Tommy, my farmer friend. He is in town for some pre-surgery tests; if all goes well, he will have hip replacement surgery soon. A few years ago, Tommy suffered a broken pelvis with complications in an auto accident. He almost died; he told me that he prayed for death. Last year he had his cancerous bladder removed and since then his pee runs into a bag. Now he is having his hip replaced. For years he has been sick, injured, or disabled, always in some degree of chronic pain and disability. But yet he has stayed engaged in life, working in his backyard garden, teaching sustainable farming techniques to the next generation, collecting recordings and tweaking his six-channel stereo system, through it all remaining upbeat and reasonably cheerful. How does he do it, I wondered.

So I asked him. Tommy answered, "That's why I get involved in all the things I do – to have something to live for – and something to leave behind when I go." Tommy taught me that the key to a positive attitude is to ignore the pain and just keep running, full speed ahead.

~ 448 ~

I went to visit Elaine.

"How's Lou?" she asked.

"Gone," I said. "Dead. Twenty-five years ago."

"John, too?"

"John, too."

"Grandpa and grandma?"

"All gone."

"My brain crazy," she told me a couple visits ago. She cannot think or walk or go to the bathroom by herself, yet she remains cheerful, grateful that she doesn't have to cook or clean or worry about anything. It doesn't matter that it took her five minutes to break into the wet-wipe wrapper. She has all the time in the world. She seems content, not struggling with her disabilities, just accepting whatever comes. There is a blessing, I guess, in the mental fog that she lives in. I suffer because I see things too clearly.

I spent an hour and a half with Elaine in a room full of disabled adults who had to be assisted with moving, eating, wiping their chins, and who could barely express themselves in words or gestures. Except for the size of the residents, this place was indistinguishable from a nursery of two-year-olds. But the experience was not depressing; it actually lifted my spirits. These are people who have nothing to do, nothing really to live for, yet they live apparently contented, in the now, without a care in the world, in a comfortable place with caring people to help them. Their bodies and minds have let go. Elaine and her friends taught me that limits and disability can be lived with. My problems, pains, and limitations are not so huge.

~ 449 ~

Eternity is stillness and emptiness. Time is motion and substance. There is a dimension, a nexus, where time and eternity meet. We do not normally know this place consciously, but we cross that boundary when we fall asleep and when we wake up, when we are born and when we die. These are the only times when we can experience that place naturally, transported by the natural flow of life.

When Lou died I was thrust there while still conscious, unnaturally. The protective psychological veil that was thrown up immediately after his dying breath was not adequate to shield me from the scorching burn as my soul tried to rush off with him into eternity. A body-mind that is alive and meant to be moving in space-time cannot withstand the stillness.

When my life slows down as it has now, when my travel through time begins to stall, I am sent back to that place and I remember the horror of being stretched across the nexus, stuck motionless in the candle flame, twisting and burning. When I am stalled in the flame, my fear burns bright. When my psyche hits this place, I become totally weak, helpless, vulnerable, out of control, like a body without a supporting skeleton, formless jelly tossed aimlessly in formless chaos, my thoughts nothing but scattered white noise, my array of ordered emotions swept away by a single nameless, faceless ocean of fear.

I lose track of the things I am living for, and the death spiral begins. I am stuck in space-time without any relevance in space or time; all of the substance of living is removed and the fear and pain lurking underneath are uncovered, like maggots and beetles under a fallen log.

While in this state I see only the downside of space-time – the limitations of life, the narrow, confining container that my body-mind is, unable to house the wide expanse of my soul. Any illusion that I am making progress toward enlightenment is shattered. (I realize at the same time that "progress" cannot really be made toward enlightenment; by another perspective it just happens in a flash of *satori*.)

The other way to consciously experience the nexus of eternity and space-time is through epiphany, as happened to me on 1/1/09. I try to remember the feeling I had that day, when nothing mattered and the world ran perfectly all by itself. I saw the music, musicians, and their instruments as one field of energy, without substance, and timeless, each moment complete in itself. Nothing was lacking, there were no limitations, all was perfect and natural – and yet I was still inside the same space-time body that so horrifically imprisons me on the other side of the veil.

My panicked state of total helplessness is the very nature of Great Void – empty, without form or substance. That which so frightens me is the very thing I saw in my epiphany that was blissfully transfiguring. I was not in control then, either, and that was fine. As in my floating dream, I was lifted out of reality, and that was fine. While I live I must keep running. When I am ready to "check out of Hotel Earth," as my friend Tommy puts it, I will see the stillness not as a horror, but as peace.

What's the difference? Why fear, chaos, and insanity in one context, and peace, order, and awakening in the other? Simone Weil said, "We only escape limitation by rising up toward unity or going down toward the limitless." Both the rising up and the going down enter a wormhole that goes to the same place. That's what life in time, in duality, is all about.

> In this sense, time functions as a kind of true alchemy—it can dissolve any experience, no matter how permanent it seems as it's happening, and replace it with another. It can turn lead into gold. – David at Raptitude, https://www.raptitude.com

~ 450 ~

MOTHERS-IN-LAW

You once said that you have trouble warming up to your mother-in-law because you don't have anything in common with her. Is the reason for this that you don't have much in common with her daughter, either? To those of us who know you well, the signs of discord are abundant and obvious. You and your wife have many years of shared experiences and bonding as a couple, but your love is not spiritually deep, and so the loving bridge from you to your wife's mother is not made.

There were never a mother-in-law and daughter-in-law with less in common than me and Lou's mother. She was two generations older than me, came from a different culture, spoke almost no English, and lived in a world that had almost no intersection with mine. Yet we had one thing very much in common – our love for Lou. Although we had almost no contact with each other, there was a warmth without words between us. At Lou's funeral we sat at the two center ends of the two front pews, together but for the deeply symbolic center aisle between us. At the end of the service I walked over to her, kissed her hand and said, choking back tears, "Thank you for your son." That's the same thing I said to your mother at her grave: "Thank you for your son." This is the loving bridge being made.

~ 451 ~

You are backing away from me again, and now denying that we are karmic lovers. Yet in that denial I hear confirmation. I thought about all the signs too numerous to count, from you and from the spirits, over the last six years clearly defining to me what we are. The implicit signs, the circumstantial evidence of all kinds from every source, all point conclusively in the same direction. Every force in my magical life has told me the unequivocal truth. Why do I question these signs? Why would I give more weight to words from your admittedly hazy perception than to these spiritual messages that come to me with the clarity of a laser? The words from your lips do not illuminate spiritual truth; they obfuscate it.

When I was drinking coffee with you last month at your house I expressed sadness that I have failed to get you to understand how I love you. You said, "But I am learning more every day." What I learned from our conversation today is that I should trust the spirits and have confidence in what I know to be true.

~ 452 ~

During your TV promo taping, the producer kept trying to get you to smile. A genuine smile is hard for you; your mouth smiles, but your eyes don't. Because I know you so well, I understand the reasons for this, the layers of sadness that weigh down your eyes.

I recall two times when I saw the weight lifted, when joy emerged from behind the dark cloud on your face. The first was in June at my house, when your countenance rejoiced at the idea of my living with you. (~388~) The second was at your house last month. (~445~) Yesterday I asked you why you ran away from me that day. You said that you weren't running away, just going about your routine tasks. Well … maybe … but I saw something different happening. Here is my view of the event:

Everyone else had left to run errands. You and I were alone in the house. You said you were going to take a shower, but then you didn't; you went outside and puttered around in the yard. I went out to my car to get a jacket. As I came back toward the house, you appeared beside the garage looking at me with that rarest of smiles – warm, impish, joyous. We met in the driveway as I was rummaging through a pocket of the jacket. As we stood together your voice took on a beautiful softness; your body relaxed into a calm and gentle posture as you leaned toward me. I remember thinking to myself that this was the warm, tender intimacy we have shared in my dreams, that we were meant to have. It was a wonderful moment of spiritual connection. I opened the door to go inside the house, and you were following me to the doorstep, but then you turned around, looked down to the ground, and awkwardly said something like, "I'll go in the other way." But you didn't go in; you walked to the post office to get the mail. What I think you were running from was the temptation to continue that beautiful intimacy inside the house, perhaps to a degree that would be improper.

This is what I saw.

~ 453 ~

I do not value my life. My physical existence is but a passing mist, quickly lost in the immense universal ether. My life is not about me; it is not mine. I exist to serve others, as my bodhisattva mission directs. I have always had faith that my life will end one way or another at the appropriate time, when my work is done. It's not important that I know the state of my health. It doesn't matter if I am harboring a terminal illness that kills me or if I am hit by a truck crossing the street. I am ready to die, but I want to die for the right reason: in peace because my life's work is truly completed, not in panic because I am desperate to escape my existential anguish.

My spiritual connections – the miracles and signs that guide every step I take – have allowed me to experience the extremes of samsara and nirvana, and thus to know the fundamental nature of my suffering. But no one else understands this, despite my best efforts to explain it. This is why I say that I am profoundly alone. This is not loneliness in the sense we usually mean it. I have friends who care for me and support me, but in this deepest realm on the edge of life and death, no one can help me. This spiritual journey must be taken alone.

~ 454 ~

All the myriad signs that come to me from the spirits, from your departed loved ones and mine, tell me that our love is a gift from them, a continuation of their love for us in this world. Lou sent you to me, and your ancestors sent me to you, to build a bridge of love connecting us to them, so that our grief over losing them could be overcome. Our love is sacred.

You are a bundle of contradictions. You deny sexual feelings to my face, but you continue to send signals that say the opposite. You played your provocative sexy song for me alone in the privacy of your hotel room. You later denied that it meant anything, but I think it did – in your impish way you were making love to me. When we play our song together – a gift directly from your mother that connects us to your ancestors of generations past – we are making love.

Your suggestion that I move to your town has been on my mind lately. Were you serious? I was shocked when you first mentioned it, and it still stands out as a most unusual thing to suggest to anyone but a karmic soulmate. Yet it is rare for me to get an invitation to your house for even a day or two, even when we have business to discuss. You keep me, someone you claim to love, at a greater physical distance than casual friends who stay at your house for weeks at a time. You complain about hosting these visitors who disrupt your daily routine, but for some reason you can't say no to them. And for some reason you can't say yes to me, your karmic love, who is meant to meld into your daily routine. You love me, but it seems you don't like me very much.

When your potentially life-threatening illness struck, you were confronted with the gravest spiritual challenge life can pose. Then your mother got sick and died. Within a few years you lost your health and the person upon whom you were most emotionally dependent. Samsara looked you in the eye and became personal. As I did when Lou died, you locked up your most painful and fearful feelings in a bunker where they wouldn't be able to haunt you or hurt you. Life went on in relative peace and calm, as long as you didn't look at those painful feelings. But eventually those repressed and denied emotions escaped the bunker and seeped back into your consciousness. The old fears and panic returned, reminding you that they are not gone, just submerged until a trigger – a sight, sound, smell, memory, or provocative event – conjures them back up again.

The only buffer against these attacks is an equally potent dose of the opposite force – the power of love, the love that is God, the most powerful force there is, a gift from our loving guiding spirits, the shining, shimmering balance to the horror of the dark side. All you have to do to achieve that balance is get out of the way and let yourself *feel*. Open the floodgates and let the healing water of the Spirit flow into the Self. Let my love flow in, let your love radiate out.

Opening yourself to our love doesn't necessarily mean doing anything different, seeing more of each other, working together more, or changing lifestyle (although such changes could eventually emerge). It doesn't mean acting on feelings of love in ways that would be improper. What it does mean is that when we do see each other, there will be joy, not tension, between us. Grief and sorrow over past losses and present limitations will lose their sting. Anger will melt away. Conversation will come easily, and no subjects will be off limits. We will be free to be ourselves, no holding back, vulnerabilities safely exposed, defensive shields down, no fear. No disappointments, no expectations, no sins, no blemishes. The dark cloud will be lifted from your face and the joyful smile will emerge, and the joy and the smile will remain even after we part company. We will both have more courage, compassion, tolerance, faith, hope, and happiness in all the spheres of our lives.

I am aware that this opening up may not be possible for you. You may not be able to make such a dramatic shift in your way of thinking, your way of relating to life and the world. Breaking old habits is hard. It could be that opening the door to let in the love would also let in the fear. That's always a risk.

You are so afraid to give this love legs. I don't blame you. It's a fearsome thing. I fully realize that we are playing with fire, with the farthest extremes of darkness and light, which is why I have held back sharing with you at this depth. Perhaps it is enough for you to know that such a powerful eternal love exists and be comforted by that knowledge, even if it cannot find expression in this life. But the miracles and signs that led me to you and keep me close are happening in this life, now, and tell me that you are meant to know this love, given to us by the grace of God, to bring peace and joy and meaning to our lives. It's good karma, the best kind.

~ 455 ~

Your ego is a sponge that can never be saturated. Your surface persona is shallow, greedy, selfish, hedonistic, full of socially unacceptable attributes. You have virtues as well, but I see past all this, beyond vice and virtue, to your buddha-nature, and that is why I say that there is no wrong between us. Those things that society would call wrong in your behavior are not wrong in my eyes, not because I don't see them or because they don't hurt, but because they just don't matter. I look at you through a different lens.

My life, the life that was mine, ended when Lou died. The life I am living now is yours, given to you to help you find your deeper spiritual self and make peace with it. But you are rejecting the gift. Your reeled me in after I took your bait, but now you are throwing me back. You leave me alone, stranded, wedged between two worlds, twisting on a string. You use my attributes of music, money, and heart when it suits you, when it brings you pleasure and not pain, all the while remaining impervious to my anguish. Is this love? Feels more like abuse. And yet … I understand.

~ 456 ~

When I talk about visions, dreams, miracles, and spiritual messages, I'm not talking about flights of fancy, vague impressions that could be interpreted many ways, creative concoctions of a fertile imagination, or fantasies about what I wish were true. The visions, intuition, knowledge, and direction that come to me from the spirit world are as true and real as anything in this material world. They reveal in this world the ultimate truth of the Dao, the spaceless, timeless emptiness of eternity. I have seen the House of Eternity with the floodlights on.

~ 457 ~

Joe has come into my life, our life, as a guardian angel. He reminds me of the old fisherman by the sea, who at the beginning of our relationship, as I was searching for direction, mysteriously appeared one evening to welcome me to my sacred place by the ocean, and whom I never saw again. (~306~) It seems that whenever I am lost in fear and struggling to find my path, an angel arises to clear the way and nudge me back on course.

~ 458 ~

I had another provocative dream last night. *I was climbing up a sheer vertical rock face, almost smooth, without many hand or foot holds. I was near the top, looking for another place to grab to pull myself up. I realized that there were no more holds except at the very top of the cliff, just beyond my reach, and it would be necessary for me to throw my leg up over my head, like a high jumper, to propel myself to the top. There was no way to go down to a safer ledge below; the only way was up. I never saw myself actually execute this maneuver, but in the next scene I was at the top. Then I saw a girl also scaling the rock and reaching the summit. But then she went back down. I didn't know if she climbed down, fell, or intentionally jumped off.*

From dreammoods.com:

> **Cliff** – To dream that you are standing at the edge of a cliff indicates that you have reached an increased level of understanding, new awareness, and a fresh point of view. You have reached a critical point in your life and cannot risk losing control. Alternatively, it suggests that you are pondering a life-altering decision. To dream that you or someone falls off a cliff suggests that you are going through a difficult time and are afraid of what is ahead for you. You fear that you may not be up for the challenge or that you cannot meet the expectations of others. To dream that you are climbing to the top of a cliff symbolizes your ambition and drive.

> **Climb** – To dream that you are climbing up something (ladder, rope, etc.) signifies that you are trying to or you have overcome a great struggle. It also suggests that your goals are finally within reach.

> **Rock Climbing** – To dream that you are rock climbing symbolizes your struggle, determination and ambition. You are not any letting obstacles get in the way of your goal. Additionally, the dream indicates that you have an edge over others.

I pay attention to dreams because they are one of the most powerful ways I receive spiritual messages, my bodhisattva dream (~256~) being the prime example. In the moments between sleeping and waking when most dreams occur, a meeting of souls can take place in the universal subconscious. It is very close to a state of hypnosis. The Ego gets out of the way and the Spirit can speak directly to the Self.

~ 459 ~

As a child I wondered if I was the second coming of Christ.[ii] Even then I felt a strong spiritual pull, the presence of the divine in me. In high school I found my love of nature, as I wept at the beauty of waves of dying grass in an empty neighborhood lot in the late autumn chill. Soon thereafter I received my calling to a career in music. (~340~) Then came the sequence of events that led to music school, getting a job that brought me to my new home, leading to Lou, love, loss, fear, surrender, and rebirth. My spiritual experiences of recent years have shown me how these threads are connected, and I realize in retrospect that the spirits have been talking to me for a long time.

~ 460 ~

You asked me for help finding a regression hypnotherapist, so I decided to try one out. While waiting for my first appointment with hypnotherapist Emily, I was sitting at a table in a public courtyard, minding my own business, reading my book. Out of nowhere a young Korean man, a college student, came up to me. There were a dozen other people at other tables nearby, but he approached only me.

"Excuse me," he said, *"May I ask you some questions for a class assignment? Only three questions."*

"Okay."

"What would you do if you had a million dollars?"

"Give it away. What else is there to do?"

"What would you do if you were president of the United States?"

"Resign. If I thought there was some way to do good for the world in that position, I might stick with it, but there's no real power. It's all illusion."

[ii] Buddhists also have a "second coming" doctrine: About 5,000 years after Gautama Buddha's life, the world will have descended into depravity, and the dharma, the teachings of the Buddha, will have been lost. Then the Buddha will return as a man named Maitreya to bring back the dharma.

"What would you do if you could go back in time?"

"You know something about the Dao, the oneness of all things?" He looked at me with a blank stare. "All roads lead back to the same source. If I could go back in time, I would do the same things again, and I would be doing exactly what I am doing now."

I felt as if I had just taken my final bodhisattva oral exam. The answers came quickly and easily to me, without thinking, as they should for someone deeply in the spirit. The young man and I thanked each other, and he disappeared as suddenly as he had appeared.

Needless to say, the hypnotherapy session that followed was a bit anticlimactic.

~ 461 ~

I have been troubled by the anger and anxiety that I sensed in you yesterday. Our love is meant to be an oasis, a place of refuge, from those emotions. I hoped to be your way out of pain, not a provoker of it.

When it comes to business, I'm very by the book, but when it comes to my personal relationship with you, there is no book. There is only love. Everything that seems complicated becomes simple. Every part of my life with you comes from that simple place.

~ 462 ~

Weird dream last night: *You put on a jacket and said, "I'm going to the store." I said, "Could I come, too?" I put on my jacket and we headed out. We found ourselves outside a grocery store on a dark, rainy night. But then you disappeared. I tried to call you on my cell phone, but I couldn't get through. I looked around for you. Then I looked down at the phone and realized it wasn't my phone, but someone else's. Then I noticed that my wallet was gone. I've been robbed. Oh damn, I'll have to cancel all those credit cards. I woke up.*

From dreammoods.com:

> **Coat** – To see or wear a coat in your dream symbolizes your protectiveness and defensive persona. You may be isolating yourself.

> **Store** – To see or be in a grocery or convenience store in your dream suggests that you are emotionally and mentally strained. Alternatively, the dream means that you are brainstorming for some new ideas or looking at the various choices out there for you.

Rain – To see and hear rain falling symbolizes forgiveness and grace. Falling rain is also a metaphor for tears, crying and sadness.

Night – To have a dream that takes place at night represents some major setbacks and obstacles in achieving your goals. You are being faced with an issue that is not so clear cut. Alternatively, night may be synonymous with death, rebirth, reflection, and new beginnings.

Cell Phone – To see or use a cell phone in your dream indicates that you are being receptive to new information. It also represents your mobility. Alternatively, the dream signifies lack of understanding. Perhaps you are having difficulties getting through to someone. To dream that you lost your cell phone represents a lack of communication.

Robbery – To dream that you have been robbed indicates that you are experiencing an identity crisis or are suffering from some sort of loss in your life.

All of the symbols in this dream interpretation seem to fit. Your jacket is your protective, defensive, isolating shield. We are at the store looking for new ideas, new choices, but you stop looking and disappear. The rainy night represents forgiveness and grace, but also sadness that no way around the obstacles is apparent. The cell phone snafu reflects our poor communication, and the missing wallet predicts an imminent crisis or loss.

This is an ominous dream. I know that our relationship is in trouble, but I take heart from the potential for a positive new beginning arising from our dark night of the soul.

~ 463 ~

You talk a good story about love, forgiveness, letting go, getting out of the way, but you don't live these principles. They are theoretical concepts for you, and you understand them intellectually, but you don't feel them; they don't emanate spontaneously from your inner being as a reflection of your realized buddha-nature. You openly admitted that your life is governed by fear, which I see expressed as selfishness, anger, and the need to control.

You try to superimpose love from outside onto your troubled self, to graft the light of love onto a tree that remains in darkness. My love is an expression from deep inside a tree that glows with its own inner light.

Anita Moorjani's book, *Dying To Be Me*, contains a wonderful description of this phenomenon:

> When we know that we *are* love, we don't need to work at *being* loving toward others. Instead, we just have to be true to ourselves, and we become instruments of loving energy, which touches everyone we come into contact with. When we are each aware of our own magnificence, we don't feel the need to control others, and we won't allow ourselves to be controlled. When I awoke

into my infinite self, I was amazed to understand that my life could be dramatically different just by realizing that I *am* love, and I always have been. I don't have to do anything to deserve it. Understanding this means that I'm working with life-force energy, whereas *performing* at being loving is working against it.[14]

I *live* love; you *perform* it.

~ 464 ~

APOLOGY AND FORGIVENESS, Part 1

I heard you speak today at a forum on the topic of forgiveness. At one point you asked us to think about an incident when we had hurt someone, and then to ask the person we hurt to forgive us. I am all for forgiveness, and I have freely forgiven others many times. But I was having a hard time today thinking of anything specific I had done that I should seek forgiveness for. Seeking forgiveness is genuine only when one genuinely believes that a wrong was committed, leading to a genuine change in behavior going forward.

Yes, occasionally my words or deeds may have hurt someone, but my actions may not necessarily have been wrong. Would I have done the same thing over again if I had known for sure that there would be hurt? In most cases, probably yes. Like tough love. Or like a doctor prescribing a treatment that seems more painful than the disease being treated. Sometimes compassionate hurting is part of compassionate helping, like psychotherapy. (The person doing the hurting is not the therapist; it's the patient hurting, and helping, himself.)

Often the truth hurts, but not as much in the end as ignorance, repression, and denial. People confronted with the painful truth often shoot the messenger; I've been shot many times. But I understand the pain that motivates the shooter, and I never even consider that there is anything to forgive.

You and I have hurt each other in this way, yet I still and always maintain that there is no wrong between us – between karmic lovers who connect directly at the spirit level. I thank you for those things you do that hurt me. I learn from them, about you and about me. There is truly nothing to forgive. I love your humor, but I love even more being with you when you are not fun, when you show me your pain, because at those times I learn how to help you. Anita Moorjani says, "As I look back on the trajectory of my life, it's crystal clear that every step along my path – both before and after my near-death experience, both those events I saw as positive and those I perceived as negative – has ultimately been to my benefit and guided me to where I am today."

It was pointed out by several speakers at the forum today that forgiveness must come from inside ourselves, offered voluntarily by us, not demanded from us by other people on the outside: "You should forgive so-and-so." Just as forgiveness happens inside us, so the perception of wrong being done comes from within us. The allegedly wrong act is only wrong or hurtful if we take it that way. Thus, the perceived "wrong" may be created as much by the victim as by the perpetrator.

Sometimes offenses are so egregious that there is little room for any interpretation but wrongdoing – genocide, for instance, or slavery. But even if someone's actions do produce in us morally righteous anger or hurt, give the emotions their due and then let them go. Anita says, "Living in the present means not carrying any emotional baggage from one segment of time into the next. Every instant is unique and can't be replicated." Don't hang on to past hurts. Let each instant begin pure and clean.

She also says, "If and when I notice negative thoughts creeping in, it seems best to allow them to pass through with acceptance and without judgment. When I try to suppress or force myself to change my feelings, the more I push them away, the more they push back. I just allow it all to flow through me, without judgment, and I find that the thoughts and emotions will pass. As a result, the right path for me unfolds in a totally natural way, letting me be who I truly am."

C.S. Lewis similarly advised a pregnant friend concerning negative thoughts, "As to wishing [the pregnancy] had not happened, one can't help momentary wishes: guilt begins only when one embraces them. You can't help their knocking at the door, but one mustn't ask them in to lunch. And no doubt you have many feelings on the other side."

You have all the pieces to the puzzle, but they are lying loose on the floor. You understand intellectually the concepts of forgiveness, caring, compassion, empathy, and love, but you have yet to put the pieces together in your own life. When you do, your spirit will shine, and you will find ways to express the eternal love that I know is inside you. All the signs and miracles of my life tell me that the reason I am alive on this earth is to help you put the puzzle together.

~ 465 ~

I finally understand the perplexing jumble of contradictions in your behavior. You are actually two different people, Dr. Jekyll and Mr. Hyde, a microcosm of dualism within your own self. Dr. Jekyll, your "good" side, is the one who loves me; sings songs about letting go, imagining peace, and treasuring loved ones; gives lovely speeches about compassion and forgiveness; shows kindness and respect; and acknowledges feelings.

Mr. Hyde, your "evil" side, is the one who uses and abuses me; seeks to control and dominate situations and people; angers quickly; snaps and snarls at those who love him; disrespects those most deserving of respect; and falls victim to greed, selfishness, and fear, trying all the while to repress those feelings.

Dr. Jekyll has visionary dreams of peace, harmony, and love; Mr. Hyde turns those dreams into tools to serve his greed and fear. Dr. Jekyll asks us in the spirit of love to seek forgiveness from those we have hurt, and then Mr. Hyde goes out and does hurtful things that are almost unforgivable. We have been seeing a lot of Mr. Hyde lately.

~ 466 ~

Your wife said to me, "Thank you for loving him." It must be the rarest thing in the world for a wife to say this to her husband's karmic lover. Testament to the awesome gift that is our rarest and most miraculous *ménage á trois*.

~ 467 ~

I had a lovely lunch today with Lou's younger brother. He said that as a young man Lou had a quick temper and angered easily. I never saw that. Divine love washes away anger.

PART 20
Loss Again
August 2012 – November 2012

~ 468 ~

Our best performance ever of our song. Then after the concert, in your hotel room with me, Joe, and your wife, your worst display of angry, cynical, drunken misbehavior I have ever witnessed. Just a few days ago you expressed a refreshing openness and willingness to explore sensitive matters in some depth. But tonight, for the first time ever, you left the company of your best friends in a sullen mood, without the customary parting hugs. Nobody provoked you. Something in you just snapped. How did the pendulum swing so far from one extreme to the other in just a few hours?

~ 469 ~

I went back to the park this morning to explore a new trail. Near the end of my journey I came upon a clearing with a nice view of the city. As I turned to walk down the path, a small bird landed on a tree branch barely five feet away from me. He showed no fear of me, even when I raised my camera to take a picture and spoke to him. "Talk to me, spirit bird," I said. "Are you a young bird, still missing your adult plumage and not yet aware that you should be afraid of people? Or are you an old bird about to die, losing your feathers and wasting away, with nothing to fear anymore from people?" We stood quietly together in communion, motionless, for a long while, about five minutes or so. Then he flew off.

~ 470 ~

Finally you respond: "Thank you for your love. I'm in the garage licking my wounds."

I express my indestructible, unconditional, compassionate love to you, and you run from it. I show you a vision of a beautiful place where peace and joy prevail, and you look away. I direct all of my resources of money, time, and skill to your service, and you disparage the gift. I present to you the medicine to cure your malaise, and you reject it.

How is it that you can be a participant in the greatest love it is possible to have and not be in a constant state of joy? How is it that you have instead sunk into the opposite state? You are now inflicting the severest cruelty on the people who love you the most – me, Joe, and your wife. Why do you punish the people who help you? Why are you not grateful, rather than brutal? I'm not looking for appreciation or even acknowledgment; my love goes on just the same without it. I am looking for understanding, a way to make sense of this baffling turn of events.

~ 471 ~

As you drift farther and farther away from me, I feel a strange new emptiness. It is like the veil that came over me when Lou died, shielding me from the psychic horror that I could not handle. But this time there is a peace about it, an emotional detachment. It is as if you are dying, almost dead, and I am dying with you, satisfied that I have done all I can do, ready to leave this veil of tears and move on to my next assignment, as C.S. Lewis wrote in *A Grief Observed*: "It was as if God said, 'This has reached its proper perfection. ... Good; you have mastered that exercise. I am very pleased with it. And now you are ready to go on to the next.'"

Except that we have not reached our proper perfection. For this to be the end of our journey together would seem to be failure – mission *not* accomplished. Peace, but with a tinge of melancholy. There must be more to us than we have experienced so far. I continue to watch and wait, keeping vigil.

~ 472 ~

It is often my job to tell people things they don't want to hear. All my life I have found myself in roles that make it my duty to take difficult stands. It is not that I choose these roles; they seem to be inevitabilities along the spiritual road that has been presented to me. I do not relish giving people bad or uncomfortable news, quite the opposite, but sometimes it comes with the territory.

As a social justice activist, I have often had to tell people things they didn't want to hear about human rights, ethics, and fairness. I speak truth to power, and I have paid a high price on several occasions, enduring harassment, rejection, threats, and intimidation. But these attacks have been balanced by the gratitude and respect that I have received from those I serve, and by the knowledge that what I did was right. There is a saying about comforting the afflicted and afflicting the comfortable. I have done both, sometimes in the same act.

As a manager it has been my job to learn about laws and regulations regarding contracts, taxes, employment, accounting, and general business practices, and to inform the leadership of my organizations when they are in danger of violating these rules – often information they don't want to hear. But even when they feel hamstrung or thwarted (usually only temporarily) by the limiter the law puts on them, they are grateful for my warnings and sleep better knowing that they and the organization will not be in trouble as a result of their actions.

And finally, as a spiritual caretaker – the most important role I play – I cannot look away from actions that reflect bad karma. The Three Poisons – described in various ways such as greed/anger/ignorance or desire/aversion/delusion – cry out to me for an antidote. I cannot feel your pain and not seek to address it. That is why I tell you things you don't want to hear. Not to hurt you or punish you or judge you, but to love you.

Think of me in the same light as the doctor who told you that you were sick. The doctor did not want you to be sick and took no joy in giving you the bad news. He was simply in a job that required him to sometimes tell people things they don't want to hear. And in giving you that news, informing you about your condition, he set the stage for treatment and a possible cure. Anger at the doctor would be misplaced; the disease was not his fault, and he provided unwelcome information with Right Intention, to be helpful. Gratitude for the doctor's knowledge and honesty, which illuminated the facts and moved toward a resolution, would be a more appropriate response.

Don't kill the messenger, kiss the messenger!

~ 473 ~

My friend relayed to me a comment made by his companion at last night's concert: "That lady [me] is a stitch!" she said.

"How do you know?" he asked.

"Just watch her. She's funny!"

I have never thought of myself as "funny." Because of my serious work and my spiritual struggle, I have viewed myself as a pretty sober, even somber, person. But at that moment I realized that I have maintained a pretty good sense of humor through it all, and it shows.

I also realized that your complaints about my angst and your rejection of my love have contributed mightily to my increasing sadness of recent months. And then I further realized that you, not me, are the somber one. You project yourself onto me. It is *your* angst that you see reflected in me.

You have a sense of humor, too, but it seems contrived and easily turns from witty and playful to sarcastic and mean. Your humor is a façade, coming from a dark place to hide your sadness. My humor is genuine, coming from an inner light that breaks through my sadness.

~ 474 ~

Tonight I attended a service at the Anglican church. While there, I stumbled upon this, a burial rite from *The Book of Common Prayer*:

> Into thy hands, O Lord, we commend thy servant, our dear brother, as into the hands of a faithful Creator and most merciful Savior, beseeching thee that he may be precious in thy sight. Wash him, we pray thee, in the blood of that immaculate Lamb that was slain to take away the sins of the world; that, whatsoever defilements he may have contracted in the midst of this earthly life being purged and done away, he may be presented pure and without spot before thee; through the merits of Jesus Christ thine only Son our Lord.

The Buddhists also have a doctrine of merits. Building merit is accomplished by performing good deeds. Merits accumulated in this life can be transferred to one's ancestors, thus helping them achieve retroactive nirvana through a ritual of merit transfer.

> "Subhuti, if a bodhisattva were to give away enough of the seven jewels to fill as many world systems as the grains of sand in the Ganges River, and another bodhisattva attained the forbearance of the selfless nature of all phenomena, the virtue of this bodhisattva would exceed that of the former. Why? Subhuti, this is because bodhisattvas do not accumulate merits." Subhuti said to the Buddha: "World Honored One, how is it that bodhisattvas do not accumulate merits?" "Subhuti, bodhisattvas do not cling to the merits they generate. Therefore I say that they do not accumulate merits." – *Diamond Sutra*

Bodhisattvas do not accumulate merits; nothing clings to their selfless nature. Their merits are instantly and automatically transferred to those they serve. My merits are already yours, as the merits of Jesus Christ have already washed away the defilements of the deceased Anglican. Your sins are washed away in your bodhisattva's sacrificial blood, her sacrificial love.

I am not like the others in your life whom you have used and abused. They get angry, get even, and get out. I will do none of that. The abuse I am taking from you now is necessary for your salvation and my enlightenment. My acceptance of this abuse without anger or protest, my practice of the 3rd Perfection of patience and forbearance, as Christ accepted his mortal suffering, is meant to show you what divine love is and perhaps awaken it in your own heart.

~ 475 ~

ON GREED

Greed is not just wanting stuff. It is a general attitude, a compulsion to draw to oneself anything and everything of perceived value – money, material objects, power, control, support, the skills and labor of other people, compliments and flattery, good health, strength, safety and security, and so on.

Greed is the first poison. It comes from a sense of unworthiness, inadequacy, incompleteness, a feeling that something is missing. Greed, desire, and covetousness are our striving to fill an empty hole, to find the missing piece. Greed leads to the second poison: the fear of not getting what we want or losing it once we have it.

Greed is overcome when you realize that as long as you are in a psychic state of inadequacy you can never be satisfied; there can never be enough, and you are a slave to your desires and fears. You can let go of greed once you know that your worth is not measured in terms of your possessions, intelligence, skills, social status, or physical attributes, and that you are complete and perfect without any of this.

All things are yours once you let go of them. I have money precisely because I don't care about having it. Money is like a wild animal; once you stop trying to catch it and are content without it, it can come to you without your bidding.

I am just a temporary custodian of my possessions. Everything I possess – my money, my car, my house, my physical body – are only on loan to me, to be used as tools for carrying out my sacred mission. They are not mine; they flow through me as my *ki*, life energy, does.

The Buddha articulated the nature of greed very well:

> If one doesn't have desire, then it is perfectly all right to own a house of a thousand stories. If one has desire, then one needs to give up attachment to even a miserable mud hut. If one doesn't

have desire, then it is all right to possess a thousand measures of gold. If one has desire, then one needs to give up one's attachment to even a single copper penny.

From greed comes grief, from greed comes fear; he who is free from greed knows neither grief nor fear.

Jesus described it pretty well, too, in these passages:

No man can serve two masters; for either he will hate the one, and love the other; or he will hold to the one, and despise the other. Ye cannot serve God and mammon. (Matthew 6:24)

If you would be perfect, go, sell what you possess and give to the poor, and you will have treasure in heaven; and come, follow me. ... It is easier for a camel to go through the eye of a needle than for a rich man to enter the Kingdom of God. (Matthew 19:21-24)

So did Wayne Dyer in *The Power of Intention*:

By staying focused on what I intend to create, by believing that the universe is all-providing, and by knowing that I'm worthy of the unlimited beneficence of the Source of being, I just keep attracting prosperity to me. And by being unattached to what shows up, which means that I have no desire for more and more, I'm able to let it go easily.

And Yoda in *Star Wars*:

Fear of loss is a path to the dark side. ... Attachment leads to jealousy, reflective of greed, that is. ... Train yourself to let go of everything you fear to lose.

And finally, Ira Gershwin and DuBose Heyward in *Porgy and Bess*:

I got plenty o' nuttin'
An' nuttin's plenty fo' me.
I got no car, got no mule
I got no misery.

De folks wid plenty o' plenty
Got a lock on de door,
'Fraid somebody's a-goin' to rob 'em
While dey's out a-makin' more.

~ 476 ~

I have failed to express in words the nature of the bodhisattva. You don't get it. But that's okay. You don't need to. While you are contemplating my strange answers to your questions, remember that you don't need to understand them. You don't need to understand a tree, even while it stands before you and states the obvious – that it is a tree. Just be grateful for the shade.

When I acknowledge that I am a bodhisattva, I am not being prideful. Every time I start thinking along the lines of, "Look at me, I'm a bodhisattva!" something happens to cut me down to size. To be a bodhisattva is not an achievement; it is a gift, a burden, and a sacrifice. My life is sacrificed to your service. The proof is in my actions in all areas of your life.

> Beware of false prophets, who come to you in sheep's clothing but inwardly are ravenous wolves. You will know them by their fruits. Are grapes gathered from thorns, or figs from thistles? So, every sound tree bears good fruit, but the bad tree bears evil fruit. A sound tree cannot bear evil fruit, nor can a bad tree bear good fruit. Every tree that does not bear good fruit is cut down and thrown into the fire. Thus you will know them by their fruits. (Matthew 7:15-20 RSV)

I am content to be led by spiritual forces. What serves you serves me. I have no horse in this race. I do not plot the course of our journey; I am but the ferryman who steers our vessel down the river, across the treacherous bar to the Pure Land, holding the rudder, keeping us to the Middle Way and away from the rocky shoals as God's mighty current carries us.

Actions speak louder than words. If you don't believe my words, then judge me, if you must, by my actions. Know me by my fruit.

~ 477 ~

We sort of agreed to disagree on the matter of choices in life. I tend to think that we are both right, but in the end it doesn't matter. It is true that we have choices; it is also true that we do not have choices, or we let others make them for us, or we choose not to choose. Some choices are obvious and easy; others are hard. Some lead down paths we have traveled before; others go into the unknown. I believe that ultimately, no matter which choices we make, including the choice not to choose, we end up in the same place. Some paths may be longer or more painful than others, that's all.

~ 478 ~

I spoke the simple, evident truth. I should be neither shattered nor elated by your response, whatever it may be. I am merely sad, and exhausted. You have become irrational, illogical, defensive, accusatory, delusional, and oblivious to anything outside yourself. You have lost your mind.

My love goes out to you endlessly in all directions, but it doesn't find you. Like a string vibrating without its resonating chamber, or a seed blowing in the wind, seeking but never finding fertile soil. Like a searchlight scanning 360 degrees of darkness but illuminating only empty space, that which it seeks to enlighten somehow always beyond its beam's reach.

~ 479 ~

You are like an air traffic controller. You manage people the way ATCs manage airplanes in flight – each person/plane on its own separate trajectory. Your goal is to keep all the people/planes out of each other's airspace, communicating with each person/plane on a need-to-know basis, only imparting as much information as necessary to keep that person/plane on the course you have set for him/her/it. You see the people around you like airplanes in the air around the airport – as potential threats, forces that, if not kept at a distance, could collide with you and interfere with you. You may occasionally allow another person/plane to approach you to provide an escort, defense, or in-flight refueling, but rarely to share in your mission as a true partner.

I am like the leader of a precision flight team. My goal is to get all the people/planes on my team to line up in perfect formation, all on the same trajectory, in constant communication with all the other people/planes. When we do aerial tricks we may veer onto different paths, but each person/plane has an equal place in the larger design which is in relation to and known by all the other people/planes. I see the people around me as integral parts of my squadron – all working together in mutual support, furthering our shared mission.

You are a one-man show. You perform as a soloist with very little sensitivity to the musicians around you, whom you consider to be mere accompanists at your command, rarely equal partners.

I am a team player. I perform in musical groups in which each player is equal to and answerable to all the others. Team play can be tedious, time-consuming, and messy, but the results are worth the effort. A team is synergistic, greater than the sum of its parts.

As fear overtakes you, you want to take over the machinery of everything around you, as a virus takes over the mechanism of a cell and turns it to its own purposes. This almost always has a deleterious effect on the body. There is a reason why a cell functions the way it does; it is part of a team, each part contributing harmoniously to the life of the entire organism when functioning properly. You override the rules of team play, as a virus overrides the DNA of its host cell. In both organisms and organizations, disease and death are often the result.

~ 480 ~

There is some frail, precious quality in untreated addicts and the mentally ill that seems to give them a special insight into other worlds. This is the quality that often makes them great artists, scientists, philosophers – a special gift they wouldn't have if not for their frailty. Would we have wanted to treat Mahler's manic-depression? Would we have gotten the same magnificent symphonies out of him? Would Billie Holiday's haunting, limpid voice have been the same without heroin? Vincent Van Gogh said, "Sometimes I hate the idea of regaining my health. A grain of madness is the best of art."

Which world is real? The manic phase or the depressed one? The drug-induced hallucination or the less colorful world seen through sober eyes? Is your addiction the vehicle for your genius, or for your destruction? Or both?

~ 481 ~

This evening at rehearsal for the church service on Sunday, my lawyer (who sings in the choir) came up to talk with me. I inquired about his daughter, "How's Katie?"

After a long pause, he said, "Have you heard about the cancer?"

"No." He proceeded to tell me that she was advised to have surgery and she was very frightened. His eyes were sad and his voice quavered; I could tell he was frightened, too. I asked, "Has she gotten a second opinion?"

"No, but two surgeons recommended that she have surgery and a round of radiation."

I said that surgeons often recommend surgery because that's what they do. "Why not get an opinion from someone who isn't a surgeon? It may not change her mind about her planned course of treatment, but she might go forward more calmly knowing that she has explored all the options."

The tension in his face relaxed and he nodded in agreement. "That's a good idea. I will suggest that to her tomorrow." He gave me a big hug and kiss and said, "Thank you so much."

~ 482 ~

There is no dependency at all in my love for you, yet I am totally vulnerable. I come before you spiritually naked and defenseless. My love opens my heart completely. You can hurt me very easily, and have done so many times. You hold my life in your hands, like holding a tiny bird. You are squeezing the life out of me; I feel my eyes bugging out.

You never have and never will hold as much power over anything as you do over me. You hold the power of life or death over me, as Pontius Pilate held it over Jesus. And as Jesus said to Pilate, "You would have no power over me unless it had been given you from above."

Your power, your power to hurt me, is not in providing or depriving me of anything; I don't need anything from you, not in money or music or business or any worldly thing. You hurt me by remaining stuck in a dark place where my love cannot reach you.

Please tell me about the things that anger you, trouble you, worry you, scare you. Helping you with all these things is why I'm not dead yet. Paul Tillich said, "There is no love which does not become help."

~ 483 ~

One may long, as I do, for a gentler flame, a respite, a pause for musing. But perhaps there is no other peace for the artist than what he finds in the heat of combat. "Every wall is a door," Emerson correctly said. Let us not look for the door, and the way out, anywhere but in the wall against which we are living. Instead, let us seek the respite where it is—in the very thick of the battle. – Albert Camus, "The Artist and His Time"

Your wife and Joe are spinning with you in the maelstrom, caught up in the soup of emotions and passions that arose with your meltdown a few months ago. (~468~) They have seen both sides of you, the good and the bad, but they are carried away in opposite directions by opposite drives. Your wife chooses to dwell on the good in you, responding to her love for you, blinded to your bad side by that love, defending you and accepting the pain of your unrepentant abuse because that is the only way she can make a life with you.

Joe chooses to dwell on the bad in you, responding to the abuse that you have inflicted on him, blinded to your good side by the pain of that abuse, criticizing you and recoiling from the pain, recognizing that while you remain in denial and unrepentant he cannot make a life with you.

I am in the middle, between the pairs of opposites, looking compassionately and dispassionately at both sides of you, in my eternal love unmoved by either your vices or your virtues. I am largely removed from the passions and the poisons, from desire for the good and aversion from the bad, looking upon the scene from an eternal perch above the fray. The battle is swirling around me, but I am in touch with your buddha-nature, which is at one with me where there is respite even in the thick of the battle. I calmly see your dual nature as equally balanced, albeit stretched across an unusually wide gulf. You have abused me, but in my practice of the 3rd Perfection, I am not wounded. I have been and will forever make a life with you, an eternal life that remains complete and constant no matter what behaviors you exhibit in this world.

I still have hope that you can change course before hitting rock bottom. You are a man of great extremes. I see it as my role in your life to help you bring those extremes closer together, closer to the Middle Way. I am holding out my hand to you, clearing the path to freedom, offering the precious gift of eternal love. But you must choose to take my hand, walk the path, and accept the gift.

~ 484 ~

I started hyperventilating. I was thinking about you, worrying, feeling the pressure of deadlines and the weight of responsibility. Or maybe it was just too much caffeine from drinking coffee all day. Whatever, I needed to get out of the house and reset my thermostat.

I went to my favorite place by the sea, near the boat harbor. Just a few people were there. I walked the length of the promenade near the ocean and then turned around to return by way of the sheltered harbor. About halfway along the pier, a cat came out of the shadows, striding up to me, looking for attention. This was not a wild feral cat like the ones I usually see on the rocks by the ocean. This cat was fat and friendly, evidently a well-cared-for resident of one of the boats. I sat with the cat for half an hour, stroking his back, neck, belly, head, flanks – whatever part was presented to me. After a while the cat walked toward a boat, mewed at me to follow, and led me home. I looked inside the boat. There was a light on and a bowl of cat food, but no people in sight. The cat jumped into the boat, ate a little bit, and came back out for more petting. The name of the boat was New Leif – "New Love."

I whispered my chant to the cat and the boats and the still water in the harbor. My breathing calmed down. I thanked the cat for giving me the attention I needed tonight, for sitting a dark hour with me. I remembered the wise saying, "Happiness: If you dwell on the past and worry about the future then you will struggle with the present." I realized that I am happy. My life at every moment is fulfilled. I am Love. I am God. I am doing all I can.

~ 485 ~

While you spend your energy in anger and fear and denial, disabling those around you who are trying to help you, seeing only treachery and incompetence in them, I am ever so competently working to enable you, to fund your legacy for years into the future, keeping faith with the task that your ancestors have sent me to do. I am more involved in your life than you are. You run away from your troubled life; I run toward it.

~ 486 ~

When I talk about the miracles in my life, I'm not merely saying, "Oh look, I found a lucky penny!" I'm talking about life-altering signs and portents that come from and lead to places out of this world. When God puts his hand on your shoulder and says, "Go this way," you don't say no.

My time, skills, money, and my love have been poured out for you and will continue to be, without limitation. I don't expect any thanks from you for my sacrificial devotion, although one would think I should be entitled to at least the same modicum of respect that you would give to any bum on the street. But I'm not getting even that. And it's okay.

PART 21

Betrayal

December 2012 – March 2013

~ 487 ~

At our meeting today the dam finally burst, the lid blew off the pressure cooker. We have been having disagreements about the business aspects of our work. Your latent fear angrily burst forth.

You accused me of once going behind your back, but you are oblivious to the many times (I count seven) when you went behind my back. I never brought up those instances, some of which caused problems for the business, but quietly smoothed them over and forgave you for them without your asking, without judgment, anger, or thought of retribution. *This is my practice of the 3rd and 6th Perfections.*

You said, "I don't want to lose control of my work." I assured you that I don't want control; I'm only trying to mindfully steer you away from dangers, trying to help you, enable you, remove obstacles, and protect you in the pursuit of your work. *This is my practice of the 4th and 5th Perfections.*

You asked, "Are you afraid that I might have you fired?" I said that if I am not fulfilling my duties in a competent and honorable manner, then I should quit or be fired. I am doing this job, very competently and honorably, out of love – not for money, title, status, or even gratitude, none of which I need. *This is my practice of the 1st and 2nd Perfections.*

But you refused to hear me and would not be moved. I had to do all the giving while you did all the taking. There was no love, no compassion, no gratitude, and no respect from you. Your façade is now totally torn off. Your anger; irrationality; arrogance; egotism; thirst for control; judging and placing blame; accusations and projections of your negativity, fear, and base motives on everyone but yourself; blindness to the many good works done on your behalf by many fine people around you, and especially to your bodhisattva's huge gifts; revealed so many layers of delusion and bad karma that I hardly know where to begin. How much humiliation and abuse can I allow myself to take? Jesus took quite a bit.

One of our mutual friends described you as a case of arrested development, stuck at a level of immaturity that most people grow out of in their 20s or 30s when they realize that the world does not owe them anything, they are not the center of the universe, and all other people are not theirs to command.

The first thing your mother-in-law said today when she greeted me was, "You're an angel, you know."

~ 488 ~

My friend Ignacio quotes Whitehead's definition of eternity as the "sum of everything, plus one." Where does the "plus one" come from? In my search for the answer, I came upon this:

> The immensity of the here and now, looking backward and forward at once, listening simultaneously to what was behind and what was ahead, and the rustling of the past, sunken into the forgotten invisibility, was rising up again to the present moment and became the simultaneous stream of creation in which the eternal rests. – Hermann Broch, *The Death of Virgil*

Thus, the "plus one" comes from within the whole, the past rising up to the present, eternally compounding, adding one to the future without subtracting anything from the past, all without reducing or increasing the whole. The future falls back and becomes the past. This aligns with the Buddhist emptiness, which contains both sides of duality, all of the infinite pairs of opposites, and the apparent creation of something out of nothing.

Think of eternity as a big globe. All matter, energy, and time – Past, Present, and Future – are contained therein and thereon. Time runs along the surface. As you spin the globe and view each frame along the time continuum through a magnifying glass, the frame you are presently viewing, that has your momentary attention, is the Present. Frames already viewed are the Past, and frames yet to be viewed are the Future. As your consciousness moves from frame to frame sequentially in one direction, Future becomes Present becomes Past. (Can time move in the opposite direction, or skip around in non-sequential frames? Who knows? Does it matter?)

Eventually you completely circle the globe, and what was Past is now again Present. Once again Future becomes Present becomes Past; Past gives way to the Present which moves on to the Future. We are living the past. History repeats itself, except that the new Present may be altered by the effect of the previous temporal go-round. Perhaps in the meantime lava bubbled up from the core of the globe to create a new wrinkle on the space-time surface. This is creativity, the "becoming" of space-time, Whitehead's "plus one," and the acts that are a "contribution to the structure of the world," as described by Robert Goldman in *Einstein's God*:

> Since it is a world of all-moments-being, rather than of each-instant-fleeting, a world in which the acts of daily living are not ephemeral but enduring, the opportunity to make life meaningful is enhanced. Every act performed is a contribution to the structure of the world—a sobering and humbling thought.

Ignacio quoted William Faulkner: "The past is never dead, it's not even past." There we have it – the Eternal Now. Joseph Campbell said that stillness is eternity, movement is space-time. The sutras say that "being" is eternity, "becoming" is space-time. All these descriptions express the same truth.

~ 489 ~

Even while I am exhilarated by my philosophical discourse with Ignacio, I have spent much of today in deep despair over you. All love and compassion have gone out of you, and I feel lost in a desert, not knowing which way to turn. But I remember the incredible timing of the signs, even in this time of darkness: Joe coming into my life to help me see our situation objectively, taking off my love-colored glasses and bringing me down to earthly reality; the movie *Flight* coming out just when I needed a more detailed picture of the addictive syndrome; and our mutual friend Walt becoming my psycho-correspondent, validating me, encouraging me, and helping me understand addiction from his family's personal perspective. The spirits are still with me, sending angels to help me, and they will guide me through this mire as they have before.

~ 490 ~

Today at the Buddhist temple my primary spirit guides were honored – Kannon, also known as Avalokitesvara or Kuan Yin, the bodhisattva of compassion; and Achala, the fiery god of purification and symbol of the eighth bhūmi. Kannon teaches gentle, compassionate, maternal love. Achala teaches firm, wise, paternal love. Together they embody enlightenment.

In consultation with my spiritual guide: *You are doing the right things … people may not confirm this to you, but the Buddha knows … your joy and gratitude in the teaching is known to your ancestors … the Buddha also feels your joy … remain steadfast in the teaching … leave the timing to the Buddha … share your grateful heart, expand your circle … be sincere … even those who do not understand will be touched by your joy … the Buddha will help you.*

"You are doing the right things." It wasn't just these words – the first ones out of her mouth – it was the tone of her voice, the certainty of it. I was startled by it. Not just a gentle affirmation of my path, but an emphatic one. Later I asked for further amplification. She said that the overwhelming message she got from me was joy (imagine that, in the midst of my deep despair!), but that I was sometimes hesitant because I wasn't getting feedback from others confirming that I was doing right. "Don't be afraid," she said. "The Buddha knows your sincerity; trust the Buddha to guide you."

Today's teaching said that Kannon hears the world's cries and helps those who suffer, but does not fulfill self-serving wishes. This puts into focus the limits of my otherwise boundless generosity.

~ 491 ~

HEALTH, Part 4

The depth of my life at the physical-spiritual nexus continues to amaze me. I wrote earlier about the hormonal shifts that revealed to me our Shiva/Shakti connection not just in the spirit, but in the body. I read on Facebook of my friends struggling with physical and emotional ailments, and I pray for their peace and return to health (however that may be defined), but at the same time I feel my health being taken out of my hands and put in the hands of great and powerful forces beyond my conscious control.

My abstention from doctors is partly due to my lack of confidence in the health care industry in the wake of Lou's unsatisfactory experience, and my distrust of medical marketing – selling us drugs and treatments that we don't need and may even hurt us, but that make big money for Big Pharma. An even more important reason is my faith that I will be taken care of by the spirits for as long as my work here on earth is unfinished. I surrender myself, body and soul, to their power.

Although I don't discount the scientific explanations for illness, I think there is a power, a realm beyond chemistry and physics, that decides who gets sick and who doesn't. Whether we call it karma, good and evil spirits, God, the Source, or whatever, there is something beyond our conscious body-mind that shapes our experiences and synchronizes them with all other experiences.

It is an incredible feeling, to feel my body healing itself, shoring itself up, fending off disease without my conscious intent, without my obsessing about my health or particularly trying to be healthy. I'm not careless about my health, but I don't fret over it, either. The engine of my old jalopy will continue to run until it has taken me to the end of the road.

~ 492 ~

Yoda said: "Fear leads to anger, leads to hate, leads to suffering." The Second Noble Truth tells us that desire – greed – is the cause of suffering. Greed starts the cycle – leads to fear, leads to anger, leads to hate, leads to suffering.

In your life I see a demonstration of this pattern: your *greed* leads to *fear* of not getting what you want or losing what you have, to *anger* over not getting what you want or losing what you have, to *hate* (manifested as abuse) of those whom you think stand between you and what you want, and thus to your present *suffering*.

With your recent metamorphosis into Mr. Hyde, I have begun to release my one remaining desire – your awakening. Although your hostile separation from me is emotionally catastrophic, I am surprisingly calm. I am letting go. The untethered feeling I first described twenty-four years ago, and which you also felt after your mother died, I now realize is the state we seek to attain, the state of our final arrival – untethered, unsupported – a state of independence from all the illusions of space-time and body-mind. After losing our tether, rather than seeking a new tether, we should seek to be comfortable and even happy in our untethered condition. Total acceptance and surrender. No greed, no fear, no anger, no hatred, no suffering. Nirvana.

~ 493 ~

Two angels visited me today, Ignacio and his wife Cecilia. They delivered Christmas cheer – cookies, a booklet about Advent, and a card. A person's character is reflected in the quality of his/her friends. I am so humbled and grateful for these friends who would write this to me:

> *Dear Betty – Blessings to you – you are a Bright Light for us – and so many others. Laughter feels good with you … May joy resound – and thank you for adding to our joy. If my words were music I would make them suitable for you to play, with a refrain that says something about peace, love, and friendship.*

~ 494 ~

What a powerful, spiritual time I had with your wife's family over the Christmas holiday. We gabbed all day and all night, and then some more. All subjects were covered. We came to a remarkable meeting of minds.

We were joined on Christmas Eve by you, your wife, and other family members. You were only half there – silent, withdrawn, sullen, awkward, and to me, cruel.

Your mother-in-law said, "He doesn't deserve my daughter." True, and neither do you deserve me or Joe or any of the other angels in your life, but God in his mercy sent all of us to be here with you. God's love does not have to be deserved.

Your sister-in-law and I had wonderful talks about all kinds of things, sacred and secular. At one point she asked me out of the blue, "Are you an incarnation of Kuan Yin?" I was startled by the abruptness of the question and did not answer for a long time. I smiled, remembering the time that our friend Susan said, "You seem to be a person who came into the world to help others," and Ignacio and Cecilia writing, "Blessings to you – you are a Bright Light for us," and the many spiritual messages and miracles through which my sacred mission became known.

Before discussing my Kuan Yin connection, I asked her how she knew the Bodhisattva of Compassion. She said that Kuan Yin had been with her in a former life, and that she feels the drive to serve others continuing in her present life. I then revealed my Kuan Yin experiences and confirmed her observation that I am indeed a vehicle of compassion in this world. Like many others, she recognized my identity without my having to say it.

~ 495 ~

Did God really appear on earth in human form? Did Jesus really raise Lazarus from the dead? Did he really die on the cross? Is there really a Holy Spirit that dwells in us and lives on after we die? Is the life of Christ to be taken literally or symbolically? Is it history or fantasy?

The answer is yes – literal *and* symbolic, history *and* fantasy. Every life is the life of Christ. We are God. We are the Christ. We are the Holy Spirit. God is eternity, Jesus is space-time, and the Holy Spirit is the bridge that connects them. Each of us will go through trials and temptations, participate in miraculous events, and suffer the same agonies of pain and separation from God that Jesus did. As we approach the end of karma, the extremes of duality become more and more stark, and the parallels with the life of Christ in our own lives become ever clearer. It is that miraculous clarity that allows me to say I am a bodhisattva with the same calm assurance as Jesus said he was the Son of God.

The Bible is an allegory, each word and deed attributed to Jesus being symbolic of thoughts and events that every human life will experience on the way to salvation/enlightenment. But the historic Jesus of flesh and blood is also true, embodied throughout the ages by the bodhisattvas, the living and breathing saviors of every faith and every age who walk among us, teach, serve, and sacrifice themselves for us.

Bodhisattvas regularly raise people from spiritual death and darkness to spiritual life and the light of eternity, but there is also an even more literal kind of physical death and resurrection. I have written in this journal about several incidents of vaginal spotting that I experienced at pivotal points in our relationship. My eternal love for you – beyond space, time, and the physical body-mind – nevertheless found literal expression in my physical being. On a few brief and fleeting occasions an old woman well beyond her childbearing years became young again, her fertile creative body symbolically returned to her in this world now. My biological creative force that was dead came to life again in the flesh.

It is not just that I wished I could have creative sexual union with you; I was and am *actually* having that union with you now, in eternity. We are karmic lovers, Shiva and Shakti in eternal embrace, actively creating, now and always. At specific junctures in this life, our eternally fertile condition manifested miraculously in me here and now, in space-time – in flesh and blood, literally.

~ 496 ~

NEW YEARS DAY

Elaine is, surprisingly, doing better. Her brain is no longer so confused. I took her some wine, and we toasted the New Year. We had a very warm and animated conversation. I was reminded of the many times before Elaine's disability when we would go together to the Buddhist temple on New Year's Day for our traditional New Year blessing.

She invited me to sit on the bed with her. She said, "I can talk with you about anything. Things I cannot talk about with anyone else. I trust you to tell me the truth."

HEALTH, Part 5

Good health, once lost, can be regained two ways – by taking treatments to fight disease, or by letting go of the desire for good health. Fighting the good fight is often appropriate, and it is the option most people choose. But fighting only at the level of the body-mind attacks the disease on only one battlefield, which may not be the one where the disease originates.

How can letting go of the desire for good health bring good health? This sounds so counterintuitive, so negative, like throwing in the towel. But it is actually the opposite – handing the towel and the battle over to God. Our desire for life and health and our fear of death and disease are more powerful forces than germs, pollutants, or a poor diet in making us sick. The place where our desires and fears are found is the main battlefield in the war, and the weapons that vanquish disease on this battlefield are not drugs and surgery, but surrender and love.

There are two opposite ways of facing serious illness without fighting it: giving up and letting go. Giving up is not the same as letting go. Giving up is saying, "I'm terminal. There's no use fighting. I give up." This is allowing death to win. Letting go is saying, "I can find peace even in the midst of suffering. I don't need to fight my own body processes; I don't need to be healthy to be happy. I can let go." This is allowing life to win.

When you no longer grasp for health in fear of losing it, health can return. Anita Moorjani, who was miraculously cured of cancer after a near-death experience, said, "Live fearlessly!" When you no longer fear illness, it loses its hold on you. Love drives out fear.

It is the same with life and death. You can give up by saying, "Fuck this lousy life, I want outta here!" Or let go by saying, "Thank you, Lord, for the many blessings that have filled my life. My work is done. I am ready to leave this world in peace and gratitude."

If health does not return in the context of surrender and acceptance, it means that life is naturally ending. When the Buddha reached that point, he refused the medicine that might have brought him back to health, knowing that prolonging his life was, at that point, pointless.

I admit that I have not yet fully mastered the art of surrender, in either health or life. But I have seen the light at the end of the tunnel and felt the peace in passing waves. The final test awaits.

~ 498 ~

I nodded off in my easy chair and had a quick dream: *I was walking down a staircase and suddenly tripped. The trip was so sudden that it startled me awake.*

From dreammoods.com:

> **Stairs** – To dream that you are walking down a flight of stairs represents your repressed thoughts. You are regressing back into your subconscious. It also refers to the setbacks that you are experiencing in your life. To dream that you slip or trip on the stairs signifies your lack of self-confidence or conviction in the pursuit of some endeavor. If you slip going up the stairs, then it means that you are moving too fast toward attaining your goals. If you slip going down the stairs, then it suggests that you are moving too quickly in delving into your subconscious. You may not be quite ready to confront your subconscious or repressed thoughts.

~ 499 ~

The relative peace that has come over me in the wake of your rejection is like the paradoxical relief one feels when one gets a terminal diagnosis. A terrible ordeal awaits me, but at least now I know what I'm up against. Now I know the full sorrowful extent of my sacred mission with you.

Joe said that you don't know what love looks like. He thinks that what love looks like to you is people adoring you and giving you what you want – a good description of your superficial conscious self. But that self, in both its past expression of love and its present expression of hate, is not the real you. I think in some far distant corner of your soul you *do* know what love looks like – it looks like me.

~ 500 ~

APOLOGY AND FORGIVENESS, Part 2

At a lecture on forgiveness I learned that there are only two things we need for happiness: forgiveness and gratitude. Forgiveness says everything was right in the first place. Whatever happened in the past was supposed to happen. Now just accept it. Forgive yourself and others.

Forgiveness takes away the power, poison, and pain of the past. It frees the present from the past. *Gratitude* frees the present from the future. We are satisfied with and grateful for what we have now, no matter what may come later.

You claim to know forgiveness and gratitude, but you continue to live in shame and remorse, still an emotional prisoner of the past and a slave to your fear of the future. Wash away all regret and fear, and replace them with love.

~ 501 ~

I was gone for thirty-seven hours, eleven of it spent in the air. I wonder if those hours at 39,000 feet weren't the most important part of trip. No place to go, a chance to be alone with my thoughts, speed and altitude bringing me closer to God.

I am reading a book titled *The Immortal Life of Henrietta Lacks*, the story of a woman whose harvested cancer cells were reproduced in vitro in 1951 and became the basis for most of the ongoing research in human cell biology. Henrietta's cells were unusual because they were "immortal," able to reproduce indefinitely, apparently not subject to the inherent limitation that normally stops cell division after about fifty generations. Many scientists considered this absence of cellular senescence in Henrietta's cells, which made huge strides in medical research possible, to be a miracle.

The author of the book, Rebecca Skloot, describes her relationship with Henrietta's daughter, Deborah:

> I was a science journalist who referred to all things supernatural as "woo-woo stuff;" Deborah believed Henrietta's spirit lived on in her cells, controlling the life of anyone who crossed its path. Including me. "How else do you explain why your science teacher knew her real name when everyone else called her Helen Lane?" Deborah would say. "She was trying to get your attention." This thinking would apply to everything in my life; when I married while writing this book, it was because Henrietta wanted someone to take care of me while I worked. When I divorced, it was because she'd decided he was getting in the way of the book. When an editor who insisted I take the Lacks family out of the book was injured in a mysterious accident, Deborah said that's what happens when you piss Henrietta off.[20]

Your mother and who-knows-what other spirits are my Henrietta, speaking to me, directing me from beyond, from a place of universal immortality. You once said you wanted me to see through your eyes. Now I ask you to see through mine. Ask yourself what magnitude of spiritual power would be required for you to believe you are a bodhisattva, an incarnation of Kuan Yin, or to compare your life to the life of Christ. That's the overwhelming force to which I am responding.

~ 502 ~

HEALTH, Part 6

If you go looking for disease, you are bound to find something that the health care industry can make money fixing. (It's like taking your car in for its 5,000-mile checkup – the car is running great, but you know the mechanic will find something "wrong.") I concluded that it is not good to know about everything that goes on inside the body; we are not always meant to know if we are sick, or necessarily do anything about it, once we know. The body, unlike a car, has a way of fixing itself if you let it. No use worrying about it or getting in the way.

Somehow I have always known that when my time comes, God will visit upon me a disease that nothing could or should cure. Until then, I will be healthy. So it has been. On rare occasions I go to the doctor to seek relief from symptoms, but I don't go looking for disease when there is no evidence for it. When the time is right, deadly disease will find me. The decay of my body, now and always in progress, will accelerate and become manifest. I will be ready.

Love of life is a form of greed. Holding life up as more sacred than death is a form of fear. Considering life sacred could also be a form of respect, as long as death is similarly respected, as long as life and death are both embraced as two sides of the same sacred coin, neither side to be craved or spurned. Karma ends when both sides of the dichotomy are recognized as the same.

~ 503 ~

Your low opinion of yourself is now coming to the front of your consciousness. All of the feelings you didn't want to talk about with me, all the secret fears you were afraid my probing would uncover, are now pouring out of you onto me in misdirected aggression, as a man who is angry with himself kicks the dog. I receive the hardest kicks because I see deeply inside you and am closest to your pain, and because I am protected – my spirit angels have prepared me for your blows.

Paradoxical as it seems, it is evidence of your spiritual intimacy with me that you project onto me your deepest pain and anguish. Your outward hate is yet another sign of your inward love – our inescapable divine love. You express to me a depth of feeling that you cannot release with any other. Not with anyone who depends on you or upon whom you depend, or with whom you must keep up the façade.

And so I say, my dear, heap upon me all the anger and hate and venom that there is in you. And when you are spent, with nothing left to heave, when you are an empty vessel, catharsis complete, when you have finally let go of the last drop of venom, when you have not one more ounce of strength to fight your demons or grasp for rescue, when there is nothing to do but surrender, my love will still be here, ready to help you fill the dark, empty vessel with marvelous light.

Make no mistake – what you are doing to me is torture, and it hurts. But I understand it, as a sacrificial lamb knows its role as a vehicle to salvation. I am and will always be, as you say, your "beautiful bodhisattva."

~ 504 ~

Life is a pendulum swing from one pole of duality to the other, or a roller coaster with crests of happiness and troughs of sadness. The journey to enlightenment is a narrowing of the arc of the pendulum swing, or a gradual flattening of the roller coaster track. Awakening happens when the pendulum, or the car on the now-flat track, stops. Arrival in eternity.

At the beginning of the journey, the pendulum of life swings over a wide arc, 180 degrees, from the first poison to the second and back again, as we run toward what we want and away from what we don't want, holding at the same time nostalgia and regret for the past along with hope and fear for the future. Sometimes, in our desire to escape the suffering and turmoil of this whipsaw, we try to jump off the roller coaster – that's the third poison.

You plummet into an abyss of greed, anger, hate, and denial, and I am helpless to stop it. How can I have come so far with you, guided here by the spirits and the power of divine love, only to fail in the end? I must remember that your journey is yours, not mine. Your choices are yours, not mine. I take my own journey and make my own choices. In the end, everything we do is right. There is no failure.

The Dalai Lama said, referring to the centuries-long oppression of Tibet by China, "I must thank the Chinese for teaching me patience." And so, I must thank you for teaching me patience. I also thank the trees, who teach me how to change the world by standing still.

~ 505 ~

You and I are like elevated train tracks or airplanes flying at different altitudes that appear to intersect in two-dimensional space, but are separate in the third dimension. The eternal place where we fully connect is invisible, like an image on the blind spot at the center of the retina; untouchable, like a hologram projected into thin air; without substance, like a black hole that is only known by its effects, its residue, the circumstantial evidence for it.

Until now I did not fully realize the gravity of your emotional and spiritual distress. I knew you were troubled, fearful, guilt-ridden, selfish, and egotistical. But I thought our music could reach beyond those obstacles, and my gifts of money and skill could free you of worldly impediments and allow your buddha-nature to emerge.

Now I see that the real obstacles to your liberation are not imposed from the outside, but from inside. There is virtually no communicative connection between your Self and your Spirit. Your physical being and your eternal soul are strangers to each other. Your Ego, which should be connecting your physical and spiritual souls, seems to be totally removed from that role, pickled in alcohol and absorbed in ego gratification, oblivious to messages from both body and spirit. Neither I nor anyone else can reach your spiritual essence via your space-time body-mind.

I am at very nearly the same place of existential anguish where I was twenty-seven years ago after the loss of Lou. But there are differences. Since Lou died, I have lived with one foot in eternity, which changes the complexion of all worldly events – balances them, evens them out. I now know that life is an illusion and that worldly attachments cannot be clung to. I now know the futility of anger and grief. I now understand the ten bhūmi of the bodhisattva, the Six Perfections, the Four Noble Truths, the simple life of unsupported thought. I now see the living as shadows of death, and the dead as shadows of eternal life.

And most important, I now have the miracles, the revelatory guideposts that have led me to this place at this time. I have seen the dancing molecules; my chanting has evoked the wind, rain, and fire gods; I have been graced with dreams and visions and spirit visitations that have given me confidence that I am meant to be where I am, doing what I was meant to do. And so I soldier on, with faith that my spirit guides will lead me again as they have led me before. There is meaning in this travail; it is the prelude to something; our story is not yet over.

~ 506 ~

A basic tenet of Buddhism is *pratītyasamutpāda*, the Twelve Links of Dependent Origination, or Conditioned Arising, which describes the circular and unending sequence of cause and effect. An aspect of this principle is interdependent co-arising: In duality, when one side of a pair of opposites arises, the other side arises with it, by mutual consent. Yin must always balance yang.

In keeping with interdependent co-rising, the Six Perfections have six corresponding vices called "demons." To be genuine, and to avoid the demons, all Perfections must be pursued without struggle or hesitancy, arising joyfully and spontaneously from the buddha-nature within. Here are the Six Perfections and the demons they can give rise to:

1) GENEROSITY – Giving, but not to the point of enabling sloth or greed. Serving, but not in service to selfish desires.

2) DISCIPLINE – Rigor, but not to the point of austerity or struggle. Not coerced, not motivated by outer expectation, but by inner conviction.

3) PATIENCE – Forgiveness, but not to the point of condoning evil. Tolerance, but not to the point of allowing or enabling abuse. Humility, but not to the point of humiliation.

4) DILIGENCE – Accomplishing, but not to the point of forcing. Swim with the current, in consonance with universal rhythms.

5) MEDITATION – Concentration, but not to the point of attaching to specific thoughts or experiences. Meditation serves as an antidote to our afflictions, clearing away attachments and defilements, but can be corrupted into becoming itself an attachment.

6) WISDOM – Knowing truth, but not to the point of closed-mindedness or pride. "Our view of how things are is not something to grasp with a tight fist." [16]

~ 507 ~

I accidently channel-surfed into a program about substance abuse rehabilitation. The speaker was a lady who is a recovering alcoholic and now works with Alcoholics Anonymous. She had some very interesting things to say, like "Alcoholics are egomaniacs with an inferiority complex." (Boy, does that ring true!) She also quoted Einstein – "We can't solve problems with the same mind that created them" – in the context of the difficulty alcoholics have asking for help. They think they can recover with the same mind and the same thought processes that got them into trouble.

But most revealing was her description of the "jumping off place," the overwhelming fear that arises when the drinker realizes that he can't live with alcohol and can't live without it, can no longer get high and can no longer get sober. That's when the alcoholic knows he can't get better on his own and seeks help.

I received this Buddhist message today: *Put yourself in another person's shoes ... learn other ways of doing things ... you are very good at helping others ... you can help in new ways.*

Okay ... I'm going to an Al-Anon meeting next week.

~ 508 ~

Last night I had a dream: *I was looking at my fish tank. It was dark, but I could see that the water was almost gone from the tank, and most of the fish were out of the tank, flopping on the ground. I tried to pick up some, but they were slippery and hard to grab. Then I looked behind me and found a big fish, not a small guppy like the others, but a round, fat fish, like a carp, a little larger than my hand. He was mostly white in color, and glowed in the otherwise dimly lit room. I picked him up and cradled him in my hands. He stopped writhing and became calm, seemingly content to lie still in my protective custody. I moved to put him back in the tank, but I realized the water level was too low for him to live there. Then I woke up.*

From dreammoods.com:

Fish – To see fish swimming in your dream signifies insights from your subconscious mind. Thus to catch a fish represents insights which have been brought to the surface. It may also imply a slippery or elusive situation.

Fish Tank – To see or clean a fish tank in your dream indicates how you have full control of your emotions. You keep your feelings in check.

Water – To see water in your dream symbolizes your subconscious and your emotional state of mind. Water is the living essence of the psyche and the flow of life energy. It is also symbolic of spirituality, knowledge, healing and refreshment.

Light – To see light in your dream represents illumination, clarity, guidance, understanding, and insight. Light is being shed on a once cloudy situation or problem. You have found the truth to a situation or an answer to a problem. If the light is particularly bright, then it indicates that you need to move toward a higher level of awareness and feeling.

Water represents the subconscious mind, that which is dark, mysterious, submerged. The shallowness of the water in my fish tank says to me that there is very little left to me that is still underwater. My subconscious is very near the surface. Since most of my fish are out of the tank, my emotions are not held in check, they are breaking loose. I try to get them back into the confines of the tank, but I am not succeeding. This is definitely a slippery and elusive situation.

You are the big, bright white fish, becoming calm in my hands. By picking you up I bring insights about you to the surface. Your bodhisattva is holding you safe in her hands, having found the truth through the prevailing darkness of fear and ignorance, preparing to move toward a higher level of awareness.

Maybe the low level of water in the tank represents freedom from past confinement. Perhaps the big white fish is not meant to return to the small walled-off space from whence he came. So where do I and my fish out of water go from here?

~ 509 ~

Today was my annual pilgrimage to the sacred hot springs. A park ranger told me a trail previously closed had recently been reopened. Almost nobody knows that this trail is now open, so I was in complete solitude. Perfect for my chants and offerings.

There is something mesmerizing about chanting in a place of such power, alone with no sound except the occasional birdcall and the incessant wind. I started my chant to your mother in fuller voice than usual. On most occasions after I deliver the line that invokes the wind god, I pause for a moment and pay attention to the wind. Often the wind god will show me a sign, usually a little gust, as happened when I presented my chant for the first time at your mother's grave. But this time, the wind suddenly stopped. I don't mean it just let up a little; the wind totally stopped. For a few seconds there was eerie calm in this exposed and normally windswept field. I asked myself, how would the wind god tell me he's listening in a place where the wind is always blowing?

~ 510 ~

SEX, Part 17

As I sat alone in quiet contemplation on a cliff overlooking the sea, I began thinking about karmic sex – karmic love, actually – sex being just one of its many symbolic manifestations.

Some descriptions of karmic love are negative, emphasizing bad karma, weaknesses and defilements of past lives revisiting us in the present, manifesting as abuse, neglect, discord, or unfaithfulness. Such relationships might be karmic, *but they are not love.* What I call karmic love, divine love, or spiritual love is categorically different, a manifestation of the Holy Spirit; God's grace, the bliss of eternity, nirvana, heaven on earth.

Love comes in many forms and degrees. But in most cases love is limited by two things: greed and fear. Dependency is the way that worldly relationships express these two poisons. What we think is a search for love is more often a search for a provider or protector.

Dependency is often an expression of greed, the first poison. We want something, so we attach ourselves to and act lovingly toward the people who can get it for us. We reel them in and keep them on the line as long as our desire is fulfilled. When the desire is no longer being fulfilled or the price of fulfillment gets too high, we cut them loose and look for a better provider.

Similarly, dependency can be an expression of fear, the second poison. We become dependent on those who protect us from that which we fear – sickness, hunger, poverty, anxiety, and pain. When we fall through a hole in our protector's safety net, we leave the relationship and look for a better protector.

Real love can exist in relationships of dependency, as long as the dependent attachment does not become abusive or exploitive and is not the sole reason for the relationship. But if one satisfies the needs of a partner out of coercion, obligation, or in expectation of reward, or if one feels angry or neglected when a partner fails to satisfy one's own needs, then the motivation for the relationship is not love.

The highest and deepest love possible, what I call karmic love, divine love, or spiritual love – the kind I have – is not just a higher degree of love than the others; it is an entirely different kind of love. It is compassionate love in communion with the eternal God-self, without dependencies of any kind. Nothing needs to be provided, no protection is necessary. All is surrendered to the love – all material, intellectual, and emotional assets, and all safety and security. Everything is given up, to the point of total self-sacrifice, without needing or expecting anything in return.

Just as love takes different forms, so does sex. Most sex is engaged in for pleasure, domination, or escape. These reasons roughly correspond to the three Buddhist poisons. The desire for pleasure is an obvious first poison motivation. The need to dominate, to exert power and control over another person, reflects fear, a second poison motivation. (Rape, and especially anal intercourse, forcing something into a place it is not designed to go, where physical resistance is met and violence is required to complete the act, is the ultimate dominance display.) Submission to this kind of dominance is also a reflection of fear – fear that something even worse will happen if one doesn't submit. And finally, there is escapism, the third poison – the ability of sex to momentarily take the mind off the day-to-day hardships of life. Sex that comes from any of these selfish motivations has nothing to do with love, and can become an addiction.

Sex in karmic love is different from any other kind, more for the other than for oneself. One's pleasure is measured in terms of the other. There is no hint of dominance; in fact, each is so submissive to the other that one's own ego disappears, melded into the other. This sex is never an escape mechanism, but rather a way to live life with even greater awareness. It casts out all the poisons.

This is not to say that true worldly loves are of lesser value. They are dualistic aspects of divine love, characterized by service to the beloved ahead of self, connecting us in the space-time continuum as divine love connects us in eternity. Like the infinitely sided polygon approaching a circle, mature worldly love can approach divine love, leading to and preparing the quantum leap to awakening.

The first step to divine love is self-love. One cannot love another until he loves himself. I don't mean in a narcissistic way, but in the sense of loving God – the God inside oneself. Fear rises up when the Self cannot see its own loving buddha-nature. Awakening to divine love drives out fear. Once one awakens to his own divine essence, it becomes possible to see it in others.

~ 511 ~

You try to make separation between us, but you can't; our music involuntarily proclaims our karmic love for all the world to hear. You try to make the appearance of closeness with your wife, with public hand-holding and praise from the stage, but these are hollow gestures, just for show. Nothing can erase the more profound gestures of disharmony that both of you involuntarily display. Imagine my angst, knowing perfect karmic love with you in eternity, yet witnessing your heartbreaking inability to fully experience even the earthly forms of love in this life.

PART 22

Unraveling

~ 512 ~

I had another provocative dream last night, a journey deep into our universal subconscious:

Scene 1: *You and I were in loving embrace. I kissed your neck, felt your cheek pressing mine. You were happy, your face lit up with that radiant smile of pure joy that I have seen so often in visions but only rarely in life. Then suddenly you disappeared into a small speck of golden light.*

Scene 2: *I was led through a doorway into a very cramped rail car, like the small one-person cars in carnival rides. As the car began to move, I looked back and saw three sinister men in scruffy black and gray clothes watching me. The front of the car was right in front of my face, as if an air bag had been deployed. I could feel the car lurch along its track, but there were no windows, so I couldn't tell where I was or where I was going. The car was not dark, however; the interior was covered on all sides with soft upholstery, brightly colored in a patchwork quilt design. My claustrophobia started to kick in a little, but I said to myself, live fearlessly! Live in the moment. I am in this car for a reason.*

Scene 3: *I am in a room with lots of people milling around, like an airport or train station. You came walking up to me, wanting to tell me something. Apparently you did not want to be overheard; you were looking around furtively at the other people nearby and beckoned me to a less crowded spot in the room. Your voice was soft, gentle, warm, not the harsh, accusatory tone you have taken of late. But then a dark, sinister man dressed in the same scruffy black and gray clothes riding in a small electric vehicle came along, backed you up against the wall and shot you with an invisible beam that turned you into a small speck of light. I chased the man in his cart down the corridor, asking, "Is this what always happens when he tries to open up with me?" The man rode away and did not answer.*

From dreammoods.com:

> **Kiss** – If you are kissing a close friend, it represents your respect and adoration for your friend. You are seeking some intimate closeness that is lacking in some waking relationship. It may

or may not signify a romantic interest for him or her. To dream that you are kissing someone on the neck or vice versa refers to uninhibited passion.

Light – To see light in your dream represents illumination, clarity, guidance, understanding, and insight. You have found the truth to a situation or an answer to a problem. Also consider the color of the light for additional significance.

Gold – The golden color reflects a spiritual reward, richness, refinement and enhancement of your surroundings. It also signifies your determination and unyielding nature.

Train – To dream that you are on a train symbolizes your life's journey. It suggests that you are on the right track in life and headed in the right direction.

Train Station – To dream that you are at a train station represents a transitional period in your life.

Black – Black symbolizes the unknown, the unconscious, danger, mystery, darkness, death, mourning, rejection, hate or malice. It also signifies a lack of love and lack of support.

Gray – Gray indicates fear, fright, depression, ill health, ambivalence, and confusion.

My kisses on your neck and your radiant smile represent our eternal spiritual union. The men in black and gray are your dark side, representing your low self-esteem, fear, anger, guilt, the part that feels rejected and unloved, that causes you to be distant and detached. The small speck of golden light that replaces your body in my presence is the vestige of your divine essence, your God-self revealed, staying with me as the sinister men zap your body away. But my ride in the train car to the station, and your presence there, says to me that the next transition in our life's journey is near, and that my next task will be to challenge the demons, the mean scruffy men. I think the three men I saw as I got into the car were the three Buddhist poisons.

This dream tells me that there is a part of you that does love me, does find happiness with me, and does want to walk the path of divine love – that's the part that enjoyed my kisses and came up to me at the station. But there is another part of you – the dark, fearful part – that shuts you down the minute you try to open up.

~ 513 ~

I sat at your mom's grave for about an hour today. Left her flowers, recited my chant, and spent a timeless moment with her. Funny how it is when you live in the moment, how the moment expands to fill all the time you can give it, all the time you have.

I said to her, "I'm doing the best I can for your son. Trying not to hurt him, but also not flinching from the difficult things that might help him." Every time I see the rock wall behind her grave, I am reminded of my bodhisattva dream (~256~) that ended with me on a raft beside that wall, asking, "If these people had one more day of life, what would they do with it?" I am living that one more day for her.

~ 514 ~

Last night my friend, a colleague in the music business, said to me, "You look happy."

Imagine … I look happy. You have ripped my heart out of my chest and it is lying on the ground, torn and bleeding … but she says I look happy. Have I found the peace that passes understanding, the calm in the midst of the storm, the perfection of the 3rd Perfection? Or am I simply insane?

Or perhaps I am truly living this life at the level of the buddha-nature, where there is no right or wrong, where everything is perfect, just as it should be. Maybe that's why people think I am happy, because at that level I *am* happy, at peace, even in the midst of incredible mortal suffering.

~ 515 ~

It would appear that your emotionally violent behavior toward me is intentionally cruel and malevolent. But I know it is not evil that drives you; it is greed, fear, and ignorance. Your wrath is not a display of strength or power, but rather of weakness. You don't understand divine love, so you fear it. You don't know how to relate to a woman as an equal, in a way that is not merely sexual, so you fear a strong, capable woman and mistake her expressions of mature love for sexual desire or dependent clinging. You are so wrapped up in your own concerns that you cannot see anyone else's concerns or be sympathetic to them.

Not only do you not know how to acknowledge our divine love and properly express it, you don't know how to offer even the most basic human friendship. You have no real friends, only drinking buddies, admiring fans, mutually self-interested business associates, and a live-in maidservant with the nominal title of "wife." You are kind and polite to these people only to the extent you have to be to keep them in your service. I have indeed uncovered a deep, deep suffering in you.

~ 516 ~

JESUS AND THE FOUR NOBLE TRUTHS

1) **All life is suffering.** "In the world you have tribulation …" (John 16:33)

2) **Suffering comes from desire.** "Each person is tempted when he is lured and enticed by his own desire. Then desire when it has conceived gives birth to sin; and sin when it is full-grown brings forth death." (James 1:14-15)

3) **There is a way out of suffering.** "… but be of good cheer, I have overcome the world." (John 16:33)

4) **Here is the Way.** "I am the Way and the Truth and the Life." (John 14:6) "If, when you do right and suffer for it, you take it patiently, you have God's approval. For to this you have been called, because Christ also suffered for you, leaving you an example, that you should follow in his steps." (1 Peter 2:20-21)

The Way out of suffering is hard. It requires more suffering before no suffering can be reached. The Way to heaven goes through hell. For those who have been called to this, to the life of the bodhisattva, the Way is found by following in the steps of Christ. But it's not easy, and few will find the narrow gate: "For the gate is narrow and the way is hard, that leads to life, and those who find it are few." (Matthew 7:14)

People sometimes think that my vision of eternity, my 1/1/09 epiphany, is some kind of blessing or honor, wishing it could be bestowed upon them, too. Perhaps they are a little angry that God has denied them this "reward" despite their lifetimes of steadfast devotion, humble service, and earnest prayer. Such visions are not earned by good works or by prayer and supplication; they are only experienced by the grace of God. Why, when, and to whom these visions appear remains God's mystery.

Those who think they might like to be called to this life, to see what I have seen, need to be careful what they wish for. These visions come at a terrible price; they are as much a curse as a blessing. Every moment of bliss in this life, even when generated by a vision of eternity, is balanced by horror of equal magnitude. People see the image of Jesus and aspire to it, wanting to possess his spiritual power, his divinity. In fact, everyone does possess that divinity, but we can only manifest it if and when we are willing to pay the same price as Jesus did – spiritual trials and tribulations, abandonment, suffering, and sacrifice.

Being exposed to the beatific vision of heaven also means being exposed to the fires of hell, to live the life of Christ in all its darkness as well as its light. It is a combination of the greatest weakness with the greatest strength – the ultimate vulnerability with the ultimate compassion for those who would exploit that vulnerability. To be mortally wounded and say, "Father, forgive them, for they know not what they do."

~ 517 ~

I got word that my farmer friend Tommy died today. He finally "checked out of Hotel Earth." Godspeed on your new journey, dear friend.

~ 518 ~

I say with great sadness that a threshold has been crossed. Your wife has also become abusive. It is not uncommon for someone who has been abused to become first a defender of her abuser and then an abuser herself. I'm surprised in this case, though, since so many decades of abuse had gone by without her turning to the dark side. I thought she had the strength to resist. But apparently she can no longer keep the ramparts up.

I am still amazed that your incredible torture has not reduced me to blind panic. I have clearly sublimated the pain. Yet there are moments when a deep melancholy washes over me, when I realize the magnitude of your suffering and my helplessness in the face of it. And yet, I abide, your bodhisattva watching over you.

~ 519 ~

While my mind remains composed, my house is in total shambles. Reflective of my life, perhaps? Inner peace, outer chaos. In the music room are stacks of old tapes and records waiting to be digitized. In the bedroom are piles of old clothes waiting to be given away. In my office are piles of old music manuscripts waiting to be transcribed into the computer. Files going back forty years await culling. In the living room are piles of old books and magazines waiting to be read, and a box of old concert programs awaiting entombment and resurrection. The dining room holds current files for current projects, sitting in boxes on the floor because there is no other place to put them.

Goethe called architecture "frozen music." My house is like that, the many facets of my life's work frozen in place. The material evidence of my life is a snapshot in time of an endless work in progress.

~ 520 ~

My dream last night: *I am swimming on the surface of a dark, tranquil pond. There is a high, steep rock wall coming out of the pond. I say to myself, "That wall is high. I don't know if I can lift myself up high enough to get out of the pond." But I try, and am successful in getting out.*

This dream sequence happened twice.

From dreammoods.com:

> **Swimming** – To dream that you are swimming suggests that you are exploring aspects of your subconscious mind and emotions. The dream may be a sign that you are seeking some sort of emotional support.

> **Water** – To see water in your dream symbolizes your subconscious and your emotional state of mind. Water is the living essence of the psyche and the flow of life energy. It is also symbolic of spirituality, knowledge, healing and refreshment. To see calm, clear water in your dream means that you are in tune with your spirituality. It denotes serenity, peace of mind, and rejuvenation.

> **Walls** – To see a wall in your dream signifies limitations, obstacles and boundaries. There is a barrier obstructing your progress.

> **Rocks** – To dream that you are climbing a rock signifies your determination, ambition and struggle. If the rock is particularly steep, then it refers to obstacles and disappointments.

~ 521 ~

Occasionally I go through bouts of self-doubt. Am I just delusional to think that I am a bodhisattva in the accelerated last stages of enlightenment? Is it just my overinflated ego overwhelming my underdeveloped humility? But then, I remember all the miracles – the countless experiences that continue to visit me while asleep and awake, the constant bombardment of spiritual messages, the deep meaning that emanates from everything I touch and that touches me – every book I read, every person I meet, every concert I play, every lecture I attend, every animal that crosses my path. It is as if I am at the hub of a great wheel, all the spokes connecting in me.

The *Daśabhūmika Sūtra*, where the ten bhūmi of the bodhisattava are described, says this about the immovable eighth bhūmi:

> Therefore, the buddhas give the enlightening beings such infinite tasks to develop knowledge, the knowledge-producing deeds effected in a single instant of which are immeasurably, incalculably greater than all former undertakings from the first inspiration up to the attainment of stability in the seventh stage. Why? Because previously it was practice undertaken *with one body*, whereas having climbed to this [eighth] stage the power of practice of enlightening beings is realized by *infinite different bodies*, by production of infinite voices, by accomplishment of infinite knowledge, by accomplishment of infinite manifestations … by infinite accomplishments of physical, verbal, and mental actions, the power of enlightening beings' practice is fully realized by immovable application.

I am more than just me. I am among the "infinite different bodies" of the eternal consciousness that is Kuan Yin. The goddess of compassion is reflected in me, acts through me, and propels me to the eighth bhūmi, where I, too, as Kuan Yin's avatar, am able to realize infinite accomplishments of compassion. It is my identification with the divine Kuan Yin – *nyuga ganyu* – that is the source of the miracles that have brought me to this place on the edge of eternity.

The eighth bhūmi is clearly a major transition in the journey to awakening. Even as creation separates us into infinite different bodies, at the eighth bhūmi we become aware of the intimate eternal connection we still have with all that is, and we begin to reunite our separate consciousness with all others in the collective unconscious.

~ 522 ~

If one understands heaven to be not a place, but a state of being – not outside oneself but inside, an internal aspect of the eternal – then the Lord's Prayer takes on wonderful new meaning:

Our father, who art in heaven …
Our father who is in the heaven within us.

Thy kingdom come, thy will be done …
May my God-self come to the fore; may my acts be the will of God.

On earth as it is in heaven …
May my life on earth perfectly reflect my concurrent life in heaven, in the spirit.

Where is heaven? Where is God? Wayne Dyer has the temerity to say, "I am God." He tells everyone else to say it, too. And believe it.

God is all around us, in everything – "out there," but more importantly, "in here," too. When you consider yourself in this divine light, everything you say and do takes on new weight. Your voice utters the word of God. Your acts are the movement of God on earth, walking among us.

All the buddhas, bodhisattvas, prophets, saints, saviors, and angels – however they may be described in various cultures and religions – are beings who allow the God within them to be fully expressed. No greed, anger, vanity, or defilement of any kind can obscure or overwhelm the eternal love that is revealed in that expression.

I don't pray or chant or meditate to ask some external power for favors. I seek to be in touch with my inner buddha-nature, my God-self, and to manifest in my life my eternal connection with all of creation. As I approach awakening, as I grow in my spiritual awareness, I pray that my words and deeds will become ever more in tune with the celestial harmony, and that I will eventually disappear into it.

~ 523 ~

Ignacio introduced me to a new personality analysis tool, the Enneagram. He said the Jesuits use it. I have spent several hours today exploring various aspects of the system, which identifies nine personality types and the interrelationships among them. Fascinating, and uncannily accurate in describing the current dysfunctional relationships around me.

The Enneagram reinforces what I have already learned about love and greed: Greed causes us to want to attract things to us, to become filled with abundance and visible in our wealth and power; greed feeds and reflects the Ego. Love, on the other hand, causes us to want to give it all away, to become empty and invisible – love feeds and reflects the God-self, the buddha-nature.

~ 524 ~

My dream last night: *I was in a hotel room, an old but luxurious hotel, with fancy doorknobs and door locks. I was wearing a dress with large brown and orange prints on a white background. I went out into the lobby of the hotel, where three ladies were admiring the dress. I saw myself and was startled to see me in the dress, which had a delicate white lace overlay. I walked over* to a store counter in the hotel and said to the sales clerk, "The three ladies would like to buy the dress."

Then I followed a hotel employee, an apparently nice man, into my room. The lights were off and it was dark. I sat on the bed. He said, "Don't you take your clothes off to have sex?" He began to lie down beside me.

I touched his cheek and said, "I didn't come here to have sex."

He said, "Why are you here, then?"

"I just followed you." I got the feeling that he wouldn't take no for an answer. He got up and locked the door. I ran into an adjoining room and tried to open the door to get out, but the door I opened went to another room, not outside. As I ran to unlock the door leading outside, I saw the man coming toward me. I woke up.

From dreammoods.com:

Hotel – To see a hotel in your dream signifies a new state of mind or a shift in personal identity.

Lobby – To dream that you are in a lobby indicates that you are trying to make something known.

Clothing – To dream of your clothes is symbolic of your public self and how you are perceived. It is indicative of the act you put on in front of others. Clothes are also an indication of your condition and status in life.

Dress – To see or wear a dress in your dream represents a feminine outlook or feminine perspective on a situation. You are freely expressing your femininity. Look up the specific color for additional significance.

> **White** – White represents purity, perfection, peace, innocence, dignity, cleanliness, awareness, and new beginnings. You may be experiencing a reawakening or have a fresh outlook on life.

> **Orange** – Orange denotes hope, friendliness, courtesy, generosity, liveliness, sociability, and an out-going nature. It also represents a stimulation of the senses. You feel alive!

> **Brown** – Brown denotes worldliness, practicality, domestic bliss, physical comfort, conservatism, and a materialistic character. Brown also represents the ground and earth.

Lace – To see lace in your dream points to your sensuality and femininity. Alternatively, it denotes tradition and old-fashioned ideals.

Buying – To dream that you or someone is buying something represents acceptance of an idea, condition, or situation.

Door – To dream that you are entering through a door signifies new opportunities that are presented before you. You are entering into a new stage in your life and moving from one level of consciousness to another. To dream that the door is closed or locked signifies opportunities that are denied and not available to you or that you have missed out on. Something or someone is blocking your progress. It also symbolizes the ending of a phase or project. If you are inside the locked door, it represents harsh lessons that need to be learned.

Rape – To dream that you have been raped indicates that you have been violated or that you have been taken advantage of. Things are being forced upon you.

I think the basic message in this dream is a reiteration of what I learned yesterday from the Enneagram – you are in deep trouble, almost into the unhealthy levels of your Type Eight, where you could do real harm to yourself and others. The impending rape in my dream might mean you are going over the edge and I will be harmed. The locked doors do not bode well. What are the harsh lessons that need to be learned? Perhaps the three ladies who are buying my dress of purity are your wife, her sister, and her mother. This is a darker, more complex dream than usual, with many layers. Let's see what happens.

~ 525 ~

Here is a description of a healthy Enneagram Type One:

Level 1 (At Their Best): Become extraordinarily wise and discerning. By accepting what is, they become transcendentally realistic, knowing the best action to take in each moment. Humane, inspiring, and hopeful: the truth will be heard.

Level 2: Conscientious with strong personal convictions: they have an intense sense of right and wrong, personal religious and moral values. Wish to be rational, reasonable, self-disciplined, mature, moderate in all things.

Level 3: Extremely principled, always want to be fair, objective, and ethical: truth and justice primary values. Sense of responsibility, personal integrity, and of having a higher purpose often make them teachers and witnesses to the truth.[17]

Here is a description of the Eighth and Ninth Bhūmi Bodhisattvas, from the *Daśabhūmika Sūtra:*

[On the eighth level] Their understanding of suchness is so complete that it overturns afflicted views, and reality appears in a completely new light. They enter into meditation on emptiness with little effort. Compassion and skill in means are automatic and spontaneous. There is no need to plan or contemplate how best to benefit others, since these bodhisattvas skillfully adapt themselves to every situation.

On the ninth level, they fully understand the three vehicles—hearers, solitary realizers, and bodhisattvas—and perfect the ability to teach the doctrine. Ninth bhūmi bodhisattvas also acquire the "four analytical knowledges"—of doctrines, meanings, grammar, and exposition. Due to this, they develop wondrous eloquence and skill in presenting doctrinal teachings. On this level they also cultivate the perfection of power, which means that because of the strength of their mastery of the four analytical knowledges and their meditation they are able to develop the six perfections energetically and to practice them continually without becoming fatigued.[11]

I was struck by the correlation between these two descriptions of spiritual elevation from two very different times, places, and cultures:

> From the Enneagram: ... make them teachers and witnesses to the truth ... knowing the best action to take in each moment ... rational, reasonable, self-disciplined, mature, moderate in all things; fair, objective, and ethical ... become transcendentally realistic.

> From the *Daśabhūmika Sūtra*: ... perfect the ability to teach the doctrine ... skillfully adapt themselves to every situation ... able to develop the six perfections energetically and to practice them continually ... reality appears in a completely new light.

The Enneagram website says that most mere mortals are unlikely to attain the healthiest Level I. Only the likes of Zen monks and Christian mystics should aspire to such perfection. But, true to my Type One perfectionism, I have higher expectations than that, especially for myself!

Do I sometimes slip into lower levels of Type One, becoming critical, judgmental, angry, self-righteous, and impatient? Of course. But I do not stay there. I recognize my own complicity in the events that provoke my negativity, and my consciousness of divine love quickly lifts me up to higher levels.

I hold back conferring the Level I or Ninth Bhūmi designation upon myself at this time, but in my understanding of "suchness" I cannot help but see my sails unfurling in that direction.

~ 526 ~

The Enneagram is truly provocative. I continue to delve into the mystery of it, the uncanny accuracy of its descriptions of personality types and relationships. In all personality types, positive movement up to the healthiest levels is a progression from self to God-self, from the narrow temporal view to the broad eternal view, from greed and fear to compassion and love.

In studying relationships between Ones (me) and Eights (you), I am struck by what a powerful combination healthy Ones and Eights can be – Lyndon Johnson (8) and Bill Moyers (1), for instance. Martin Luther King, Jr. (8), had a picture of Mahatma Gandhi (1) on his office wall, and gave his life practicing the principles of nonviolent civil disobedience that he learned from Gandhi.

But only healthy Eights can know love; an average or unhealthy Eight is still intimately involved only with himself. To an unhealthy Eight, other people are only objects, pawns on a chessboard, loveable only so long as they are useful. An Eight can only know true love when he has overcome his fear of exposing his vulnerability.

From enneagraminstitute.com:

> Beneath their imposing exterior, Eights often feel hurt and rejected, although this is something they seldom talk about because they have trouble admitting their vulnerability to themselves, let alone to anyone else. Because they fear that they will be rejected (divorced, humiliated, criticized, fired, or harmed in some way), Eights attempt to defend themselves by rejecting others first. The result is that average Eights become *blocked in their ability to connect with people or to love,* since love gives the other power over them, reawakening their Basic Fear [of being harmed or controlled].[17]

One of the most haunting things I read about Type Eight is, "For Eights to allow their hearts to come forth, ironically, is one of the most courageous things they can do." Is it any wonder, in light of these insights, that you don't know how to love me (or anyone)? Thanks to my powerful visions, I know that you *do* love me in the deepest part of you, and at first your heart did courageously come forth with me, but your frightened self now has your heart and your love locked in a dark prison.

I can see that your torment is meant to propel my spiritual growth, but shouldn't you grow, too? How can I rise to heaven if you are still in hell? I feel like Clarence, the angel-in-training in *It's A Wonderful Life* – I can't get my angel wings until I help you get yours.

~ 527 ~

GOOD FRIDAY

I know you are out there crucifying me. I have received reports that you are undermining my credibility with our musical and business associates – lying about me, casting unfounded aspersions on the quality of my work, questioning my integrity, exerting your power and forcing your will by going around me and trampling over me. You are sinking ever deeper into hostility and delusion.

I have been your staunchest ally, but now you are turning me into an enemy. An Enneagram article about addiction says this about an average Type Eight addict: "At Level 5 he often takes disagreement as a threat to his security, and is particularly threatened by those who are not afraid of his potential angry ranting or confrontational explosions, or who have an equal intelligence and are not afraid to express it."

I am guilty on all counts. As your fear welled up, you came to see our disagreements as threats. I told you, lovingly, that I am not afraid of your angry ranting, and I have expressed my equal intelligence in many ways on many occasions. But I am not your enemy. I am not trying to control you. I am not a threat to you. I'm trying to help you and support you. Even now, in spite of the torture you inflict, I am working to preserve and protect the good things that you have achieved. My indestructible love, totally forgiving and compassionate, continues to serve you, working for your salvation regardless of your destructive behavior.

The Enneagram Institute says that Ones like me have a problem with relationships when they insist on being right at the expense of their connection with the other. Jesus insisted on being right with the Pharisees and the Romans at the expense of his relationship with them, and they killed him for it. I insisted on being right – doing what is right – in my work with you, and you are symbolically killing me for it. Jesus and I simply bore witness to the truth as we felt we had to, living as directed by a higher power. Jesus must have been a One.

~ 528 ~

EASTER

Jesus is said to have performed miracles and endured terrible physical suffering as proof of his divinity. But did the miracles really happen? Assuming the suffering really happened, what is the meaning of it?

Buddhist lore describes the Buddha in terms amazingly similar to Christian lore about Jesus. Buddhist literature is filled with stories of elevated beings who performed supernatural acts:

> All the eminent monks of great virtue in the past were able to predict what day they would die, and even on the brink of death their bodies were as soft and supple as a baby's. Others who were even more lofty turned into a field of light, and their human forms disappeared. At most all they left behind were a few pieces of fingernail, or a lock of hair as a memento. In the tradition of Chinese Buddhism, it is said that those individuals who have reached this stage [the Fourth Dhyana] sometimes choose to walk with their feet one inch above the earth, so they do not harm any living beings.[21]

Jesus walked on water and disappeared from his tomb; Buddhas walk above the earth and disappear into a field of light.

There are also gory stories of disciples who "cut off his arm" to demonstrate the seriousness of their commitment to the dharma, and whose lives were horribly sacrificed in the practice of the Perfections:

> In the "Jātaka Tale, Patience Teacher Birth Story" (*Khantivādin Jātaka*), a jealous king repeatedly asked an ascetic what the ascetic taught, to which the ascetic replied, "Patience," which the ascetic further defined as "not to get angry when injured, criticized or struck." To test the ascetic's patience, the king had the ascetic struck two thousand times with a whip of thorns, had the ascetic's hands and feet axed off, cut off the ascetic's nose and ears, and then kicked the ascetic in the heart. After the king left, the ascetic wished the king a long life and said, "Those like myself do not feel wrath." The ascetic died later that day.

This story demonstrating the ultimate practice of the 3rd Perfection bears a striking resemblance to Christ's crucifixion, including the divine element of forgiving his tormentors.

Are these stories, Christian and Buddhist, factual retellings of actual events, or hyperbole to make an extreme point and emphasize the stories' relevance beyond space-time reality, using physical symbology that we can understand in this physical world to communicate a message of great intensity from beyond the physical plane?

The Sunday school group at church has been arguing about the importance, or not, of Jesus' resurrection being a real physical event. I am naturally lining up with the side that gives physical reality no importance, the underlying meaning of the story being the important part. The life of Christ, from his alleged virgin birth to the resurrection, is a great parable, not needing reality in this dualistic world to convey its eternal message.

Mythologist Joseph Campbell's "hero's journey," beautifully depicted in the movie *Finding Joe*, is the life of Christ (and also of the Buddha). At the core of the hero's journey is the cycle of *separation*, *initiation*, and *return*. It could be said that Jesus had two hero's journeys, first when he was separated from society after his baptism, was initiated by the temptations of Satan in the desert, and then returned to teach. This was his worldly journey, in duality.

His second journey was even more powerful, his journey into eternity: He was separated from his disciples and followers, who rejected and humiliated him, and even from God – My God, my God, why hast thou forsaken me? – during the horrible initiation rite of crucifixion. The resurrection is his triumphant return, this time not to the world but to God, having slain all his dragons and having shown us how we can slay ours, too.

Neither birth nor death are real; they are both just milestones, blips on the chart, in the continuous and unending worldly manifestation of eternity – the constant rising up and falling back of the dancing molecules. When the bodhisattva's work is done, the blips stop; he jumps off the wheel of samsara, ends his cycle of reincarnation into the world of dualism and karma, and becomes a buddha. Resurrection.

At the end of the movie *Ben-Hur*, after Judah Ben-Hur had witnessed the crucifixion, he said, "I felt his voice take the sword out of my hand." To feel – as I have – love so great that it takes the sword out of your hand even in the midst of mortal suffering, to the point that you can say, "Father, forgive them, for they know not what they do," is a life-transforming experience. Once you know that kind of love, there can never be anger or vengeance or hatred ever again.

~ 529 ~

ON THE MYSTIC EXPERIENCE

Am I a mystic? More from the Enneagram people, written as if the author had my personal experience in mind:

> Prerequisites for mystical awareness—openness, patience, inner silence, humility, reverence for mystery, the ability to "not know"—as well as a deep hunger in the heart that can only be filled by the divine. With the mystic's vision comes an unshakable knowing of the objective reality of what he or she has experienced. (When you are in a mystical experience, you know it is real and is, in fact, much more real and objective than what we usually take to be reality.) As a result, the mystic's heart and mind are clarified and made joyous—and, paradoxically, her commitment to benefit this world becomes deeper.

> *Equanimity* gives us the inner peace and space to taste and digest our experiences, even painful ones, without being "storm-tossed" by every feeling. With Equanimity, we find purpose and meaning in even the greatest human sufferings.

> Once Equanimity has given us emotional stability and a kind of fearlessness in the face of human suffering, then *Compassion* can go to work. Compassion allows our hearts to go out to others who are still enveloped in their own ignorance and self-created suffering. Compassion engages our heart, connecting us to the suffering of others—indeed, to all human suffering—although without a hint of superiority or detached distance. Ironically, if Equanimity frees us from the sting and debilitations of suffering, Compassion throws us right back into the middle of the action—into the "eye of the storm" of human suffering.

> *Engagement* impels us to throw ourselves into the fire of grace, seize the experience, and definitively take it into our hearts. Engagement allows me to not blink, and to make the mystical experience "my own"—without the ego claiming it for itself. This Virtue enables me to fully embrace the experience, to be permanently changed by it, and to put it into action in the world.

> *Truthfulness* entails being humble about our experience. The truth is that we did absolutely nothing to "earn" what we just experienced, and we may not even understand what has just happened to us. Truthfulness affirms that "the finger of God has touched me"—and I don't understand it or know what to do about it. Truthfulness admits that we are speechless and clueless in the face of mystery.

> Finally, *Courage* is related to the other two Virtues. We need courage to admit that we have had a mystical experience, and also that we are called to live in a different way. Courage emboldens us to realize that mystical awareness involves responsibility—the responsibility to bring my experience of the divine reality into the world. It takes enormous courage to realize that the future will have to be different from the past, now that I have seen something of ultimate reality. In view of what I have just experienced, I need to re-evaluate all of my actions and habits.[17]

My *Equanimity* allows me to calmly endure your torture and remain engaged in service to you. My *Compassion* connects me to your suffering and makes it mine. My *Engagement* puts the mystical miracles of my life into action and brings them to bear on your life. My *Truthfulness* keeps my ego in check, reminding me that the finger of God points the way, and divine love is at the heart of the mystery. My *Courage* keeps me from running away from the mysterious divine reality and from my responsibility to bear witness to the truth as it has been revealed to me.

~ 530 ~

I am just finishing Martin Heidegger's *An Introduction to Metaphysics*. It was a hard read, a complicated subject made more difficult in translation. But it was worth the effort.

> Historical science after all investigates the temporal, while philosophy investigates the timeless. Philosophy is historical only insofar as it—like every work of the spirit—realizes itself in time. For us history is not synonymous with the past; for the past is precisely what is no longer happening. And much less is history the merely contemporary, which never happens but merely "passes," comes and goes by. History as happening is an acting and being acted upon which pass through the *present*, which are determined from out of the future, and which take over the past. It is precisely the present that vanishes in happening.[18]

Here is another fabulous description of the timelessness of eternity. Although the last sentence would seem to contradict the ever-present "now" of the Buddhists, it actually confirms the same underlying idea. Prior sentences make the point that past, present, and future are relative to each other only in the temporal historical context. They tumble over each other and become indistinguishable in the philosophical timelessness. History is "an acting and being acted upon" – cause and effect – karma.

> Consequently a fundamental characteristic of the essent [existing thing] is *to telos*, which means not aim or purpose, but end. Here "end" is not meant in a negative sense, as though there were something about it that did not continue, that failed or ceased. End is ending in the sense of fulfillment. Limit and end are that wherewith the essent begins to *be*. It is on this basis that we must understand the supreme term that Aristotle used for being, *entelecheia*—the holding (preserving)-itself-in-the-being (limit). That which places itself in its limit, completing it, and so stands, has form, *morphe*. Form as the Greeks understood it derives its essence from an emerging placing-itself-in-the-limit.[18]

Things begin to *be* when they have form. "The earth was without form and void, and darkness was upon the face of the deep. ... And God said, 'Let there be light,' and there was light. ..."

The *polemos* named here is a conflict that prevailed prior to everything divine and human, not a war in the human sense. This conflict, as Heraclitus thought it, first caused the realm of being to separate into opposites; it first gave rise to order and rank. In such separation cleavages, intervals, distances, and joints opened. In the conflict <setting-apart> a world comes into being. (Conflict does not split, much less destroy unity. It constitutes unity, it is a binding-together, *logos*. *Polemos* and *logos* are the same.)[18]

"… and God separated the light from the darkness. … And God made the firmament and separated the waters which were under the firmament from the waters which were above the firmament." (Genesis 1:2-7)

Both Heraclitus and Genesis express a Western metaphysical philosophy of creative conflict, of "becoming," the emerging of space-time form and duality out of the eternal formless unity of the void – without destroying the unity. Form comes into being by placing and completing itself in the limit defined by the cleavages and spaces created in the primordial conflict between opposites.

From Parmenides: But only the legend remains of the way (along which it is disclosed) how it stands with being; on this (way) there are many indications: how being, without genesis, is without destruction, complete, alone there without tremor and not still requiring to be finished; nor was it before, nor will it be in the future, for being present it *is* entirely, unique, unifying, united, gathering itself in itself from itself (cohesive, full of presentness).[18]

This is exactly what I saw during my 1/1/09 epiphany – "being," without genesis, without destruction, gathering itself in itself from itself. The question of *ex nihilo nihil fit* ("nothing comes from nothing" – Parmenides' philosophy of "being") or *creatio ex nihilo* ("creation out of nothing" – Heraclitus' philosophy of "becoming") is moot; they are both true. Parmenides and Heraclitus simply saw the same reality from different angles, one from timeless eternity, the other from temporal duality.

I am exhilarated by my ability to grasp the meaning of these complex passages, synthesize them with other knowledge, and relate them to my own experience. By some miraculous and mysterious force, seminal wisdom from many diverse ages and cultures is finding its way into my consciousness all at once, like a grand confluence of mighty rivers.

The sails of the eighth and ninth bhūmi bodhisattva seem to be fully unfurled, resolute in their purpose, immovable and inexorable even in the face of the searing spiritual wounds you inflict on me – perhaps *because* of them.

~ 531 ~

Ignacio and I continue our ongoing tussle over free will vs. predestination, process in time vs. stasis in eternity. In my 1/1/09 epiphany, as powerful as the dancing molecules – matter dissolving into energy before my eyes – was the sensation of timelessness, each infinitesimal moment complete unto itself, not needing any past or future. The concept of "process" had no meaning. There was no need for me to impose my will upon life, no desire to do so, no possibility of doing so. Everything was perfect as is; there was no way to improve it and no will to change it, only the desire to be in harmony with it, which I already was and could not help but be.

In this world things process, evolve, and change like the patterns in a kaleidoscope. But at the same time, the stillness of eternity also exists. As in a kaleidoscope, all the pieces of the universe already exist along with the potentiality for all their infinite patterns, complete and perfect, in the fully lit House of Eternity. (~435~/~437~/~441~)

Another way to envision the coexistence of free will and predestination is to think of life as channel surfing on the television. We can exercise our free will to pick any channel we want, to linger on a channel with a program we find interesting, or to continue surfing. Perhaps we stay with a channel for a while, see a preview of coming attractions, and are pleased to discover that a program we want to see is coming up next.

Although we may have been surprised in the present moment to find out about this future program, there is a place where preset future programming can be known in advance – in a logbook, a TV Guide. We can know the future by looking in the logbook, which is like a catalog of all the contents of the House of Eternity, the Akashic Records of TV. All the programs on all the channels are listed – all those playing now and to be played in the future. We can even go backward into the past to find the programs that were previously played.

Our exercise of free will in the present moment allows us to choose which channels we will watch, to select our own unique path, our own Way, through the infinite smorgasbord of preset channels and programming available in the TV House of Eternity.

~ 532 ~

Jesus said: I am the Way, and the Truth, and the Life. No one comes to the Father except through me. (John 14:6)

Lao-tzu said: The Way (Dao) that is named is not the Way. (*Dao De Ching*)

Most Christians say that to be born again in the Spirit, to come to the Father, we must "believe" in Jesus Christ, a man with a name. We must follow a named Way, which Lao-tzu said is not the Way. How can Jesus and Lao-tzu be reconciled?

> In the beginning was the Word, and the Word was with God, and the Word was God ... And the Word became flesh and lived among us ... The law indeed was given through Moses; grace and truth came through Jesus Christ. No one has ever seen God. It is God the only Son, who is close to the Father's heart, who has made him known. (John 1:1 ... 18 RSV)

Jesus is the unnamable Way put into words, and flesh. The minister said, "Jesus did not come to save, but to reveal." Jesus came to bear witness, to reveal the truth, to make the unseen God visible. What was the Word,[iii] the truth that Jesus revealed? Jesus came to spread the good news, that salvation can be had not by good works and following the old Law of Moses, but simply by faith and grace: "I am the resurrection and the life. Those who believe in me, even though they die, will live, and everyone who lives and believes in me will never die." (John 11:25-26)

Who or what is the "I" and "me" that Jesus refers to in this passage? Not Jesus the man, the flesh and blood mortal, the words of whom would be no weightier than those of Elijah or Moses. The divinity of Christ, the Word that is Christ, the Truth which is truly worthy of our faith, trust, and surrender, is revealed in the *life* of Christ – the "process" of Christ – which, like the life of the Buddha, is a journey to resurrection and bliss through spiritual solitude, searching, surrender, suffering, and sacrifice. The Way and the Truth and the Life of Christ, like the Middle Way of the Buddha, points the Way that is the unique, indefinable, unlimited, unnamed personal journey that each of us must take to enlightenment and eternal life.

> To preach Christianity meant primarily to preach the Resurrection. ... The Resurrection is the central theme in every Christian sermon reported in the Acts. The Resurrection, and its consequences, were the 'gospel' or good news which the Christians brought: what we call the 'gospels', the narratives of Our Lord's life and death, were composed later for the benefit of those who had already accepted the gospel. The miracle of the Resurrection, and the theology of that miracle, comes first: the biography comes later as a comment on it. – C.S. Lewis, *Miracles*

Preaching on the existential miracle of the resurrection is just scratching the surface; the *meaning* of the resurrection – as Lewis says, "its consequences" – not the event itself, is the heart of the teaching. But the narrative gospels – the fable and legend of Jesus the man – are

---

[iii] The original Greek word for "Word" (λόγος logos) as used in John 1:1 is sometimes translated as "true account" or "truth." In Islam, another name for Allah (kalimat Allāh ["Word of God"]) is "Truth" (ٱلْحَقّ 'al-Ḥaqq).

also important because they teach us the *whole* life of Christ, physical and metaphysical, actual and allegorical, the Way to the eternal life that the resurrection represents. They bring Christ down to earth and make his life journey relatable and relevant to ours.

~ 533 ~

Thinking about Noah's Flood and rainbows: God is Light. Rainbows are the splitting of invisible white light into the spectrum of colors. Therefore, life is a rainbow – eternity broken up into a temporal spectrum of discrete space-time objects and events. As with all the Bible's miracle stories, this is an allegory, with meaning beyond the words. Surely the laws of physics that create rainbows were not different before and after the Flood. What symbolically happened with the story of the Flood was the arrival of a new perspective on duality.

Being cast out of Eden showed Adam and Eve the dark side of duality: "… in pain you shall bring forth children … By the sweat of your face you shall eat bread until you return to the ground." (Genesis 3:16-19) The message from God with the post-Flood rainbow was that there is a bright and beautiful side of duality, too. An angry and judgmental God can also be merciful and forgiving. If life can be said to be a blessing, it is because life gives us a particular vantage point from which to see the otherwise invisible eternity in its component parts, in all its beauty and all its horror, in movement through time and space.

~ 534 ~

At various junctures in this journal I have questioned myself. When I describe myself as a bodhisattva, living the life of Christ, I sometimes wonder if I am in some kind of grand delusion. Am I fooling myself, misreading the miracles, engaging in a self-indulgent ego trip, adopting a status for myself that I wish were true but is not, succumbing to selfish desires, not transcending them?

> The Pharisees and Sadducees came, and to test Jesus they asked him to show them a sign from heaven. He answered them, "When it is evening, you say, 'It will be fair weather, for the sky is red.' And in the morning, 'It will be stormy today, for the sky is red and threatening.' You know how to interpret the appearance of the sky, but you cannot interpret the signs of the times." (Matthew 16:2-3 RSV)

The people around me are skeptical; they do not understand my interpretation of the signs, as the Pharisees did not understand the signs of the times, of Jesus' life as the fulfillment of ancient prophesy. And so, when I begin to doubt myself, I remember the signs of my times – the miracles, the revelations, the epiphanies, the serendipities that propel me forward.

Why is it that the threads of the last fifty years of my life are now spontaneously coming together before my eyes, without my looking? Why is it that without my intention, without my effort, the flower opens before me? What force has compelled me to write hundreds of pages in this tome chronicling my spiritual journey, having the unintended effect of infusing my spiritual development into every aspect of my life?

> In this seventh stage [the seventh bhūmi] all elements of enlightenment are fulfilled moment to moment by the establishment of all qualities of buddhahood. What is the reason for this? All the elements of effort to evoke knowledge that are accomplished by enlightening beings in the first through seventh stages are *accomplished without effort* beginning in the eighth stage, and on until the final end. – *Daśabhūmika Sūtra,* from the *Avataṃsaka Sūtra,* Book Twenty-Six, "The Ten Stages"

Without intention, without effort, I live every moment in the dharma, in the spirit. In the end, I do not read the signs; they read me. I do not live my life; it lives me.

~ 535 ~

> We are just an advanced breed of monkeys on a minor planet of a very average star. But we can understand the universe. That makes us something very special. My goal is simple. It is a complete understanding of the universe, why it is as it is and why it exists at all. If you understand how the universe operates, you control it in a way. – Stephen Hawking, *Der Spiegel* (17 October 1988)

Stephen Hawking suffers from ALS and is almost completely paralyzed. His advanced monkey body is useless to him, a heavy, limiting weight impeding his physical function in the world. He is able to control almost nothing in his life. But he controls his mind, and he has discovered that understanding brings a kind of control. I am in awe of him, of his ability to create a new world for himself inside his head, where his spirit and intellect can fly free and unfettered.

You want control because you are afraid to be without it. I understand what motivates you; I am not afraid of you. Because I am not afraid of you, you can't control me, and are therefore afraid of me, afraid that I will control you.

The irony is that I don't want to control you or anything else. Knowledge is power, but also peace. I live as though what ought to be actually is, as I see life in my visions – as Hawking lives in total control inside his head.

PART 23

Sacrifice

April 2013 – July 2013

~ 536 ~

There was a board meeting of our business organization yesterday, without me, that turned into a Betty vilification fest. You want me out, and are actively working against me. You have co-opted the weaker members of the team into supporting you. Your wife is a victim of Stockholm syndrome (the captive befriending and defending her captor) and cannot stand up to you. Joe was my only advocate.

It became a matter of personal loyalty – a choice between you and me. At your wife's urging, the board decided to ask me to resign. There was no criticism of my work; the board's only rationale for my dismissal was that you can't seem to get along with me. They are giving in to the bully and sacrificing me in doing so.

I understand my dream now, with the nice man, the locked doors, and the imminent rape. (~524~)

~ 537 ~

The land of Judea is occupied by Rome, and ruled by a distant emperor who enforces his tyranny vicariously through a cruel and ruthless army.

Last year our board member Susan said to me, "You seem to be a person who came into the world to help others." She had seen my bodhisattva nature, so I confirmed it to her.

Last Christmas your wife's sister asked me if I am Kuan Yin. I said, "I am."

Now your wife betrays me. Susan says, "Give us Barabbas."

Another board member cries, "Crucify her!"

Only Joe, my Nicodemus, defends me before the Sanhedrin. The board president says, "This woman has done no wrong," but, afraid to defy tyrannical authority, condemns an innocent woman to spiritual death and washes his hands of the matter.

I say, "Father, forgive them, for they know not what they do."

Some people say love is hard to define. No, it isn't, not really. My life defines it.

~ 538 ~

Nothing belongs to me. Every edifice that man creates crumbles into dust.

The cat who cheered me up at the boat harbor last year is gone. (~484~) I looked for him the last several times I went there, but neither the cat nor his boat of residence, New Leif, was in evidence. I guess the boat found a new docking place and moved away. The cat, like the old native fisherman whom I saw there only once, was a spirit sent to guide and comfort me when I needed it.

I await the new spirit guide who must surely be coming to lift me out of this new nightmare.

~ 539 ~

As the Buddhist minister began her esoteric chanting, I felt a sudden tingling near the top of my spine, in the back of my neck. It was confined to a specific area of maybe two inches square, was quite intense, and lasted for about thirty seconds. I suspected that it could be the site of a chakra. This description seems to fit the bill, from Cyndi Dale's *Complete Book of Chakra Healing*, concerning the back side of the throat chakra:

> The back side of the fifth chakra is the center through which we channel thoughts, ideas, and concepts from other beings, other dimensions, and other aspects of ourselves. We receive information through the back of the neck, and then pass it along through our conscious, vocal front side … Often seen as the "seat of the soul" because it provides us with guidance from and for our soul self.[19]

Ah yes, spiritual messages enter at the back of the neck. As I type this, I am feeling it again.

I spent this morning in session with a psychologist. The psychologist suspects that your anger comes from unresolved issues with your mother. The Buddhist minister says it's with your father. Either way, you are blind with rage at me over something I cannot control. But then, that's the lot of the bodhisattva – to serve as a receptacle or resonator for another's pain.

~ 540 ~

Had another dream last night: *I was with a group at a rustic retreat, sitting on the side of a smooth road with low stone curbs. A lot of people were rushing past me, and I had to hold my computer and other belongings close to protect them. I seemed to be thinking about getting the information out of the computer into another device.*

The road led into a cabin where I was staying, into the kitchen. I left my computer by the side of the road and entered the cabin. There were two people in the cabin who had taken over the place while I was gone. They were anxious for me to leave. I gathered up my stuff and looked for my round loaf of bread. I asked to get back what was left of it. They reached up to a high shelf and brought down half a loaf. I noticed that the air holes were very large, almost more air than bread. They had eaten all the other food I had in the cabin.

I took the bread, gathered up my computer, still intact, from the side of the road, and headed down the dark road. As I walked, some friends joined me and showed me a newspaper with happy pictures of past events.

From dreammoods.com:

Computer – To see a computer in your dream symbolizes technology, information, and modern life. New areas of opportunities are being opened to you.

Road – To see a road in your dream refers to your sense of direction and how you are pursuing your goals. If the road is winding, curvy, or bumpy in your dream, then it suggests that you will encounter many obstacles and setbacks toward achieving your goals. If the road is dark, then it reflects the controversial or more frightening choices which you have made or are making.

Cabin – To see or dream that you are in a wood cabin indicates that you will succeed via your own means. It suggests that you are self-reliant and independent, yet still remain humble. You prefer the simpler things in life.

Kitchen – To see a kitchen in your dream signifies your need for warmth, spiritual nourishment and healing. Alternatively, the kitchen represents a transformation. Something new or life altering is about to occur.

Shelf – To see a shelf in your dream suggests that there is something you need to put aside right now. You need to put your ideas or plans on hold. Alternatively, the objects on the shelf may refer to some aspect of yourself that you have forgotten or neglected.

Food – To see food in your dream represents physical and emotional nourishment and energies.

Bread – To see bread in your dream represents the basic needs of life. Bread may signify the positive qualities and great things you have learned on your journey of life.

Newspaper – To see or read a newspaper in your dream signifies that new light and insight is being shed on a waking problem that is nagging on your mind. You are seeking knowledge and answers to a problem. Pay attention to the dream as it may offer a solution. Alternatively, reading the newspaper implies that you need to be more vocal. You need to express yourself. It is time to make the headlines.

You and your wife are the two who have taken over my kitchen and evicted me. I am resigned to leaving, but I am taking with me only a portion of my bread, my basic nourishment, which is full of holes. This is what is coming off the shelf, what is left of my psyche, which I have neglected while caring for you. Although the road is dark, it is smooth and only slightly curvy. I think the computer represents the information I am holding, my insights into you. My concern about getting the information out of the computer and reading the newspaper at the end may represent the publishing of this journal.

~ 541 ~

All of my advisors came to the same core understanding of our situation, saying that your problem with me has nothing to do with me or anything I have done, inside or outside of our business relationship. They said in their various ways from their various disciplines that you are waging an internal battle with yourself, even going back to troubles in past lives and the lives of your ancestors, and you have chosen me to be the receptacle for your anger, fear, frustration, and grief. Given the spiritual depth of our relationship, I do not find this surprising or unexpected.

What I did find surprising and unexpected was the board's decision to give in to intimidation, to make the victim pay a second time for the abuse perpetrated against her. Like a rape victim who is raped the first time by her rapist and then a second time by the court that finds her rapist not guilty. Like trying to end slavery by killing the slaves.

I ask myself how I contributed to the discord between us and what I might have done differently to have prevented it. Sure, I could have acquiesced to your every whim and desire (you demanded no less), and that would have prevented the discord. But what would have been gained by doing that? I came into your life to help you break out of your self-destructive and abusive mold, not to enable it. My mission is not to make peace; it is to reveal truth. My life as a truth-teller has always come with great pain and strife; there is no way around it.

Martin Luther King, Jr., described the situation well in his description of "positive peace," from his letter to fellow clergymen written in the Birmingham jail:

> I have almost reached the regrettable conclusion that the Negro's great stumbling block in his stride toward freedom is … the white moderate, who is more devoted to "order" than to justice; who prefers a negative peace which is the absence of tension to a positive peace which is the presence of justice … Actually, we who engage in nonviolent direct action are not the creators of tension. We merely bring to the surface the hidden tension that is already alive.[22]

It is not lost on me that Martin Luther King was assassinated. So was Gandhi. The messenger is often killed.

~ 542 ~

For the last couple of weeks, I have been conferring with trusted friends and advisors of various psychological and religious persuasions, weighing their words along with my own thoughts, searching for the best way to handle my ousting from your business.

At first, I considered requesting an audience with the board, or perhaps with board members individually, hoping to present a defense and possibly get them to rethink their course, for the good of the organization. But then I realized that what happened to me at the board meeting was not about me, and any defense of me would be irrelevant.

Then I thought about writing the board a letter describing in detail the many layers of harm being done to many people and to the organization, hoping that if they understood the bad karma they created, they might be able to avoid creating more in the future. But then I realized that the board had been thoroughly alienated from me and would not hear anything I might say.

Then I thought, why would I want to continue a working relationship with people who don't want me, who have been poisoned against me? How can I be effective in an environment of disrespect, dishonor, and humiliation? I realized that I must go. So I will.

A very, very negative peace. For now. Until the resurrection.

~ 543 ~

Today I wandered around the zoo, pondering my dilemma and what to do about it. I sat on a bench in a quiet corner for a long time, reflecting, contemplating, meditating, ruminating.

A zookeeper drove by a couple times in his electric cart and the second time asked, "Are you okay?"

I answered, "I'm fine, just resting, relaxing."

"You look very relaxed," he said.

~ 544 ~

What is the meaning of sacrificial offerings to God? Most people say it is to atone for sin or appease God. Perhaps, but I think it is for something else. A sacrificial offering, a gift that represents a true sacrifice, a painful loss on the part of the giver, is a tangible sign of spiritual growth. Why was Cain angry with Abel, angry enough to kill him? Because God favored Abel's offering over Cain's. What made Cain's offering insufficient?

The quality of a sacrifice is measured in the willingness to give up something of great value, not just any old fruit from the harvest or sheep from the flock, but the finest unblemished fruit, a perfect lamb, even unto one's own child (Abraham and Isaac) or one's own life (Jesus). The sacrificial object itself is not what is being measured, but rather the spirit of the giver and the degree of poverty, loss, pain, or humiliation he is willing to endure in making the sacrifice.

A sacrifice is not just a gesture of atonement, appeasement, or supplication – it is a significant step away from greed, attachment, and possessiveness, and toward unsupported thought, toward divine love and the eventual surrender of everything. "Greater love has no man than this, that a man lay down his life for his friends." (John 15:13)

~ 545 ~

Ignacio's group had a lively discussion on the work of Rupert Sheldrake, who questioned several of the dogmas of science, one being that *"nature is purposeless."* What is the purpose of nature, of life – in particular, of the bodhisattva's life of service and sacrifice? What is the point of improving one's life, even finding nirvana or helping others to do so, when there must always be a balance of yin/yang in the dualistic world? No matter how many buddhas are elevated and taken off the wheel of samsara, other souls are backsliding and making bad karma, and more generations of earthly creatures are constantly being reborn. Evil can never be eliminated or even reduced, except as good is also reduced to maintain the required balance.

An answer came to me when we looked at another questionable dogma: *"The total amount of matter and energy is always the same."* I equate Einstein's $E=mc^2$ – the relationship of energy, matter, and time – to the spiritual relationship of eternity and duality. Today it dawned on me that the goal of a life of service, good works, and building merit is not to make life better or happier, but to bring all separate creatures in the dualistic world back into the oneness of eternity. Perhaps the total amount of matter and energy *can* change: As more *arhats* are made and elevated, as their matter and energy are evaporated into the emptiness of the Dao, fewer souls are reborn into the human and lower realms.

By transmuting Einstein's equation, I see a spiritual metaphor. Over the immensity of time and space, matter and energy – the physical manifestation of dualism in the world – are reduced and dissolved together into pure light: $E/m=c^2$. Einstein said that mass and energy are really the same thing. (~429~) Mass, or matter (m), is low-frequency energy with form and substance in space. Energy (E) is the collection of high-frequency, formless forces in space. Time, represented in this equation by the speed of light (c), is the continuum in which forms and forces ebb and flow and coalesce into discreet temporal objects and events.

Energy and matter can together increase ($3E/3m=c^2$) or decrease ($2E/2m=c^2$). As m approaches one (1), the universe contracts. As m approaches zero (0), matter disintegrates and energy dissipates; the creation unwinds. When m equals zero, the universe is destroyed, imploded into the eternal nothingness from which it came. The laws of the physical world no longer apply. The left side of the equation $E/m=c^2$ goes away entirely, and everything becomes pure light. The mass of a photon, a quantum of light, is zero.

I have no idea if this analysis has any scientific validity, but as a spiritual metaphor for the interconnectedness of science, philosophy, and religion, it resonates with me. It describes the end of creation with the same elegance as Parmenides and Heraclitus described its beginning. (~530~) I think Einstein the Philosopher is smiling.

And another questionable dogma: *"Telepathy and other psychic phenomena are illusory."* I have long questioned this one; virtually every page of this journal is spawned by my personal experiences from beyond the physical senses. It is tangible substance that is illusory.

~ 546 ~

A few years ago I wrote about the idea of joyous suicide (~316~), a self-inflicted death when life is felt to be completely fulfilled, all life's work done. I am now considering that all death is a form of suicide. A terminal illness is the body telling itself to shut down, to kill itself. Falling victim to an accident or even being murdered is in a way a self-inflicted wound, your karma having put you in a place and time and circumstance where you would be in harm's way.

> Some events you produce willfully, and some events you draw to you—more or less unconsciously. Some events—major natural disasters are among those you toss into this category—are written off to "fate." Yet even "fate" can be an acronym for "from all thoughts everywhere." In other words, the consciousness of the planet. – *Conversations with God* [23]

~ 547 ~

Two motorcycles churned up the hill, destroying the tranquility for miles around. They buzzed through the park, roared down the road to the overlook, and finally stopped in the parking lot below my nest. One motorcyclist said to the other, "I thought we'd be going somewhere interesting," and they sped off out of the park.

The sounds of birdsong, the fragrance of the forest and spring blossoms, the panoramic view of the city from high above, the squirrel who stands up to eye me from just below the mound where I sit, the fine powdered pollen from pine cones wafting in the air and between my fingers, the elevated thought that comes to me in the quiet still air – after two hours sitting here in the same place I still have not lost interest.

~ 548 ~

Last year around this time, as the anniversary of Lou's death approached, I went through a very rough time. I came to you for support, comfort, compassion. I exposed my vulnerability and my innermost torment to you, my best friend. I did so because that's what best friends do. I wanted a friend. You thought I wanted sex.

This year, despite your cruel estrangement from me, I am strangely calm. Through my current travail I have learned that our love came to me not to bring me comfort or support (or sex), but rather the intense suffering necessary for me to reach higher levels of spiritual awareness. Thank you for the suffering. It will either kill me or propel me to the tenth bhūmi.

You complain that I only speak from my own perspective. That's because my own perspective is the only one I have. Nevertheless, I do believe that my perspective encompasses a wide angle, and includes a large part of your suffering. I *do* feel your pain most acutely. I only speak the truth as I know it, only when I feel I must, and without harmful intention. But you do not believe my truth and are hurt and angered by it, despite my assurances of goodwill. You accuse me of not seeing things from your perspective, but every time I ask what things look like from your perspective, you refuse to answer. When I ask you what I am seeing incorrectly from my perspective, you refuse to answer.

You are unable to see things from my perspective. I think you are also unable to see the truth that is already inside you – your karma – the role you played in bringing my uncomfortable truths forth and in generating your angry and fearful responses to them. I shine a light on your karma, both the good and the bad, and hold a mirror up to you. You welcomed me into your fold to nurture the good karma with my music, money, and skills, but now you reject me because the bad karma has come to the fore. I have unwittingly lifted the lid on the trash can of your life and you recoil at the stench that is released. But you do not realize that the stench is not coming from me, the messenger, but from you. You cannot get rid of it by pushing me away. You cannot run from it; it follows you everywhere like a smelly shadow.

My first conscious breakthrough in understanding sociopathy came when I saw through my dear friend James' obnoxious, almost abusive, rudeness. Other people were offended or angered by him, but not me. I understood him in the deepest, most compassionate way, and loved him regardless of his behavioral dysfunction. I realized at that time that my increased ability to perceive and understand antisocial behavior at such a deep level was a quantum leap toward awakening. In retrospect I can see that experience, like every other pivotal experience in my life, as tailor-made preparation for what I am facing now. How did the Past know what the Future would hold?

> In the Buddhist tradition there are many stories, called Jatakas, of the previous lives of the Buddha. As a bodhisattva, he practiced inclusiveness and forbearance. There are stories of him smiling while his body is being sawed into pieces. As a young boy I read the Jatakas and I could not understand how a human being could be that patient and forgiving. I was too young to understand that the Buddha was able to practice that way because he had the eyes of understanding and could see the causes and conditions that had led to the cruelty and inhumanity of the person who was harming him. "The ability to see" is the raw material in a bodhisattva that leads to great compassion. ... When we are able to love others in spite of their misdeeds, we are already a bodhisattva. – Thich Nhat Hanh, "When We Look Deeply"

Thank you for the suffering, for my next quantum leap.

~ 549 ~

Soldiers come back from war profoundly changed. They have seen life with all façades, pretenses, stripped away. Some grow from the experience; others are crippled by it. So it will be with me. I can feel myself growing and being crippled at the same time.

I told a mutual friend about my being fired from your business. She said, "This is for the best. The gods have taken you out of a bad situation for your own good. They will bring you back when the time is right."

"New beginnings are often disguised as painful endings," said Lao-tzu. Another aphorism: "Sometimes when things are falling apart they may actually be falling into place."

~ 550 ~

Ernest Hemingway said, "The best people possess a feeling for beauty, the courage to take risks, the discipline to tell the truth, the capacity for sacrifice. Ironically, their virtues make them vulnerable; they are often wounded, sometimes destroyed."

I have a feeling for beauty, as you have heard in my music. My courage in taking risks, so evident in my discipline of truth-telling, has led to incredible sacrifices of money, property, heart, and spirit. You have exploited my virtues and vulnerability, and wounded me deeply.

But I am not destroyed. I am incredibly saddened by your mistreatment of me; never before had I worked so hard for people I love so much. You are my family, and now I am an orphan. Yet I love you still. The signs, visions, and miracles that led me to this place give me the strength to weather this storm and shake off all feelings of anger and vengeance.

> You have heard that it was said, 'An eye for an eye and a tooth for a tooth.' But I say to you, Do not resist one who is evil. But if any one strikes you on the right cheek, turn to him the other also; and if any one would sue you and take your coat, let him have your cloak as well; and if any one forces you to go one mile, go with him two miles. Give to him who begs from you, and do not refuse him who would borrow from you. (Matthew 5:38-42 RSV)[iv]

Ignacio helped me understand Jesus' advice to "turn the other cheek" as a form of passive resistance, not a sign of meekness or weakness, but a dynamic assertion of the truth by bearing witness to it. When an aggressor exerts force against a nonviolent opponent to accomplish his

---

[iv] The Buddha offered the same advice: "Conquer the angry one by not getting angry; conquer the wicked by goodness; conquer the stingy by generosity, and the liar by speaking the truth." (Dhammapada 223)

ends, the aggressor is shamed. Jesus, Gandhi, and Martin Luther King didn't fight, but they didn't go away, either. They took all the punishment that their oppressors could dish out, much of it in the public eye, and by so doing bore witness to the truth. Eventually the aggressor sees the evil of his actions in the suffering of his victim, and in the revulsion to his demonstrated abuse reflected back to him by those who witness it.

In the short-term, you go on as before, apparently unharmed by your shameful actions, while I am devastated. But in the fullness of time, the situation will be reversed. My suffering through this injustice will send me to higher levels of spiritual elevation, while you will feel the effects of the bad karma you have made for yourself, karma that will follow you wherever you go in this life and thereafter. If you believe the teaching that you have received from the Buddhists, you know the truth of this.

Years ago I wrote, "I have known for some time that the first stage of wisdom is the abandonment of the expectation of justice." (~27~) My current travail has served to deepen my understanding of this truth. Unmitigated injustice is spiritually intentional; it has a divine purpose; it is an essential experience on the path to awakening.

> When we touch the center of sorrow, when we sit with discomfort without trying to fix it, when we stay present to the pain of disapproval or betrayal and let it soften us, these are the times that we connect with bodhichitta. – Pema Chödrön

~ 551 ~

I feel like a zookeeper who tenderly and affectionately cares for the venomous snakes in the Reptile House. Normally the affection is mutual, and the keeper loses her fear of the snakes. But then one day a snake bites his loving keeper. The bite hurts, and the venom penetrates deep into the system. And then the vicious snake's mate turns on the keeper, too, and bites her. The effect of the double dose of venom sends the keeper into convulsions of pain, and the powerful venom causes lasting, maybe permanent, maybe fatal, damage to the keeper's vital organs.

Will I recover? My spiritual grounding provided the antivenin that saved my life, but I can't seem to shake this gnawing, numbing, paralyzing residue of deep, deep, deep sadness. The saddest part is that it is no longer safe for me to approach the dear ones whom I still love and once held close. I would rather die from my wounds than live like this. The one reason that I still linger in this life is the possibility that my work with you is not yet done, and the time may come when I can safely hold you close again.

~ 552 ~

This morning at the temple I felt another wave of the deep terror that ran through me in the years immediately after Lou's death. What still terrifies me, what jumped up uninvited into my consciousness this morning, is the question of what is beyond God, beyond the Dao, outside the emptiness. Where did the nothingness from which something came, come from? Trying to wrap my mind around that idea is to experience the ultimate untetheredness – there is no higher mathematics or physics or philosophy or religion that can offer any guidance whatsoever in that deepest, darkest chasm. There are no signposts, no supports, and no guardrails there.

The human imagination has tackled and conquered such difficult concepts as imaginary numbers, the fourth spatial dimension, quantum mechanics, and the oneness of the Dao, but no mind that I know of ever comprehended in thoughts or words this most formidable question. No mind was ever meant to, and trying to do so is the road to insanity, running the spiritual train off the track.

I had to get up and leave the service for a moment, walk around outside, reorient my mind to the world again, and push the reset button. For an instant my mind broke loose from its harness and ran free into forbidden country. It took me a while to round it up again and put the blinders back on.

~ 553 ~

A recent newsletter from the Buddhist temple said, "Because of great wisdom, the enlightened one does not linger in the illusory world of birth and death, and because of great compassion, he does not linger in the world of enlightenment. Because the path has no end, he continues to strive even after he has attained enlightenment."

This so precisely states what I have been saying so imprecisely for years. I have talked about being split between two worlds, about the companion forces of wisdom and compassion, about the bodhisattva's understanding of suffering in this world, accepting it with patience and tolerance, knowing the peace that awaits in the other world.

ON JEALOUSY AND ENVY

Ignacio taught me another thing today: the difference between jealousy and envy. Jealousy is saying, "This is mine and you can't have it." Envy is saying, "That is yours and I want it (or resent you having it)." Two sides of the coin of greed.

Our goal is to turn jealousy into generosity: "This is mine; I freely give it to you." And envy into admiration: "That is yours, the fruit of your life, not mine." Or more deeply: What is mine only appears to be mine. I am merely a temporary custodian of all that I hold – money, possessions, friends, thoughts, health, life. My life's work is not to hoard whatever assets I have and accumulate more, but to let flow from my reservoir whatever of my assets are necessary to carry out my mission of service, even unto the depletion of those assets, even unto death.

And the converse is also true: What appears to be yours is really also mine. Even while truly owning nothing, everything is ours – our responsibility. When someone gains or loses something of value – property, fame, status, health, wealth – we share in the credit or blame to the extent that we influenced that person in a positive or negative direction. No man is an island, and everyone is everyone else's keeper.

> "For the kingdom of heaven is like a householder who went out early in the morning to hire laborers for his vineyard. After agreeing with the laborers for a denarius a day, he sent them into his vineyard. And going out about the third hour he saw others standing idle in the market place; and to them he said, 'You go into the vineyard too, and whatever is right I will give you.' So they went. Going out again about the sixth hour and the ninth hour, he did the same. And about the eleventh hour he went out and found others standing; and he said to them, 'Why do you stand here idle all day?' They said to him, 'Because no one has hired us.' He said to them, 'You go into the vineyard too.' And when evening came, the owner of the vineyard said to his steward, 'Call the laborers and pay them their wages, beginning with the last, up to the first.' And when those hired about the eleventh hour came, each of them received a denarius. Now when the first came, they thought they would receive more; but each of them also received a denarius. And on receiving it they grumbled at the householder, saying, 'These last worked only one hour, and you have made them equal to us who have borne the burden of the day and the scorching heat.' But he replied to one of them, 'Friend, I am doing you no wrong; did you not agree with me for a denarius? Take what belongs to you, and go; I choose to give to this last as I give to you. Am I not allowed to do what I choose with what belongs to me? Or do you begrudge my generosity?' So the last will be first, and the first last." (Matthew 20: 1-16 RSV)

This parable explains how envy can confuse generosity with apparent unfairness or injustice. The householder, like the good shepherd, treated each member of his flock equally in terms of each worker's humanity, regardless of the amount of work he did. It appears from this parable that Jesus was a socialist, even a communist: From each according to his ability, to each according to his need.

~ 555 ~

You said, "I don't want to lose control of my work." But I wonder, do you now or did you ever really have control of your work? Who will have control of it when you are dead? What makes it "your work"? I heard you give a speech about getting the ego out of the way and allowing the music, the creative inspiration, to come from beyond and simply flow through you. None of our work is really ours, and we are presumptuous to think that we ever really control it.

~ 556 ~

Ah, so you shall be sure to be misunderstood. Is it so bad, then, to be misunderstood? Pythagoras was misunderstood, and Socrates, and Jesus, and Luther, and Copernicus, and Galileo, and Newton, and every pure and wise spirit that ever took flesh. To be great is to be misunderstood. – Ralph Waldo Emerson

Ah, I'm in good company, then. Misunderstood – and feared. Therefore vilified, nullified, crucified.

I am remembering the deaths of Gandhi, Galileo, Jesus, Socrates, Martin Luther King, Jr. Each one is honored and revered now for the very achievements that precipitated their deaths. By the time they died, they had either accomplished their great work of destiny or set the wheels in motion for the goal to be reached after their deaths. Has my life of service achieved enough yet for my death to be at hand?

In the movie *Gandhi*, Mirabehn said just before Gandhi's assassination, "He thinks he has failed." Even though the independence of India had been accomplished, the Hindu-Muslim discord of India-Pakistan cast a shadow of failure upon him. That is where I am now. Because you cast me out, I feel as though I have failed. But has my truth-telling in your life set into motion a new awareness that, while you now deny it, will surface later, as Galileo's revealed truth became undeniable after his death?

~ 557 ~

I am reading the autobiography of an immigrant fisherman. He left his native land at the age of sixteen with only a grade school education, but with wisdom and diligence he became a very successful businessman and a pillar of the community in his new home. Before he embarked on his new life, he received wise counsel from his teacher, who said:

> You must utilize your luck when you go abroad to earn your fortune. When you feel that luck is with you, you must advance ten miles instead of one. But if you intuitively feel that luck is not with you, you should not advance. For example, you are sailing with the wind and want to go east, but with interference from the wind, you have difficulty proceeding. In such a case, drop your anchor and rest. Eventually the wind will stop and another wind will blow from another direction. When the new wind blows, raise your sail ten feet instead of one. Advance at full speed. You'll succeed in business if you keep this in mind.

This story clears up the confusion that is raised when I talk about activity vs. passivity, letting go vs. holding on, leading life vs. being led. There are two opposite kinds of activity and two opposite kinds of passivity. The sailor's wisdom above describes the skillful use of action/activity and inaction/passivity.

The unskilled use of passivity is to retreat from life, to give in to apathy and ignorance – to stay at anchor even when a good wind is blowing. When I say that we should learn to let go, I don't mean to withdraw from life and just watch it go by. Even while watching and waiting, there should be mindfulness, constantly observing, taking it all in, gaining the knowledge and wisdom to know when the good wind is rising and it is time to set sail.

The unskilled use of activity is to force whatever you think you want, unmindful of your place in the universal harmony, the effect of your actions on others, or the nature of obstacles in your path. When spiritual teachers suggest using the power of intention or positive affirmation, they are not encouraging you to pursue a future that is not meant to be, or delude yourself into thinking you are what you are not. The object is to entertain all possibilities, to completely open up to the universal energy and let it point you in a positive direction. When that direction is revealed, commit to it fully. Unfurl your sails ten feet instead of one.

All of life is the exercise of the paradox, the conundrum, of volition vs. predestination. Do we make life happen, or does it just happen on its own? Act, but don't do so out of reflexive greed or desire. Wait, but don't do so out of paralytic fear. Finding our true destiny requires our active participation. Sometimes that participation is mindful inaction.

~ 558 ~

I am remembering the day at your mother's grave when I chanted for her, when I called to the wind god and the wind blew, and when I called to the rain god and the rain fell. (~268~) Most people would say that the wind would have blown and the rain would have fallen, anyway, without my chant. Maybe … but I understand how it is that those who chant up the sun at sunrise know for a fact that the sun wouldn't rise but for the chant.

~ 559 ~

There are two Gods described in the Bible. The one true God – the God that Jesus embodied, that his life exemplified – rises above and beyond judgment, vengeance, condemnation, rewards, punishments, and glorification. The verses below are reflective of this God, the Source:

> But I say to you that hear, Love your enemies, do good to those who hate you, bless those who curse you, pray for those who abuse you. To him who strikes you on the cheek, offer the other also; and from him who takes away your coat do not withhold even your shirt…. Judge not, and you will not be judged; condemn not, and you will not be condemned; forgive, and you will be forgiven. (Luke 6:27-37 RSV)

> But when they heard it, they went away, one by one, beginning with the eldest, and Jesus was left alone with the woman standing before him. Jesus looked up and said to her, "Woman, where are they? Has no one condemned you?" She said, "No one, Lord." And Jesus said, "Neither do I condemn you; go, and do not sin again." (John 8:9-11 RSV)

By loving his enemies, not seeking vengeance, and not condemning, Jesus was acting as God the Source – not judging, only loving. This is the love of God, *agape*, the highest form of spiritual love.

The other God in the Bible is an anthropomorphic representation, a limited God created by Man in the image of Man. This is the God that expresses human emotions and attributes like vengeance, mercy, anger, forgiveness, wrath, and conciliation. I suspect this image was created by Bible authors to paint a picture of God that people from polytheistic cultures like those in Egypt, Babylon, Greece, and Rome could relate to, whose gods possessed similar human characteristics, to make a bridge from the familiar to the unfamiliar, from the known to the unknown. This human-like image of God, what I call "Santa Claus for grownups," was created with the best of intentions, but down through the centuries it has become gravely misunderstood and mistaken for the real thing.

~ 560 ~

Today I had my second session with hypnotherapist Emily. I wanted to see if she had some guidance for me in dealing with your rejection. But before that, I stopped at a nearby eatery for lunch. As I sat at a table outside, a lone dove walked along the ledge behind me. I had finished eating and had no food to offer, or anything else to attract the bird. We made eye contact. "Is that you, Lou?" I asked, remembering that Lou had told me doves were the spirits of ancestors.

Then the bird stopped and sat down just a couple feet from me. We continued together in silent communion for a long time, at least a minute. The bird was firmly planted and did not move, even allowing me to take its picture. Eventually the dove flew over to a table a few feet away to beg for food, but I had gotten the message. Doves are spirit messengers.

~ 561 ~

MY MYSTIC JOURNEY WITH KATHY, Part 1
On Time and Space and the Trinity

My niece Kathy asked me about my view of the Holy Trinity, and requested that I cite scripture to validate my view. Okay … here goes:

When I was a young student in catechism class, we were taught that the Trinity was like H_2O in three forms: ice, water, and steam. Not a bad analogy, except that it does not take into account the simultaneity of space-time and eternity. H_2O cannot be ice, water, and steam at the same time in duality, but can be in the one timeless moment of eternity.

Journey back to the Garden of Eden, the place of unity. (Actually, we don't have to journey very far; we are already in the Garden and always have been, we're just blind to it in the dualistic world into which Adam and Eve were cast.) When Adam and Eve ate of the Tree of the Knowledge of Good and Evil, they became "as God," with knowledge of duality – good/evil, naked/clothed, pleasure/pain, beauty/ugliness, happiness/sadness.

> So when the woman saw that the tree was good for food, and that it was a delight to the eyes, and that the tree was to be desired to make one wise, she took of its fruit and ate; and she also gave some to her husband, and he ate. Then the eyes of both were opened, and they knew that they were naked; and they sewed fig leaves together and made themselves aprons. (Genesis 3:6-7 RSV)

Remembering that the creation story is an allegory, we realize that Genesis refers not just to nakedness of the body, but also of the soul. Adam and Eve covered their bodies with fig leaves, and also covered their souls – their indwelling God-selves – with ego, their newfound awareness of a self separate from God.

> Then the Lord God said, "Behold, the man has become like one of us, knowing good and evil; and now, lest he put forth his hand and take also of the tree of life, and eat, and live forever;" therefore the Lord God sent him forth from the garden of Eden, to till the ground from which he was taken. He drove out the man; and at the east of the Garden of Eden he placed the cherubim, and a flaming sword which turned every way, to guard the way to the tree of life. (Genesis 3:22-24 RSV)

God knew that Adam and Eve would need to feel the pleasure and pain of duality before they would be ready to return to the Garden via the Tree of Life. Jesus arrived to show them – us – the Way back to the Garden.

The Tree of Life, the fruit of which enables us to live forever – to have eternal life – is the cross of Jesus, from which he returned to the right hand of God the Father, to the Garden, to the place of unification of the pairs of opposites. This is also the Buddha's bodhi tree, under which he was enlightened and returned to the emptiness of the Great Void where all is one. With his sacrifice, Jesus sheathed the cherubim's flaming sword and gave us access to the fruit of the Tree of Life, and with it entry back into the Garden, into consciousness of eternity and oneness with God.

> And the people came to Moses, and said, "We have sinned, for we have spoken against the Lord and against you; pray to the Lord, that he take away the serpents from us." So Moses prayed for the people. And the Lord said to Moses, "Make a fiery serpent, and set it on a pole; and everyone who is bitten, when he sees it, shall live." So Moses made a bronze serpent, and set it on a pole; and if a serpent bit any man, he would look at the bronze serpent and live. (Numbers 21:7-9 RSV)

> Jesus said, "No one has ascended into heaven but he who descended from heaven, the Son of man. And as Moses lifted up the serpent in the wilderness, so must the Son of man be lifted up, that whoever believes in him may have eternal life." (John 3:13-15 RSV)

Moses lifted up the fiery serpent on a pole, so that all those who saw it might have physical life. Jesus, the Son of man, was lifted up on his pole so that whoever believes in him might have eternal life.

The symbolism of the serpent, the Garden of Eden tempter, is not lost on me. We "pray to the Lord, that he take away the serpents from us" when we recite the Lord's Prayer: "Lead us not into temptation but deliver us from evil." When Jesus gave us the Lord's Prayer, did he know that he would be the one to deliver us from evil, our bronze serpent on a stick?

Looking deeper into the metaphor of the serpent in the Garden of Eden, usually thought to be a metaphor for Satan, we see that the serpent was not really evil, not a liar and deceiver, but more of a mirror, a revealer of the other side of the dual/eternal coin. God said, "You may freely eat of every tree of the garden; but of the tree of the knowledge of good and evil you shall not eat, for in the day that you eat of it you shall die." (Genesis 2: 16-17)

But the serpent said, "You will not die. For God knows that when you eat of it your eyes will be opened, and you will be like God, knowing good and evil." (Genesis 3: 4-5) Both God and the serpent told the truth – God warning of the physical death of the body in the realm of duality, and the serpent explaining that in the eternal realm they would not die, but would gain consciousness of duality, of good and evil, like God.

Fire and flame are important symbols in many cultures and religions. The cherubim guard the Tree of Life with a flaming sword; Adonai was the name given to the voice of God who spoke to Moses from the burning bush; the Holy Spirit came to the disciples as a flame – some churches keep a flame burning constantly in the sanctuary as a symbol of the ever-present Holy Spirit:

> When the day of Pentecost had come, they were all together in one place. And suddenly a sound came from heaven like the rush of a mighty wind, and it filled all the house where they were sitting. And there appeared to them tongues as of fire, distributed and resting on each one of them. And they were all filled with the Holy Spirit and began to speak in other tongues, as the Spirit gave them utterance. (Acts of the Apostles 2:1-4 RSV)

Now let's visit Albert Einstein and the realm of science.[v] Einstein's Theory of Relativity was not just a breakthrough in physics; it was a scientific explanation of the Trinity. It ties together the fire symbolism and the relationship of matter, energy and time.

The trouble with the ice/water/steam analogy is that unlike H_2O, the three persons of the trinity exist simultaneously at all temperatures, in all space and time as well as in eternity. As Einstein proved, matter, energy and time are unified at the speed of light. Therefore, God (eternity) is expressed in space-time as light – electromagnetic radiation. Jesus said, "I am the light of the world; he who follows me will not walk in darkness, but will have the light of life."

---

[v] Science and art are friends of religion, all searching for the same truth. If science and religion appear to conflict, it is because we are misunderstanding either the science or the religion, or both. Truth is true from all perspectives. When we feel the celestial harmony unifying these companion pursuits, we will have found the truth. "Science without religion is lame, religion without science is blind." – Albert Einstein

(John 8:12) At the speed of light, past, present, and future are one; time is compressed into one singular, infinitesimal, eternal moment. This is what I call God.

Psalm 139 contains this wonderful exposition of the oneness of past, present, and future:

> Before a word is on my tongue you, Lord, know it completely.
>
> My frame was not hidden from you when I was made in the secret place, when I was woven together in the depths of the earth.
>
> Your eyes saw my unformed body; all the days ordained for me were written in your book before one of them came to be.

Now we can put the pieces together. Space-time (Jesus) is a perspective within eternity (God), differentiated in duality but not in eternity. The force that connects space-time and eternity is the universal energy, the light, the flame, of the Holy Spirit.

To put it simply, I think of God as a symbol representing the central foundation, the Source, from which all things emanate. Jesus – and us – are among those emanations. All things arise and descend, live and die, come and go, move from reality to illusion and back again, but are always and eternally connected through all space and time by the Holy Spirit. I see the Holy Spirit as a bungee cord that keeps living beings in touch with God as they are sent out of the Garden into the space-time world. Eventually we all reach the limit of the bungee cord's elasticity and are snapped back into God.

C.S. Lewis describes our snap-back to God, where we are and always were:

> No possible complexity which we can give to our picture of the universe can hide us from God: there is no copse, no forest, no jungle thick enough to provide cover. ... In the twinkling of an eye, in a time too small to be measured, and in any place, all that seems to divide us from God can flee away, vanish, leaving us naked before Him, like the first man, like the only man, as if nothing but He and I existed. – C.S. Lewis, *God in the Dock*[15]

~ 562 ~

Another dream: *I was standing on the balcony of a high-rise apartment or hotel room, very high up, looking out toward the ocean in the distance. There was darkness over the ocean, and I heard strange rumblings, portents of disaster. Suddenly something seemed to fall from the sky into the ocean, parting the waters like a knife. As a huge wall of water moved toward me, I put my hands together in prayer and waited for the end. I felt the building shudder and shake in this cataclysm, but before the building fell, a big bright ball of light emerged from the upper right corner of my view and flooded the scene with its light. I woke up.*

From dreammoods.com:

Ocean – To see an ocean in your dream represents the state of your emotions and feelings. It is indicative of spiritual refreshment, tranquility and renewal. If the ocean is rough, then the dream represents some emotional turmoil.

Sky – To dream that something is falling out of the sky signifies your pessimistic attitude.

Wall of Water – To dream that a wall of water is coming towards you implies that your emotions are welling up and can potentially close you off to others.

Catastrophe – To experience a catastrophe in your dream represents sudden instability and upheaval in your waking life.

Light – To see light in your dream represents illumination, clarity, guidance, plain understanding, and insight. Light is being shed on a once cloudy situation or problem. You have found the truth to a situation or an answer to a problem. Also consider the color of the light for additional significance. If the light is particularly bright, then it indicates that you need to move toward a higher level of awareness and feeling. Bright light dreams are sometimes common for those who are near death.

The ocean of my emotions is a source of power and spiritual refreshment, normally tranquil, but objects falling from the sky and the wall of water are indicative of bouts of turmoil. Your casting me out has indeed caused much turmoil, and your continued estrangement makes me anxious and pessimistic. But the big ball of light indicates that my pessimism and anxiety will be dispelled in a flood of illumination and insight, perhaps bringing me to a higher level of awareness. Or perhaps it is spiritual death and rebirth, wiping my slate clean. If actual physical death, then I have done all I can in this life.

In recent days some beautiful people have entered or become more prominent in my life – Emily, Lori, Rita – all in relation to you. They are a therapist, a filmmaker, and a beautician, all motivated in their respective occupations by a desire to bring out the beauty in the world. These ladies have brought me peace and understanding, revealing themselves to be kindred spirits in love, devotion, and loss. They are protecting me, holding my tether, buffering me from the turmoil. Their presence in my life at this time leads me to believe that the bright light of my dream is one of illumination, not death.

~ 563 ~

ON JUDGMENT

Even though Jesus said, "Judge not, lest ye be judged," Ignacio asserts that Jesus himself judged. I can think of only one circumstance in which Jesus might be considered to have been judgmental: when he called the Pharisees "vipers" for their hypocrisy (Matthew 23), and for their evil words (Matthew 12). But was that really judgment? There is a difference between judging and bearing witness to the truth. In a court of law, lawyers present the facts in evidence, and then a judge weighs the evidence, draws conclusions from the evidence, and makes a judgment.

Jesus did not judge; he merely stated the facts. He did not judge the adulteress whom he rescued from those who would have stoned her according to the Law of Moses. He did not judge Matthew for being a tax collector, working for the oppressors. When he overturned the tables of the moneychangers in the temple, saying, "Is it not written, 'My house shall be called a house of prayer for all the nations'? But you have made it a den of robbers," he was not judging, just stating the self-evident truth. He made observations, not judgments.

He did not judge the Pharisees, either, but rather allowed their own actions to judge them. Jesus said, "You brood of vipers! How can you speak good, when you are evil? For out of the abundance of the heart the mouth speaks." (Matthew 12:34) Jesus did not judge them to be evil; they had already been shown to be so by their own words and deeds. He was carrying forward the logic that naturally flows from simple observation, that the evil heart speaks evil, not good. A tree is known by its fruit. (Matthew 7:15-20)

Jesus did not even judge Judas. He simply said, "What you are going to do, do quickly." (John 13:27) Jesus knew that the karma of life would continue as it was meant to – God's perfect perpetual motion machine – regardless of any judgments he might or might not make. One is judged, one's karma is determined, one is tried, convicted, and punished by one's own being, not by any external authority.

So it is with my life. Being cast out by you, like the betrayal of Jesus by Judas, is something that had to happen in order for me to find the path to higher levels of awakening. It is my crushing sacrifice of salvation and purification. I do not return your evil with more evil. I do not judge you, only love you. Your own actions judge you, revealing the self-evident truth, the true abundance of your heart.

Knowledge is possession of the truth; wisdom is knowing how to use that knowledge, exercising restraint in drawing conclusions or making judgments based on what is almost always incomplete or conflicting data. The distinction between truth-telling and judging is a subtle one, but it must be made. Know the truth, bear witness to the truth, but let Judgment Day come on its own.

PART 24
Dreams and Visions
July 2013 – October 2013

~ 564 ~

MY MYSTIC JOURNEY WITH KATHY, Part 2
The $12,000 Dream

A few weeks ago, when I learned of Kathy's planned missionary work, I was moved to invite her into discourse with me on spiritual matters. We have had a few communications since then on the nature of God, the Trinity, and other religious topics. She seems to have become more open to such discussions in recent years.

A few days ago, I sent Kathy a $5,000 check to support her upcoming ecumenical evangelical adventure. This appeared today on her blog:

> *On Monday night I dreamed that I would discover that my mission account balance had risen to $12,000. An additional five thousand-some dollars had just poured into my account between the time I'd left for camp and the time I returned.*
>
> *I promised myself to not get overly excited about this dream.*
>
> *The next couple days passed pretty peacefully, and I returned home. When I got back to my apartment I decided to go through the mail I'd amassed from the week. It consisted of sales flyers, a couple letters, and what have you. And then there was a check. In the amount of $5,000.*
>
> *Suffice it to say, as of this writing, I have $12,255 in my account.*

Sometimes I feel as if my mind – conscious, unconscious, subconscious – is not just my own. Through it, God speaks to me and through me. It is without boundaries or limits, extending into other beings through space-time and into the Great Void. My life is an out-of-body experience.

I admit to having become somewhat complacent about the myriad miracles piling up in my life, but I confess, this one really caught my attention.

~ 565 ~

While waiting for a plane at the airport I felt a new sensation, that of being outside the world looking in on it, as if through a portal from another dimension. It was as if someone else was looking at the world through my eyes, as if another self had been superimposed on top of my own conscious self, as if someone was watching me watching the world around me.

I sense that I am not just a person, but also a portal through which the universal mind of God is revealed, filtered through my particular perspective. I am a spiritual conduit, a channel, a synapse, a cosmic connector the meaning of which I am just waking up to.

"Remember me," said the Buddha, "as the one who woke up."

~ 566 ~

When I say that I might be crazy or demented, I wonder if am paying myself a compliment. What "normal" people consider to be mental illness might actually be a special and privileged awareness, a portal to reality that only "crazy" people can access. I have previously alluded to the allegedly impaired mental states of Gustav Mahler and Billie Holliday as possible assets in their creative pursuits. I like to talk with such otherworldly people; I am fascinated by them. I want to know what they see. I want to glimpse the alternate reality that they attach to, detached as it is from my reality.

My sister-in-law Elaine is a perfect example. She had a brain injury that seems to make her befuddled and confused. Yet she says some astonishing and strangely insightful things to me, as I described earlier in this journal. Perhaps when she asks questions like, "Is John dead?" or "Did Lou die?" she has not lost her memory. Perhaps she isn't sure about their physical whereabouts because her mind has entered a realm where they are still speaking to her.

~ 567 ~

When you combine all the colors of the rainbow as beams of light, they merge into invisible white light. But when you combine all the colors of the visible spectrum as paint on a palette, they merge into a black blob. Black and white can both be described as either the absence of any color or the presence of all colors. A wonderful paradox!

A black hole contains the complete white light spectrum, but the light does not illuminate the world because it cannot escape the black hole. Black is white, white is black. Full is empty, empty is full.

The Great Void contains all things. Matter, energy, and time are one. Contraction and expansion: The universe contracts into a tiny speck and then explodes in the Big Bang, over and over again.

Nothing escapes from a black hole, not even light. Look for the wormhole that goes through the black hole to the other side. There the light of compassion shines over the whole universe and washes everything with its glow. Love is the light, the electromagnetic force that draws all into the Dao.

~ 568 ~

AT IGNACIO'S CABIN

Last night as I was working at the computer, a fly landed on my keyboard. I brushed it off, but it landed only a few inches away on the computer screen. It seemed lethargic, perhaps not fully functional in the cold air, or perhaps it was sick and dying. I lifted it onto my finger and looked closely. It seemed okay, rubbing its back legs together, apparently content to just sit on my hand. I thought to myself that I could easily crush this insect and be done with it, but something stopped me. To swat a fly is okay in a fair fight when the fly has a reasonable chance to escape, but to kill a wild creature who is doing no harm and who has put itself at your mercy, defenseless, would be wrong.

I then began to marvel at the situation – the rare occurrence of a fly sitting still on my hand, allowing itself to be touched. One does not often get such an opportunity to commune with a fly up close. After a short time I got up and took the fly to the door, hoping it would fly away. But no. I attempted to move the fly from my finger to a wooden beam outside the door, but it wouldn't go. At one point I thought I had succeeded, but as I went back inside I saw the fly still on my hand. I tried again, and I guess it worked that time.

It can now truly be said of me, "She wouldn't even hurt a fly."

~ 569 ~

When I arrived at the bus terminal a few days ago, on my way to spend some time at Ignacio's cabin, another bus was there at the same time with a picture of Jesus and an advertisement on the side saying, "… out of darkness into His marvelous light." (1 Peter 2:9) When I left the same terminal today, there it was again, if not the same bus, at least the same ad.

As soon as I arrived at my new mountain destination, my host took me aside to explain the current emergency. "We've been trying to get a hold of you for days, but your phone doesn't answer and I guess our emails aren't getting through, either. We wanted to inform you of the wildfires in the area and warn you not to come." I explained that for the last week I had been out of cell phone and internet communication. "We have been under an evacuation notice for several days, and many of our people have left. Just last night, though, we had a big rain, which saturated the forest and quelled much of the fire. Just today, the evacuation order was downgraded to a warning. The fire is not out and may flare up again, but the authorities say that now it is okay to stay here if you feel safe."

I was tempted to tell him, "God doused the fire to clear the way for my coming." I don't really believe that the forces of nature adjust themselves to my timetable, but I have to believe that there is something that connects me to them. Virtually all my serendipities, going back to my calling in music almost fifty years ago, to the moose coming to me within seconds of my agreeing to be happy without seeing one, to the synchronized responses of fire, wind, and rain to my incantations, are a matter of exquisite timing, pieces falling into place in perfect sequence, like a cosmic ballet. Now, with Kathy's $12,000 dream, Jesus Christ on the bus coming and going, forest fires in retreat as I advance … well … I couldn't make this stuff up.

~ 570 ~

I am watching a raptor in the sky. A hawk, perhaps, circling ever higher and higher, riding the updrafts. In the course of about a minute he has become a tiny black speck against the white clouds and blue sky. Now he is above the clouds; I cannot see him at all.

Why would a bird fly so high? There is no food up there. Just because he can? Just for the joy of it, as I enjoy flying alongside the clouds in an airplane?

I spent my first morning in the mountains communing with nature, starting with the underground varmint who lives outside my cabin, some kind of ground squirrel or gopher, I guess. The birds caught my eye – robins, bluebirds, swallows, sparrows, and hawks. Then I moved to the lake. A snake slithered out of my way as I walked down the path, along which I also observed butterflies, honeybees, and bumblebees making their daily rounds in search of nectar. I sat for a while on the dock, where I was greeted by all manner of bugs – dragonflies, damselflies, horseflies, regular ol' flies, gnats, and water striders. There were also bigger critters: a family of five ducks, and fish jumping at the bugs. I thought of a Tibetan poem that says everything comes from the Great Void "as from the surface of a clear lake, there leaps suddenly a fish."

Nature shows us how God's universe works, how the process of life, everything in flux, in constant motion, all together creates a seemingly static equilibrium. Each species evolved in relation to all the others, each finding a niche where it could live and let live. Inanimate objects are also players in the drama. The sun, moon, rocks, water, and air – all the matter and energy of the universe – are interwoven into life. Geology and astronomy as well as biology measure the time of life.

In nature there is birth and death, beauty and ugliness, light and dark, pleasure and pain, just as there is in the human realm (which is a subset of nature), yet the net result of all this activity, creativity, and intensity is one harmonious whole in the stillness of eternity. When you add together all of the struggle and striving in the world and look down from above upon the still lake and serene mountains at sunset, there is only peace.

~ 571 ~

I spent the day at the creek. I sat on my favorite sitting tree and watched the grass grow for a while. I walked all the way to the back of the valley. Butterflies – white, orange, yellow, and brown – followed and led me everywhere. A brown butterfly buzzed my head and sat for a few seconds on my chest. I was wearing a yellow shirt; perhaps he thought I was a flower?

I capped off the day with a burger and a beer at the local bar. I had two very pleasant conversations, one with a bicycler named Ralph who is in the midst of his transcontinental trek. We had a lovely time talking about our life adventures, my vocation and his avocation in music, our similar vagabond views at this late stage of life. (He is the same age as me.) I paid for Ralph's beer and burger, telling him that I had just spent two weeks staying with friends, not having to buy food, while he has weeks more to go on his journey, paying for food all the way. He thanked me and we shared a warm hug as he left.

The other conversation took place as I was walking out of the bar going back to my lodging. The young lady who had waited on us inside was outside on a smoke break. She called to me as I walked away, thanking me for covering Ralph's tab and for visiting the bar on this, her last night on the job. She is leaving town and the bar business to pursue her pre-law degree. She told me about her year-and-a-half-old son and her plans to live with her sister near the college to cut down on expenses while she is in school and working a better job in a law office or in government, she hopes. I wished her well and told her I was honored to have eaten one of her last burgers. "You flip a mean burger," I said, "I know you will do as well in law."

Why do people spontaneously open up to me and offer their stories? Does my compassionate heart show on the outside?

~ 572 ~

My dream: *Someone comes running toward me saying, "The baby needs help!" I enter a bright, white room, light streaming in from two large windows. Your sister-in-law is sitting by the windows, smiling, while a baby is crying on the bed. There are children sleeping on the floor in the corner. Someone else is tending to the baby. The baby looks at me, in distress. It has a strange, old face, with large, dark lips.*

From dreammoods.com:

> **Window** – To see a window in your dream signifies bright hopes, vast possibilities and insight.
>
> **Baby** – To dream of a crying baby symbolizes a part of yourself that is deprived of attention and needs to be nurtured. Alternatively, it represents your unfulfilled goals and a sense of lacking in your life.
>
> **Lips** – Lips are a means of communication as reflected in the familiar phrase "read my lips." To dream that you or someone has black lips suggests that you are refusing to say anything about a particular situation. You are remaining completely silent.

Who is the baby who needs help, but remains silent?

~ 573 ~

Viktor Frankl, a psychiatrist, neurologist, founder of the Third Viennese School of Psychotherapy, and a Holocaust survivor, wrote this amid the horror of a Nazi concentration camp:

Occasionally I looked at the sky, where the stars were fading and the pink light of the morning was beginning to spread behind a dark bank of clouds. But my mind clung to my wife's image, imagining it with an uncanny acuteness. I heard her answering me, saw her smile, her frank and encouraging look. Real or not, her look was then more luminous than the sun which was beginning to rise.

A thought transfixed me: for the first time in my life I saw the truth as it is set into song by so many poets, proclaimed as the final wisdom by so many thinkers. The truth—that love is the ultimate and the highest goal to which Man can aspire. Then I grasped the meaning of the greatest secret that human poetry and human thought and belief have to impart: *The salvation of Man is through love and in love*. I understood how a man who has nothing left in this world still may know bliss, be it only for a brief moment, in the contemplation of his beloved. In a position of utter desolation, when Man cannot express himself in positive action, when his only achievement may consist in enduring his sufferings in the right way—an honorable way—in such a position Man can, through loving contemplation of the image he carries of his beloved, achieve fulfillment. For the first time in my life I was able to understand the meaning of the words, "The angels are lost in perpetual contemplation of an infinite glory." [24]

Jacobo Timerman dealt with his suffering in prison the opposite way, by avoiding thoughts of love and beloved. The "intoxication of tenderness" only added to his suffering; remembering love and beloved only made his imprisonment, its isolation and separation, more painful.

I began my spiritual journey at the beginning of this journal where Timerman was, aching from the loss of love, fearing the intoxication of tenderness and wanting no more of it. But my spiritual journey cranked into high gear when karmic love entered my life a second time and I made the jump to Frankl's vision, to the "contemplation of an infinite glory" that rises above and beyond worldly pain. Even with nothing left in this world, I know bliss. I have seen your luminous smile.

And even while I twist in my own sea of pain, my greater sorrow is for you, for the hurt that you have inflicted on yourself. I dream of the day when God will fulfill my vision and allow me to see your awakened face finally glowing with our shared love, turning the bad karma around. But for now I am patiently waiting, satisfied with miracles and my eternal vision, like the angels "lost in perpetual contemplation of an infinite glory."

~ 574 ~

You no longer believe that I am who I say I am. Perhaps you think I am deluded and that I glorify myself. Okay, let's assume for the moment that you're right. Like those in *The Miracle On 34th Street* who thought that Kris Kringle was delusional because he believed himself to be

Santa Claus, you doubt that I am Kuan Yin. But if I am delusional, what's the harm? You have benefitted greatly from my loving service, whatever the source of it may be. Is that so horrible? Like Kris Kringle's, my alleged delusion is a delusion for good.

But what if you're wrong, what if I am indeed who I say I am? What if you are the one who is deluded? Your cruelty would be unjustified and unskilled in any context, but how much worse that you reject and vilify your own bodhisattva! How bad can karma get? Your delusion, your doubt and the fear of me that it creates, has brought and will bring suffering – to me, to your family, to your business, but mostly to you, in the bad karma that you create for yourself.

Joe and I – the truest friends you ever had – are now outcasts, but we are not gone, thanks to the saner members of your family who want our help and are grateful for it. I am thinking we are still attached to you, if only tangentially, for a reason. God wants us standing by; we are the reserves who will be called up to active duty when the crisis hits. "They also serve who only stand and wait," wrote John Milton.[vi]

~ 575 ~

The fear is back. A disturbing dream interrupted my sleep.

I can't think my way out of fear. I recited mantras to lead myself into a better mental state: "Live fearlessly!" "What is there to be afraid of?" "All is illusion." "Whatever happens, it's okay." "This, too, shall pass." "Live in the present, don't worry about the future." But logic, reason, and common sense are of no use against illogical, irrational, nonsensical panic.

I can't reminisce my way out of it, either. I tried to conjure up the sensations of peace that came to me during my floating dreams, my epiphanies, and at every other miraculous juncture in my life. But to no avail. Like logic and reason, all comforting memories are swept away by the fear, vanishing like "an ant in the mouth of a furnace," as C.S. Lewis put it.

I have made incredible strides in my spiritual journey, but still, there is only the thinnest veneer covering my Achilles' heel. That my terror can still be triggered so easily means that I am still clinging. What is it that I so fear to lose? God sends me an occasional nightmare and a remedial dose of icy fear to remind me that I still have a ways to go.

[vi] Sonnet 19: "When I consider how my light is spent"

~ 576 ~

APOLOGY AND FORGIVENESS, Part 3

There is a fine distinction between apologizing and seeking forgiveness – actions that come from the wrongdoer; and forgiving and seeking an apology – actions that come from the wronged. Apology comes from the wrongdoer, for the benefit of the wrongdoer, whether or not there is forgiveness forthcoming from the person who was wronged. Forgiveness comes from the wronged, for the benefit of the wronged, whether or not there is an apology from the wrongdoer.

What is going on when the wrongdoer seeks forgiveness from the wronged, or the wronged seeks an apology from the wrongdoer? The wrongdoer seeks forgiveness to validate and justify his guilt, his belief that he committed a wrong act. The wronged seeks an apology to validate and justify his anger, his feelings of hurt over what he believes to be a wrong committed against him.

When I tell you that there is nothing to forgive, I am not belittling your sincere desire for forgiveness. I am simply declining to validate your guilt. In all cases of apology and forgiveness there is an assumption by the apologizer and the forgiver that something happened that was wrong. *But there is no wrong between us.* No guilt, no shame. I am inviting you to go with me to the place where concepts like right and wrong, sin and repentance, are irrelevant; where there is no scoreboard, no one keeping a tally of good or evil deeds; where everything just … is. By not seeking an apology from you, I am saying the same thing.

My lack of apology to you despite your demand for it reflects my faith in the rightness of all that has happened. I can't say that I should have or would have done anything differently. If I had thought what I did was wrong, I wouldn't have done it. In the big picture of karma, cause and effect, we share responsibility for the hurtful things that happen to us. We share in the causation; I have repeatedly brought hurt upon myself with my truth-telling. Unskilled behavior can cause hurt, but sometimes skilled behavior can, too. Hurt resides not in the act, but in the one acted upon.

> When the man's cousin learned that he had become a monk, he cursed the Buddha to his face. The Buddha only smiled. The man became even more incensed and asked, "Why don't you respond?" The Buddha replied, "If someone refuses a gift, it must be taken back by the one who offered it." Angry words and actions hurt, first of all, oneself. – Thich Nhat Hanh[25]

I am sad that you were hurt or angered by things I said or did, but I can't control the arising of these feelings in you. Your hurt is yours. Extracting an apology from me won't take away your hurt. I can't keep you from feeling hurt or angry if the seeds of those feelings are in your consciousness. I can only react with compassion, love, and understanding, and move you to take back your gift of anger. And then let it go.

~ 577 ~

HEALTH, Part 7

A few nights ago, I woke up at around 5:00 a.m. with an aching pain in my lower back, hips, and the back of my thighs. No matter which way I turned, I couldn't seem to get rid of it. I got up and walked around, did some computer work, and it seemed a little better, but when I tried to go back to sleep the pain was still there. Finally around 8:00 a.m. it went away, almost as suddenly as it appeared. I've been fine since.

Where did this pain come from, arising suddenly from nowhere and disappearing just as suddenly? I couldn't think of any exertion or injury that might have caused it. I wonder if the pains and fears that suddenly arose in me over the last few days were really my own. Am I actually feeling someone else's fear, carrying someone else's pain? Having someone else's dreams, tapping into someone else's spirit, as Kathy's $12,000 dream (~564~) tapped into mine? Am I Kuan Yin, hearer of the world's cries and sufferer of the world's pain – pain of the body and of the spirit?

A while ago I saw a movie titled *Resurrection,* about a young woman who discovered she had miraculous healing powers. She claimed no religious connection to this power and was run out of town as a heretic. There was a scene in the movie in which she took upon herself the spastic contortions of another woman, releasing the woman from suffering by bringing it upon herself. She was eventually able to expel the affliction, and she also returned to health.

I would be glad to take your suffering upon myself if I thought I could relieve you of it. But your fear blocks my healing energy. I can't drag you kicking and screaming into nirvana; you must want to go there. Before you can be in the place of no suffering, you must say yes to suffering.

> The ego says, "I shouldn't have to suffer," and that thought makes you suffer so much more. It is a distortion of the truth, which is always paradoxical. The truth is that you need to say yes to suffering before you can transcend it. – Eckhart Tolle

~ 578 ~

I got up at 6:00 a.m. to greet the fire god at first light. I went outside to the edge of the hot springs. Everything was covered in fog so dense I could not see more than a few yards past the ledge. I began my chant. As the last syllables left my lips, I looked up toward the steam vent. Through the fog I could see a vertical rainbow beginning to emerge from the clouds above the vent, as if to connect earth and sky. And then, in a matter of just a few seconds, the fog lifted entirely and I could see smoke rising from the vent, the rainbow reaching down to meet it. This complete transformation from total fog and darkness to clarity and light took place in less than a minute and occurred just as my chant was ending, as if my chant had set it in motion. I marveled at the spectacular scene before me and the speed at which it was revealed. How is it that such things can be, I asked myself.

I know – the fog would have lifted and the rainbow would have appeared even if I hadn't been there chanting. But I *was* there chanting, calling to the gods at precisely the moment of their arising. This is what I mean by miracles being a matter of exquisite timing. My life is in synchrony with the forces of nature and the power of the spirits. These miraculous events, now so numerous in my life that I can't count them, are how I know I am at the right place at the right time. They give me assurance that I am on the right path, and the strength to withstand the blows I must take on my spiritual journey.

The messages are consistent. The priests and deities at the Buddhist temple and at the Christian church, the native gods, and the spirits of nature all agree. With all these powerful forces arrayed for my guidance, support, and protection leading me – grabbing me by the scruff of the neck – there can be no doubt or hesitation. There are no choices to be made. Who am I to say no to them?

~ 579 ~

Following the Five Precepts, practicing the Six Perfections, and walking the Eightfold Path is not the result of intention. Skillful thoughts and actions come spontaneously, without trying, once the buddha-nature is released from the clutches of the Three Poisons and can be freely and fully expressed.

Just as sitting in meditation does not make a buddha (~295~), so following rules that mimic the Buddha's behavior does not make a buddha. Trying to be good does not make one good. Performing love, acting out the behaviors of love, as Anita Moorjani pointed out (~463~), does not make one loving. Love, goodness, compassion, and wisdom come from inside; they cannot be acquired from outside. Buddhahood cannot be purchased with money or good works or even sacrifice, if that sacrifice does not come forth on its own from an enlightened inner wellspring.

And yet – a flower is composed of nothing but non-flower elements. (Another way of saying, "You are what you eat.") A buddha is composed of non-buddha elements. And yet – both a flower and a buddha contain the entire universe, deriving their suchness from everything that is. In my 1/1/09 epiphany I saw the musicians "as much created by their music as the creators of it." A buddha is as much created by his good works as the creator of them. We are all one force field, interconnected through all space and time. I make and am made by all that is.

~ 580 ~

When I left Ignacio's cabin after my visit there last summer, I resolved to give Ignacio and Cecilia a fairly large amount of money to express my gratitude for my stay there. I planned to give them a check at church today. After the service, before she knew about the money I had for them, Cecilia walked urgently over to me and said, "I have much to tell you; there have been devastating floods in the mountains where our cabin is. Many people have been stranded or evacuated. Fortunately our friends and relatives are safe, but destruction of the forests, homes, and property is huge."

I had thought that one thing Ignacio might do with my money was fix the plumbing in the cabin. Now it appears that there will be much more to fix.

On the very day that I gave Ignacio the check, I heard about the devastation of the flood. The spirits told me to write a check, and then within hours of writing the check the reason for it was revealed to me. Like Kathy learning in a dream about my gift to support her evangelical mission before she had actually received the check. And like the money I gave to your wife, which I had determined to give her before she asked for it.

What did I say about miracles and exquisite timing? What moves me to give away money simply for the joy of it, in the spirit of pure gratitude and generosity, in practice of the 1st Perfection, without knowing the ultimate purpose for it, even before the need for it has arisen? This phenomenon is a perfect demonstration of the juxtaposition of past, present, and future that happens at the nexus of space, time, and eternity. My actions in the present presage an unknown but already-gestating future.

I told Ignacio and Cecilia, "You are not allowed to refuse this gift. This is God working in our lives." God said to me, "Give Ignacio the money," and so I did.

~ 581 ~

SPEAKING IN TONGUES

> Now the whole earth had one language and few words. And as men migrated from the east, they found a plain in the land of Shinar and settled there. And they said to one another, "Come, let us make bricks, and burn them thoroughly." And they had brick for stone, and bitumen for mortar. Then they said, "Come, let us build ourselves a city, and a tower with its top in the heavens, and let us make a name for ourselves, lest we be scattered abroad upon the face of the whole earth." And the LORD came down to see the city and the tower, which the sons of men had built. And the LORD said, "Behold, they are one people, and they have all one language; and this is only the beginning of what they will do; and nothing that they propose to do will now be impossible for them. Come, let us go down, and there confuse their language, that they may not understand one another's speech." So the LORD scattered them abroad from there over the face of all the earth, and they left off building the city. Therefore its name was called Babel, because there the LORD confused the language of all the earth; and from there the LORD scattered them abroad over the face of all the earth. (Genesis 11:1-9 RSV)

The many different religious beliefs, and their scriptures, doctrines, and interpretations which are often misunderstood, represent the scattering of people over the earth and the confusion caused by the different languages, literally and figuratively, that they now speak.

Getting to heaven by simply building a tower was too easy, and God couldn't let that happen as long as Man wanted to "make a name for ourselves." Man had to let go of self, come to God from a place beyond words, language, and self. Pride comes before a fall, and so the Tower of Babel fell, the city around it was never finished, and the people again fell from grace.

But then … the Holy Spirit came along to make the Word heard in every language, so that all people, no matter how scattered, could know the Way for Man to regain unity with God:

> When the day of Pentecost had come, they were all together in one place. And suddenly a sound came from heaven like the rush of a mighty wind, and it filled all the house where they were sitting. And there appeared to them tongues as of fire, distributed and resting on each one of them. And they were all filled with the Holy Spirit and began to speak in other tongues, as the Spirit gave them utterance.

> Now there were dwelling in Jerusalem Jews, devout men from every nation under heaven. And at this sound the multitude came together, and they were bewildered, because each one

heard them speaking in his own language. And they were amazed and wondered, saying, "Are not all these who are speaking Galileans? And how is it that we hear, each of us in his own native language? Par'thians and Medes and E'lamites and residents of Mesopota'mia, Judea and Cappado'cia, Pontus and Asia, Phryg'ia and Pamphyl'ia, Egypt and the parts of Libya belonging to Cyre'ne, and visitors from Rome, both Jews and proselytes, Cretans and Arabians, we hear them telling in our own tongues the mighty works of God." And all were amazed and perplexed, saying to one another, "What does this mean?" (Acts of the Apostles 2:1-12 RSV)

What does this mean? It means that the language barrier God created has now been removed. The gospel is for everyone and must be accessible to everyone. The Word is out, in all languages. He who has ears to hear, let him hear.

~ 582 ~

I have been reading a collection of writings by Thich Nhat Hanh, a Vietnamese Zen Buddhist. Thich joins Dietrich Bonhoeffer, Jacobo Timerman, Charlotte Joko Beck, and me in our less-than-hopeful opinion of hope:

> When I think deeply about the nature of hope, I see something tragic. Since we cling to our hope in the future, we do not focus our energies and capabilities on the present moment … Hope becomes a kind of obstacle. If you can refrain from hoping, you can bring yourself entirely into the present moment and discover the joy that is already here.[25]

And imagine my joy in reading that Thich agrees with St. Augustine, Einstein, and me about space, time, and relativity:

> Doan knew that neither matter, space, nor time can be observed independently of the other two. He knew that a line between the past and the future, called the present, is normally assumed. But in his study of Relativity, he discovered that the span of the present varies with the distance in space between the observer and the phenomenon observed. The present might be a short span of time, but it can also be measured in years, or even tens of millions of years. Someone on the Earth watching a falling star may not know that from other points in the universe the star has not yet fallen, or it may have fallen millions of years before. The present is not a universal entity. It can also be identified with the past or the future. – Thich Nhat Hanh, from the short story "Peony Blossoms"[25]

~ 583 ~

Another provocative book has crossed my path: *How To Know God*, by Deepak Chopra. He describes seven stages to knowing God, each stage going farther into the inner self and coming closer to the ultimate mystery. The seven stages roughly correspond to the seven chakras.

I found myself identifying with Stage Five, "God the Creator," where the creative arts arise, where intention manifests in actual events, where dreams come true. I was reminded of the fantastic sequence of events that led me to my life in music, to Lou, and to you – a fifty-year-long chain of events that began with my school music teacher and then took me around the world, enveloped me in three different world cultures, and brought me two karmic loves. And the journey isn't over yet.

Stage Six rang a bell for me, too, the stage where miracles occur, dualism ends, and love takes over. And again, as did Thich Nhat Hanh, Chopra ties together light, love, Einstein's relativity, quantum mechanics, and God at Stage Six:

> "I" am not even the mind, only the light. My identity floats in a quantum fog as photons wink in and out of existence. I feel no attachment to any of them. They come and go; I am not even troubled by having no permanent home. It is enough to be bathed in the light.

> Of the million ways you could define enlightenment, identifying with the light is a good one. Miracle workers do more than access energy patterns. As the Vedas say, "This isn't knowledge you learn; it's knowledge you turn into." Jesus spoke in parables but could easily have been literal when he declared to his disciples, "You are the light of the world."

> When he realizes that he is bathed in light, the feeling that comes over a miracle worker is one of intense love. This is because he is absorbing the qualities of spirit that the light contains. When Jesus said, "I am the light," he meant, "I'm totally in God's force field." [26]

It seems that knowledge is being handed to me on a silver platter. Miraculous forces bring a book, a movie, a song, a new friend, or a learning experience to me at just the moment I need the specific insight that these sources provide. Critical information seems to come mysteriously and serendipitously to me at just the right time. The books I recently read on metaphysics, existentialism, and Zen had been on my bookshelf for thirty years, slumbering, waiting for the right moment to be awakened in my life. I don't remember how the Chopra book came into my possession or why it percolated up to the top of my reading pile when it did. An angel gave it to me, no doubt.

Deepak Chopra says, "The saints of Buddhism, who are called bodhisattvas, are sometimes portrayed looking over their shoulders and beckoning with a smile, as if to say, 'I am going over the threshold. Don't you want to follow?'"

You are constantly in my thoughts and my heart. I await the day when you will want to follow me over the threshold.

~ 584 ~

A TRIBUTE TO IGNACIO

In *How To Know God* by Deepak Chopra, of all the overlaps in my experience with his, the most striking is addressed in his chapter on synchronicity – coincidences that really aren't.

> Jung invented the term *synchronicity* to cover these "meaningful coincidences," and the term has stuck even though it doesn't cast much light on the mystery. What outside force can organize time in such a way that two things meet, like the Titanic and the iceberg, with such a sense of fatefulness?
>
> My own life has been touched often by synchronicity, so much so that now I get on an airplane expecting the passenger in the next seat to be surprisingly important to me, either just the voice I need to hear to solve a problem or a missing link in a transaction that needs to come together.[26]

Ignacio, when I read Deepak's statement above, I realized that the stage was set for our spiritual connection years earlier when I "coincidentally" sat next to your brother Carlo on an airplane. I didn't really know you then, I just knew of you and your association with the church. Through Carlo I learned more about your life of service and your bout with cancer. I resolved at that time to get to know you better. I don't recall exactly when I started frequenting your theology discussion group, but that was certainly a factor in bringing our respective spiritual journeys into synchronicity.

On to our epiphany. (~232~)

First, the date – January 1, 2009.

> **9/11** – the day of terrorist attacks.
> **911** – the phone number we call for help.
> **1/1/9** (911 in reverse) – the day I felt terror dissolve in the peace of eternity; the day my help arrived.

And then, your sermon. Delivered in my ancestral mother tongue – connecting this experience to my genealogy and the Christian culture of my youth. Then you referenced the soprano aria in the upcoming Bach cantata, in which the name of Jesus is invoked – connecting this experience to the culture of my creative musical profession, my God-directed calling. *My vision happened during this very aria.* And then you tied the Bach/Picander text of the aria to the Japanese Buddhist Shinran, who taught that salvation could be had by simply reciting the name of Amida – connecting this experience to my adopted Buddhist culture. Earlier that day I had attended the New Year's Day service at the Buddhist temple where I recited the name of Amida.

At the time of my vision I was not consciously aware of any of these wondrous serendipitous connections, or of the 911/119 play on numbers. But in retrospect I can see that all the major events of my life, even before my life began, were all threads of a single fabric that *you* wove together for me on that day. Yes, as you said, my epiphany would not have happened had the seed not already been sown in me. But you were the catalyst, applying the water and fertilizer that allowed the seed to sprout. Or, as I quipped to you at church, "God may have set up my pins, but you rolled the ball that knocked 'em down!"

I wanted to tell you all this because I wonder if you know who and what you are. You have spent your life quietly serving God and man, doing good, but I don't think you fully appreciate the magnitude of your spiritual power and influence. You are indeed an angel, a saint, a bodhisattva, not just blessed by God, but anointed by God to do his very special work. This doesn't mean that you can't or don't make mistakes – I give everyone some breathing room from perfection, including myself. But what some people call mistakes, or sins, are simply part of the inevitable duality of things as they are supposed to be. In the end all things are right.

Jesus said, "Either make the tree good, and his fruit good; or else make the tree corrupt, and his fruit corrupt: for the tree is known by its fruit." My awakening is the good fruit falling from your tree. I can't claim to completely know why you survived cancer, but I do know that one reason was to be my bodhisattva, my ferryman, to guide me to the far shore, to the Pure Land. This is synchronicity manifesting in your life as it is in mine, the eternal God operating through your physical being. Of this I have no doubt. You continue to elucidate, enliven, and enlighten me through your theology discussion group, coffees with Cecilia, adventures at your cabin, and many other ways.

And so I bow to you in *gassho*, with my hands above my head, in recognition of and gratitude for your revealed buddha-nature, your God-self made known to me in the miracles you work in my life.

~ 585 ~

Last night's dream: *I am approaching a steep, rocky slope. I come to the base of a sheer cliff, seeing two paths. One goes off to the side along a flat trail with plants along the sides, like a dry river bed, into the dark unknown. The other goes straight up, and requires finding tenuous hand and footholds around sloping rocks jutting out and obstructing the passage. I opt for the steep assent and succeed in getting to the top.*

This dream sequence repeats, but this time my friend Joe is following behind. As I begin to climb the rock wall again, I notice that the handholds are not secure. I test one, and sure enough, a large rock becomes dislodged and falls away. Other rocks are also loose. I consider going down to try the alternate route into the dark unknown. I woke up as I was looking down toward the smoother, darker path below.

From dreammoods.com:

> **Cliff** – To dream that you are climbing to the top of a cliff symbolizes your ambition and drive. The dream may parallel your desires to achieve success and to be at the top of your profession.
>
> **Climb** – To dream that you are climbing up something (ladder, rope, etc.) signifies that you are trying to or you have overcome a great struggle. It also suggests that your goals are finally within reach. Climbing also means that you have risen to a level of prominence within the social or economic sphere.
>
> **Rock Climbing** – To dream that you are rock climbing symbolizes your struggle, determination and ambition. You are not any letting obstacles get in the way of your goal.

Apparently I succeeded in overcoming a great struggle with the climb that got me to the top of the cliff the first time, but the same route will not work to solve my current problems. I need to look down farther into my subconscious and try the other path into the unknown.

Lump in throat, yawning, gulping for air, loss of appetite. My fear has been percolating up again. Little bouts of it, just enough to put me on edge but not quite into a panic. I don't know why. Something is going on in my body – my karmic sore throat, a lingering bronchitis, the mysterious pain in my hips, my bouts of uneasy restlessness. Is this disease my own, or am I feeling the pain of my loved ones, or am I responding to the misery of the entire world?

~ 586 ~

SIN, Part 1

What is sin? As a child I was taught that we are all sinners who have fallen short of the glory of God. We need the salvation offered by Jesus if we are to be forgiven our sins and go to heaven. In church I learned the Ten Commandments, and at home my parents taught me the Golden Rule.

The world presents so many tempting ways to be bad, and yet, I was a good girl. Occasionally I did something wrong and I knew it, but often days, weeks, even months would go by without my committing any sin that I could think of. No mean, angry words or deeds, no lying, no swearing, no coveting, certainly no murder or thievery. I received much more praise than criticism in my young life. Didn't my overwhelming honesty, diligence, and goodness more than make up for the occasional minor lapses?

It didn't take me long to become skeptical about the nature of sin and the motivation of organized religion in preaching salvation. The Church has a product to sell. People must be made to believe they are sinners so that they will seek the Church's salvation, just as people who are told they are dirty will be motivated to buy soap.

> "We are selling the greatest product on earth. Why shouldn't we promote it as effectively as we promote a bar of soap?" – Billy Graham, *Saturday Evening Post*, 1963

The Buddhists take a softer approach. Their view is that there is no right and wrong, but rather skilled and unskilled behavior. We are not sinners by nature, but we create our own karma by the choices we make in our own lives. Deepak Chopra writes:

> In one phrase—"As you sow, so shall you reap"—Jesus stated the law of karma quite succinctly. He had no intention of getting away with wrongdoing but instead pointed to a higher spiritual rule: your actions today define your future tomorrow. Regardless of whether an act is deemed good or bad, this higher rule can't be sidestepped. By stage four there is enough insight to realize that all past actions have a way of coming home to roost. This dynamic turns out to be more important than identifying sin.[26]

At the mystical level of both Eastern and Western viewpoints, sin is not simply or easily defined. Sometimes saying or doing the right thing nevertheless hurts. And sometimes what seems wrong in the present will emerge as right in the future. "In everything God works for good with those who love him, who are called according to his purpose." (Romans 8:28)

I recently read a story about a priest who struggled to advise newly released prisoners how to provide for themselves when they were unable to get a job and had no other means of support. Rejected and condemned by society, all that was left to them was a life of crime. In hopes that the most heinous crimes could be avoided, his reluctant advice was to shoplift – not from small family businesses but from large ones that would not suffer too much from the loss – and to take only what they needed. How could this priest justify suggesting that ex-cons break the Eighth Commandment? His explanation shows how sin is colored by its context:

> What, then, of the Eighth Commandment, "Thou shalt not steal"? Is this advice to usurp the authority of Almighty God?
>
> No. Not the God who is born of Mary. For ours is a God, Mary tells us, who has "lifted up the lowly; he has filled the hungry with good things, and sent the rich away empty." (Luke 1:52-53) The mother of Christ reminds us what Jesus shows us: that God's love for the poor and despised—and who in our society is despised more than a newly released prisoner?—outweighs the property rights of the rich. – Rev. Tim Jones, "Desperation Theology," *Harper's Magazine,* March 2010

Is telling the truth wrong if it causes suffering? Is lying wrong if it spares someone from suffering? Is silence wrong if it leaves a condition of suffering unmitigated? The answer to all these questions is the same: yes, no, and maybe. Each person's karma will see a different effect from the same act. Each person marches to his own drummer. In the end, all things are right.

Out beyond ideas of wrongdoing and rightdoing,
there is a field. I'll meet you there.

– Rumi

~ 587 ~

My Buddhist message today: *Your heart is in turmoil … you want to help others, to fix things, but you need to trust in the spirit guides … they are waiting for you to reach out to them … increase your faith and you will be immovable, like Achala.*

Deepak Chopra says: "What is the mark of someone who moves very quickly on the path? It may seem to be a paradox, but the more turbulent you are inside, the faster you are moving. Ferment is good. Not buying into your own story is good. Krishnamurti used to say that discontent was the flame of the seeker."

I am nothing if not turbulent.

~ 588 ~

ATTACHMENT/DETACHMENT, Part 1

A physician and counselor to the dying described the painful and peaceful sides of aloneness this way:

> Our language has wisely sensed the two sides of being alone. It has created the word "loneliness" to express the pain of being alone, and it has created the word "solitude" to express the glory of being alone. I am delighted to announce that loneliness can be conquered by those who can bear solitude.

I have written often about the solitude of the bodhisattva. This solitude should be a blessed thing, a place of inner peace needing no attachments, where one finds contentment and fulfillment within oneself. It is a state of eternal detachment from the tug of worldly desire that tortures those who are lonely for their attachments. Loneliness is attached aloneness, solitude is detached aloneness.

I have had many moments of doubt concerning my bodhisattva status, wondering if maybe I am really only prideful or deluded. Each time I resolved my doubt by remembering all the miracles, visions, dreams, and epiphanies. But the one piece of evidence that trumps all the others and totally convinces me of my awakening is the nature and power of my love — immovable, irreversible, incorruptible, impervious to assault, indestructible, without a trace of doubt or hesitation. It is the compassionate loving-kindness of the Buddha, the love of God.

To love in this way is breathtaking in its beauty, but frightening in its power. I have written much about both sides of this coin, and also about what an arduous, difficult path this love is in the dualistic world. To love so completely and be driven by it to confront the sorrows of the world, yet remain detached from worldly desire, not succumbing to the attractions of the first poison, is an extreme challenge. Equally challenging is avoiding the pendulum swing to the second and third poisons, squelching or denying love in fear of its power or the suffering it brings, or refusing to live it and act on it lest impure attachments or aversions be formed.

To love without attaching is very hard, perhaps impossible while we are alive. Desires will always arise in the body-mind; that is the nature of life. Removing all desire is not really possible; trying to do so is taking the third poison, denying desire rather than removing it.

We are attached to food because we need it to survive. If we eat not out of desire for a pleasurable culinary experience (first poison) or for comfort, to quell emotional pain (second poison), but simply to survive, then attachment to food is healthy, just an unavoidable component of duality in this life. The Buddha said, "If one doesn't have desire, then it is perfectly all right to own a house of a thousand stories. If one has desire, then one needs to give up attachment to even a miserable mud hut." My food analogy can be put in similar terms: "If one doesn't have desire, then it is perfectly all right to have a pantry full of food. If one has desire, then one needs to give up attachment to even a miserable crust of bread."

Loving attachments, if for the right reasons, for the benefit of the other, not oneself, not produced by or producing a clinging dependency, do not cloud eternal love; they are earthly manifestations of that eternal love, the expression of high spiritual love through the lower souls. To paraphrase the Buddha again: "If one doesn't have desire, then it is perfectly all right to share your life with the object of your love. If one has desire, then one needs to give up attachment to even one fleeting moment together."

~ 589 ~

My love is like an ocean that flows over everything, into all the nooks and crannies. My reverence extends also to plants and animals, even inanimate objects like rocks and rivers, all of whom are embraced by this love. I greet the flowers and trees that I pass along the side of the road. I say hello to my favorite rock on the trail to the hot springs; I stop to admire the moss that grows on it and stand in awe of the iridescent shades of green, brown, and gold that it becomes when the late afternoon sun hits it.

~ 590 ~

PRIDE AND THE EGO, Part 1

"Ego" is a very dangerous word. It means lots of different things. My definition of "ego" is that which connects, but often puts obstacles between, the body-mind and the buddha-nature/ God-self. In Buddhist terms, this is the part of us that succumbs to the Three Poisons and perpetuates the cycle of dependent origination. In Judeo-Christian terms, this is the part that stands separate from God, often in defiance of him.

Those who speak of annihilation of the ego, of no-self, of no-mind, are not talking about abandoning intellect or turning off the thinking mind; they are talking about release from the bondage of fear and desire, allowing the God-self to enter into consciousness and set the stage for awakening. The Buddhist principle of unsupported thought and the Christian principles of poverty, chastity, and obedience are the physical effects of this letting go of ego. Of course, ego – in the sense of our self-identity – cannot be let go until we reach *anuttara samyak sambodhi*, but to the extent that we recognize the ego's daemonic operation in our lives, we can push it to the side and give our buddha-nature a path to come through.

~ 591 ~

MY LOVING ANGELS

Like Lily in the movie *Julia*, I am passed from one guardian spirit to another in the course of my dangerous journey, each one guiding me through a segment of the trip. I am beginning to make sense of the progression of loves in my past, a long series of spiritually meaningful connections – my parents, siblings, Lou, the twins, Archie, and James – seeing how each one advanced me one more step along my journey.

I can see in retrospect that each of these experiences was a kind of training, divine preparation for my second great karmic love, who would present all the opportunities, temptations, and challenges of the loves who came before. And now, my newest angels are sent to guide and support me through my second loss – Joe, Walt, Ignacio, Cecilia, Rita, and most hauntingly, Emily. They are my sangha, my spiritual family. Our souls connect.

I am stunned by the quality of these angels who have been sent to me at this critical time. I must be at least an eighth bhūmi bodhisattva to warrant being sent such magnificent spirit helpers. What level of spiritual elevation is required for a minister to minister to other ministers? To preach to other preachers? Who hears the Pope's confession? These fabulous souls hear my confession, and I hear theirs.

I see now how my Temple of Awakening is constructed. My two karmic loves are like two mighty columns standing in my Gothic cathedral. Between them are smaller supports that brace the walls and balance the structure – the flying buttresses, you might say. These are the angels who have propped me up and kept my structure from collapsing in the wake of devastating losses. After Lou died, it was the twins, Archie, and James who gave my love vent and brought me back to life. After your rejection of me came Joe, Ignacio, Cecilia, and Emily to rescue my tortured soul. They helped me to see beyond my own pain to the karmic inevitability and rightness of all that happened. I am now shored up, ready for the next act of this fabulous drama that is my spirit-filled life.

PART 25
Love Again, Again
October 2013 – November 2013

~ 592 ~

It's happening again. As Emily and I share more and more of our inner selves with each other, I find myself rejoicing in the throes of another mighty eternal love flowing through all my souls with reckless abandon. I remember the signs that accompanied my first two meetings with Emily – the questioning Korean student (~460~) and the dove visitation (~560~) – and I realize that God was the matchmaker who brought us together.

I have seen Emily's soul, heard her cries, felt her pain. She is inside me, and I am inside her. I feel my own eternal joy coming back to me in her fabulous smile; I hear it in her infectious laughter. In her tears I see my own sorrow reflected back to me. Looking at her I see the face of God – my own God-self looking back at me.

Here I am again in existential anguish. I live with her in love that knows no bounds in eternity, but is bound on all sides in space and time. As I find joy in love once again, my sorrow over its inevitable loss arises by the same proportion. It is my curse, that I love too well.

~ 593 ~

SEX, Part 18

My love rampages unimpeded through me. My spiritual love for Emily now sends shock waves through my body-mind. This is no small love; once again my body chemistry is changing, and in a way that reflects the gender of my new love. The physiological changes that were wrought in me as I found new karmic love with a man – the vaginal spotting – reflected the fertility of the male-female creative reproductive union. Now my love for a woman expresses in my body with a return to pre-menopausal levels of vaginal lubricant – reflecting not the reproductive aspect of sex, but rather its sensuousness – sexuality that is anticipatory, in readiness for creative union, reflective of the warm, welcoming, caressing, specifically feminine quality of sex. This phenomenon blows my mind.

With the mystical signs that preceded my previous visits with Emily, the spirits were consecrating us, heralding our relationship to the heavens. Ours is the most sacred of connections. How fabulous is this? I didn't think the miracles could get any more wondrous, but they did.

~ 594 ~

I had another animal encounter today. I was sitting at a picnic table reading a book at my favorite place in the park. Out of the corner of my eye I saw an inchworm (a very small one, more like half-an-inchworm) inching its way toward me. Wanting to spare the critter being inadvertently smashed between the pages of my book, I put my finger down in front of him, he climbed onto it, and I moved him to another separate plank on the tabletop where he would be out of danger.

A few minutes later, I noticed him again making his way toward me, reaching out to the plank where my book was, but he was unable to span the distance. A foot or two away along the tabletop there was a connecting bar between the planks, and he was making his way toward it. Sure enough, he traversed the connection between the two planks and was once again on my plank.

Why did he come back? I had no idea, but I decided to watch to see what would happen next. He made a beeline to my coffee cup; I moved it so that he wouldn't become part of my liquid diet. His next move was to my pencil, which he explored for a few seconds. Then on to my book. I let him climb onto the open page of my book, then, onto my hand. After a minute or so of wandering around my fingers, he found a sheltered spot on my palm, just below the knuckle of my first finger.

He stayed there, and stayed, and stayed. I continued reading, moving my hand only just enough to turn the pages. The inchworm sat affixed to my hand, apparently content there, for over an hour. Eventually I finished reading and had to leave. I regretted parting company with my new friend; I marveled that this tiny creature and I could have found a place of peace together, a momentary juncture connecting our disparate worlds. I gently urged him back onto the tabletop, watched him inch away, and bid him adieu.

Anyone can have this kind of experience. All it takes is patience and resisting the initial impulse to squish the bug as soon as it appears. Gustave Flaubert said, "Anything becomes interesting if you look at it long enough." I would go farther and say that anything becomes a part of you if you commune with it long enough. Awareness, mindfulness, is the source of magic. A magical life evolves in its own good time if you just watch, wait, and stay out of the way.

~ 595 ~

HALLOWEEN

Without meaning to be, I was Emily's therapist today. She is full of love, but afraid to give it life, to be vulnerable, to be hurt. She wants to detach. I know how she feels. Been there.

We enjoy each other's company. In our deep conversations we laugh, play, cry, and reveal ourselves. Even though she won't say it, I think she loves me. She looks forward to our meetings, as I do. She is moved by my writing. She is a very private person, but she exposes her personal sorrow and pain to me. She teases me with her Halloween witch hat and playfully dodges my camera as I try to take her picture. She lets her hair down with me, literally and figuratively. She says that I am beautiful – anyone who sees me as beautiful could only be looking through love-colored glasses.

Her deflector shields are up. Her scrim is much thinner than the heavy armor of The Unnamed One, but it serves the same purpose. She is taking the third poison. She is a trained actor; I sense that her professional therapist persona is an act, a well-constructed façade hiding a deep, deep pain.

She is a spectacular person, physically beautiful, with an intelligent, sensitive, engaging personality. What a waste that she buries her precious love inside her, depriving herself and others of the exuberant expression of her eternal essence. But she allowed me to see a tiny piece of it, and that was enough to bind me to her forever. Our fabulous spiritual potentiality makes loving her especially exhilarating – and excruciating. I am stunned and numbed by it.

Perhaps one day she will be where I am, not wanting to be vulnerable but unable to resist the pull of karmic love, its inevitability. I tried to protect myself as she is now, but eventually love had to find its way into and out of my heart. All I can do now is allow my deflector shields to drop and once again open myself to love and all the vulnerability that comes with it. Resistance is futile. Pleasure is pain is the bliss of eternal love in space-time.

~ 596 ~

ALL SAINTS DAY

I have been studying the photographs I took of Emily yesterday. I am haunted by one of them. Most of the shots showed her happy persona, laughing, smiling. But in one of them her façade is torn off. Her hair is down, her countenance is dark; her pain is showing. I have shed tears over this picture.

Yet her joy shines through in the other photos. It is infectious, and takes my sorrow away. In loving her I once again reach all the heights and depths of the greatest love it is possible to have.

Yesterday she said that sex was as close as humans can get without actually being inside each other. Normally that would be the case, but my love is not normal. She is inside me now. I feel infinite tenderness, empathy, closeness with her in the spirit realm, yet I am still separate from her in space-time. I am stretched to the nth degree across an infinitely wide chasm. This is the existential anguish I repeatedly refer to, the rubber band being drawn to infinite tautness.

~ 597 ~

ALL SOULS DAY

The three days of Hallowmas are said to be a time when the veil between the material world and the spirit world is thinned, when dead saints and souls can reach more easily to those on earth. In my dreams and visions my soul reaches to Emily in the universal subconscious, and we are one. The spirits have reached deeply into us.

~ 598 ~

Many years ago, when I was a child, my mother bought a small white figurine. She didn't know what it was; she just thought it was pretty. Many years later, I retrieved the figurine from the few belongings that my father had kept after Mom died. Just recently I realized that the figure is Kuan Yin. The Goddess of Compassion has been with me a lot longer than I thought.

~ 599 ~

I want to tell Emily about the fabulous effect she has had on me, in all its intimate detail. Thanks to her, I have turned a corner in my spiritual journey. But I don't want to hurt her or take her down dark roads she doesn't want to travel. So I hold back. I have seen her pain and fragility; I must not add to that. She wants to detach; I must respect that. This is the big lesson

I learned from The Unnamed One. Awakening, mine and hers, cannot be forced or rushed. A person cannot go farther than she can go.

At first I thought that my love for Emily was of the same nature and degree as my love for the twins. Now I wonder if it is much more, if she is perhaps the third great karmic love of my life, here to rescue me from the second one, her incredible lightness counterbalancing his darkness with equal power and authority. There can be no doubt that she is a divine vehicle, leading me through the last stages of my spiritual journey in this life.

I am numbed by the power of our iridescent karma. But I am all too aware of the darkness that lurks on the other side of the light. Once again, euphoria gives way to despair.

~ 600 ~

SEX, Part 19

I imagine Emily is wondering if I am sexually attracted to her. The answer is yes, of course. How could I not be? But I don't think I know how to have sex with her. My fantasies of sex with the twins always hit a roadblock when I tried to imagine what happens below the waist.

But in fact, I have already had sex with her. I have been to that place where I love her, where I am with Lou and The Unnamed One, where all is light, oneness, perfection. In the spirit realm everything works, and everything fits. Somehow, even between two women, our sexual union is perfect, constant, and timeless. It is that condition in the spirit that creates the feelings, sensations, and physiological transfiguration in the body. My body is awakened and responds to a pre-existing eternal state of being.

Sexual attraction that arises in the physical plane is a function of biology, the progression of a genetically programmed sequence that goes something like this: *delightful sensory input – bodily instincts awakened – hormonal excitation – passionate emotion – seductive behavior – sex.*

Physical manifestations of spiritual love look and feel much the same, except that the delightful input is *extrasensory,* eternal *divine love* is awakened, the passionate emotion reflects *compassionate empathy,* and the seductive behavior is *in service to the seduced.*

The Physical Soul is the seat of all passion, feeling, and emotion – pleasure, pain, joy, sorrow, love, hate, anger, affection, envy, gratitude. The Intellectual Soul is devoid of passion; it only thinks, analyzes, synthesizes. The Physical Soul says, "Emily is beautiful." Then the

Intellectual Soul asks, "Why do you think Emily is beautiful? What is the meaning of beauty? What action, if any, should be taken in response to this realization of beauty?"

The Spiritual Soul does not think or feel. It only loves. When that divine love flows to the lower souls, the powers of the intellect and the body-mind are turned to its service. The intellectual soul gives voice to spiritual love in metaphorical words and works of art. The physical body-mind turns its biological mechanisms to giving form, substance, and kinetic motion in this world to the formless, ephemeral and latent loving energy of God. It makes of the earth a heaven.

Alfred North Whitehead said that music is the sound of feelings. When those feelings are generated by the compassionate love of the spirit, the music created in the intellectual soul and brought to life through the physical body-minds of musicians is the voice of God.

~ 601 ~

Last night I had a short, strange dream in which someone said, "Congratulate Ian, it's his anniversary." I shook Ian's hand and asked, "What anniversary is it?" "Kristallnacht," he said. I couldn't figure out how Kristallnacht could be a cause for congratulations.

The next thing I knew, my clock radio woke me up. The news was on. The announcer said, "Today is the 75th anniversary of Kristallnacht …" At that moment my little dream flashed back to me.

Of course I knew about Kristallnacht from my study of history, but I did not know the exact date of it. I still don't know how my friend Ian, an Irish Catholic, is connected to that event, if at all. But it seemed that somehow in the universal subconscious my Jewish friends were calling to me.

There is another explanation: Perhaps I was not fully awakened at the moment my clock radio came on. Perhaps my dream happened as the radio announcer was giving a preview of the stories to follow and said the word "Kristallnacht" at the moment I heard it in my dream. But no matter. Either way, a marvelous interface between the conscious and subconscious is revealed.

~ 602 ~

When you have lived long enough, you begin to see patterns emerging. I am now seeing that before and after my awakening to each of my karmic loves – Lou, The Unnamed One, and now Emily – there have been two harbingers before or at the time of awakening, and two aftereffects.

The harbingers:

1) A sequence of serendipitous events that brings me and my beloved together, and
2) Spiritual signs or messages that herald, validate, sanctify, consecrate, and cement the relationship.

The aftereffects:

1) Significant unintentional weight loss, and
2) Sexual arousal (reflecting not the urge for pleasure, but for eternal oneness, not dependent on gender or other physical attributes).

The harbingers are occurrences in *time* – events that give me direction and confidence going forward, propelling me along the sacred path. The aftereffects are occurrences in *space* – changes in metabolism and body chemistry, in the material substance of my body.

I have lost about ten pounds since my love for Emily was awakened.

~ 603 ~

Last night my friend Marilyn expressed sympathy for the hurt that I suffered from The Unnamed One's cruelty. She wished that I had not experienced it. I thanked her for her kindness, but said that his rejection and my hurt were part of our karma, necessary for both of us: for me, to clearly see behind his façade, to fully understand that greed and fear, not love, were the prime motivations behind his behaviors both positive and negative toward me; and for him, to come face-to-face with a love unlike any other he has known, so great that his demons could not subdue it, that withstood his unleashing the beast within and yet still endures.

But in a deeper way, I am not to be pitied in my suffering. I hear the world's cries and suffer with the world in compassionate love. I take upon myself the sins of the world, the pain of others. I must accept the vulnerability to suffering and sacrifice that this assignment entails.

My suffering reflects dualistic balance; it is the worldly price I must pay to be the vessel and vehicle for the eternal love of God.

The serene countenance we see in images of Amida, Kuan Yin, and the Christian saints is not calmness in the realm of eternity; it is euphoric anguish in the realm of space-time, Christ's divine rapture in the midst of incredible worldly suffering, a transcendent ecstasy of pain mitigated by spiritual endorphins. It is not being at peace in the Great Void; it is being at peace in the midst of the sorrows of the world, in the eye of a hurricane with pain swirling all around.

Rumi said, "The cure for the pain is in the pain."

Albert Camus also described this condition very well: "Let us seek the respite where it is – in the very thick of the battle."

C.S. Lewis said something similar: "Silences in the physical world occur in empty places, but the ultimate Peace is silent through the very density of life."

As did Thai Buddhist monk Ajahn Chah: "Looking for peace is like looking for a turtle with a mustache. You won't be able to find it. But when your heart is ready, peace will come looking for you. Peace is within oneself, to be found in the same place as agitation and suffering. Where you experience suffering, you can also find freedom from suffering. Trying to run away from suffering is actually to run toward it."

Suffering does not stand in opposition to joy. Suffering doesn't have to end for there to be joy; they both arise together from the same source. We want to overcome, to extinguish suffering as if that could bring joy. Wisdom asks us to find peace – and joy – in the very thick of the battle.

PART 26
Epiphany Again
November 2013 – December 2013

~ 604 ~

I was sitting at the computer flipping through the photos I had taken of Emily on Halloween. The aria "Sheep May Safely Graze" from J.S. Bach's "Hunting" Cantata was playing on the radio. Suddenly I landed on the one photographic image of Emily that captured her deep psychic pain. The moment the sound of the music and the image of her face were joined, all the pieces of the puzzle came together. A complete mosaic was built from which the most intense all-embracing love emerged. My mind let go and God took over.

First I felt Emily's crushing pain rush into my soul, and I bore the heaviness of her suffering. Then emerged a vision of perfect healing and reconciliation in love and lightness as I saw her pain gloriously released. Our souls were joined together in the place where all is perfect, all sin and sorrow washed away. In an instant I descended into hell and arose to heaven; I took Emily's suffering upon me and then saw her resurrected in peace and light.

Tears welled up. I was entranced; another still deeper level of compassionate love was awakened in me. My love poured out of me to her unimpeded, without limit. It was God's love, flowing through me to her. There was a moment of rapture when the euphoria was so sublime that I actually thought, "Is this it? Am I going over the edge to *anuttara samyak sambodhi* – unexcelled complete awakening?" Not since my 1/1/09 epiphany have I felt so close to the ultimate Source, here where Emily has guided me.

The text of the Bach aria is:

Schafe können sicher weiden,	Sheep may safely graze,
Wo ein guter Hirte wacht.	Where a good shepherd watches over them.
Wo Regenten wohl regieren,	Where rulers are ruling well,
Kann man Ruh und Friede spüren	We may feel peace and rest
Und was Länder glücklich macht.	And what makes the countrymen happy.

This Bach aria and the meaning of its words are as spiritually prophetic as the aria that awakened me on 1/1/09. I am Emily's good shepherd, watching over her as she safely grazes in our happy field of peace and rest.

On 1/1/09, I was awakened to the timeless and formless nature of all things. This time I was awakened to the bright light of eternal love that brings all time and form together. Of course I have known about spiritual love for some time, thanks to Lou, having felt it being given and received inside my own being, but today I felt it as an overwhelmingly powerful universal force permeating everything, revealing itself to me in a great flood of compassion that passed from the Source through me into every nook and cranny, and into Emily.

The feeling of this love is not simply one of overwhelming happiness or peace. It contains all feelings, both peaceful and turbulent – the extremes of pleasure and pain, joy and sorrow, juxtaposed upon each other, simultaneous but still separate, together but distinct – the ultimate intensity, the ultimate tension, ever so close but not quite ready to implode into nothingness. All I can do is sit dumbstruck, numb, limp, empty.

~ 605 ~

No one should ever have to feel such excruciating love. I wish everyone could see the incredible beauty I have seen, but I would never wish for anyone to see the incredible pain that accompanies it. My ecstasy comes from both the pleasure and the pain, from the exquisite tension between them as they are stretched to their ultimate extremes.

The two sides of the dualistic dichotomy are like an equally balanced equation: X (pleasure) divided by Y (pain) equals 1. For every measure of pleasure there is an equal measure of pain. Enlightenment will come when the values of X and Y become so large that they burst their uppermost limits and melt into the singularity of one.

Leaving the Garden of Eden and entering space-time is nuclear fission, splitting the atom apart. Returning to the Garden is nuclear fusion, bringing the pieces back together again. Scientists say that nuclear fusion is what powers the sun and gives us … Light.

~ 606 ~

Last night I played one of the best concerts of my life. My spiritual power, energy, *ki*, was flowing through me. The notes played themselves. There was energy, feeling, sensitivity, spontaneity as I have not felt in performance for many years. Once again I feel the spirit coming through me into the music. Performing is fun again. Emily has reawakened my musical genie.

I have seen her buddha-nature. I have seen her perfection. Tears well up in my eyes again and again as I am caught up in her pain and her joy. In loving her, my buddha-nature has been released from its bondage of sorrow and now flows again through my music, my laughter, my tears. In loving her I find myself moving ever closer to the precipice where the extremes of pleasure and pain merge into peace.

Each of the major synchronicities, epiphanies, and *satori* that I have experienced push the reset button of my life. Each time I start over, I am born again at a higher level of consciousness, into a state of heightened awareness – of "awake"ness.

~ 607 ~

My love does not require anything from Emily, in the doing or not doing. I am sitting under my bodhi tree doing battle with Mara. I don't expect this to be easy. Emily would not be helping me if she made the battle easier. She perfectly fulfills her role in my life just by being herself, saying and doing only what comes naturally from her heart. Everything happens as it is supposed to.

I hold on to the memory of our time together after I leave her company; the joy continues to resonate. But the experience that created those memories is in the past, just an echo, not real anymore. When I am in her presence – seeing her, hearing her, touching her, smelling her, (will I ever taste her?!), sharing her thoughts and feelings – it's real, a total sensory feast moment-by-moment in space-time. I am living her, experiencing her fully in the Now, in Technicolor, like seeing the House of Eternity all lit up, all its contents brightly illuminated. When I leave her, I revert back to the severely limited view of the world which is all that the light from my small candle will reveal. All the glorious contents of the House of Eternity is still there, but mostly invisible with the flood lights turned off.

This phenomenon occurs anytime a pleasurable sensation is withdrawn, as when the taste of delicious food lingers on the tongue and then disappears, or when pain medication wears off and the sensation of pain returns. The whipsaw from the joy of the present moment to the despair of losing the moment is unavoidable in this dualistic world. In space-time everything is always changing. Nothing lasts. What has held me together so far through the space-time whipsaw is my vision of the eternal moment of the Dao, from whence my love springs, where our connection never ends.

My joy in being with Emily and my sorrow in being away from her are the same emotion – the two opposite sides of eternal love as it is manifested in the dualistic world. In the context of my spiritual love, my joy with her is not happiness, and my sorrow without her is not sadness. It is much more than that. When I am with her, I am returned to the Garden of Eden, back in physical space-time communication with God; when I am without her, I am again cast out of the Garden.

In space-time, in the dimly lit House of Eternity, there is occasionally a portal through which the entire expanse of eternity can be seen, a window that lets in the Light of the Dao to fully illuminate the House of Eternity. For me, Emily is such a portal. When I am with her, time stops and everything is bathed in divine light. When I leave her and return to consciousness in the temporal world, the portal closes.

The blind poet John Milton described it well in "On His Deceased Wife:"

> Methought I saw my late espoused saint
> Brought to me like Alcestis from the grave,
> Whom Jove's great son to her glad husband gave,
> Rescued from Death by force, though pale and faint.
> Mine, as whom washed from spot of childbed taint
> Purification in the Old Law did save,
> And such as yet once more I trust to have
> Full sight of her in Heaven without restraint,
> Came vested all in white, pure as her mind.
> Her face was veiled; yet to my fancied sight
> Love, sweetness, goodness, in her person shined
> So clear as in no face with more delight.
> But, oh! as to embrace me she inclined,
> I waked, she fled, and day brought back my night.

I slumber in Emily's presence and see again my eternal bliss. When I awake to life without her, I lose my sight.

~ 608 ~

ATTACHMENT/DETACHMENT, Part 2

My battle with Mara is about wanting to detach, to end the anguish of the dualistic extremes. It is my attachment to non-attachment. The desire to detach can be itself an attachment; a dose of the first poison presents itself, co-arises, as we take the second poison. There is also a fine but critical distinction between compassionate detachment as a protective measure and taking the third poison. Avoiding becoming embroiled in another's pain can easily slip into denying one's own pain. We must stay in the game. Somehow we must learn to be as comfortable with pain as we are with pleasure. Stop jumping from the frying pan into the fire and back again. Just sit in the fire.

Compassion means "suffer with." But we cannot "suffer with" and be detached. To "suffer with," you must feel the pain – be attached. Now I get it. Until now I had thought that as I progressed to higher and higher levels of awakening my suffering over the dualistic extremes would be resolved. But no. My suffering must not be allowed to end. If it did, my bodhisattva license would be revoked. To remain in the world, hear the world's cries, and serve those who suffer, the bodhisattva must be one of the sufferers – attached, vulnerable, feeling the pain as her own, not just looking down upon others from a position of detachment. To live in full knowledge of the most extreme pain of life and willingly accept it, joyously and lovingly accept it, is to be the Word made Flesh, to be a bodhisattva.

> Detachment is the absence of a need to hold on to anyone or anything. It is a way of thinking and being that gives us the freedom to flow with life. Detachment is the only vehicle available to take you from striving to arriving. – Dr. Wayne Dyer

Wayne describes detachment in the positive sense of letting go and just going with the flow. When we detach in this way, stop striving for pleasure and just flow with life, we are free to accept the compassionate attachments of divine love that naturally present themselves to us once we have arrived.

I came to this realization while walking down the street toward my favorite lunch place. A new calmness came over me, a new sense of peaceful acceptance of the pain of life. I felt a new love for everything around me; I had to resist the urge to spontaneously wrap my arms around the man standing next to me, a complete stranger, waiting for his lunch.

> "The sin is mine. By the law of perfection I must be free of all human attachments. But I forgot the law. I delighted in your delight; I looked to be with you 'til I died. Now I am punished with sorrow, for you are taken away from me, and perhaps I shall not find my river." – Tibetan holy man (Peter O'Toole) in the movie *Kim*

To paraphrase the Buddha: If one doesn't have desire, then it is all right to attach with joy and sorrow in compassionate love. If one has desire, then one needs to give up one's attachment to even one moment of delight. Kim returned to his holy man in the end, and was with him when he died. And the holy man found his river.

~ 609 ~

Emily said that she isn't perfect. I know that, but her imperfections are nevertheless vital ingredients of her perfection, like the teacup in the Japanese tea ceremony, which must be an original one-of-a-kind handmade cup, complete with asymmetries and natural variations in color and texture, giving the cup its own special character. Its flaws are part of its unique beauty, shared by no other cup in the universe. If Emily were perfect, she wouldn't be perfect – a unique, one-of-a-kind jewel.

~ 610 ~

ATTACHMENT/DETACHMENT, Part 3

I see that I have used the words "attachment" and "detachment" in three different ways. Perhaps it would be good to clarify those differences.

The First Way, the usual way these words are used, is to equate attachment with the first poison: covetousness, desire, dependency, possessiveness; and detachment with the second poison: fear, anger, hatred, aversion; or with the third poison: delusion, apathy, ignorance, avoidance. Both attachment and detachment are defilements, unskilled behavior, in this context.

The Second Way is to depict attachment as the oneness of all things in eternity, and detachment as the separation of all things in space-time. Attachment and detachment are not behaviors in this context, merely descriptive of the context. The tension between these two conditions is the main source of my existential anguish: to have seen the eternal oneness, to have actually experienced being united – attached – with my loved ones there, and yet be stuck in limited space-time separation – detached – from them.

When I described the nature of my divine love earlier, I said, "My attraction is more than lust or affection. It's a call to join our buddha-natures in the oneness of the Dao." This is natural and unavoidable attachment, reflective of the yearning in every soul to return home, to the Source, to the eternal oneness. The detachment of space-time is also unavoidable, and can be seen as a good thing, in that it enables us to see the infinite pieces of the eternal oneness spread out in all their glory, like all the colors of the rainbow inside a beam of white light. There is a fine line to walk, though – the Middle Way – between and among these separate components of eternity, lest one fall victim to attachment/detachment in the meaning of the First Way.

The Third Way is attaching to or detaching from the very nature of life, embracing or spurning the joy and suffering of life, engaging in or retreating from life itself and the lives of others. Attachment in this way is the very condition of being alive, being attached as interconnected jewels in Indra's Net. As this meaning applies in the personal sense, detaching would be taking the third poison, jumping off the merry-go-round of life – avoiding all pleasure and pain, all winning and losing, by not playing the game. Attaching, playing the game of life, is skilled behavior, detaching is unskilled.

As this Third Way applies more broadly, however, it is recognition of the passionate attachment that is life and the dispassionate detachment that is eternity. In the constantly flowing energy of space-time there is always movement; positive and negative charges create constant interactions among the jewels of Indra's Net, attractions and repulsions, and passions. In eternity all is stillness; the polar opposites of the material world dissolve into a singular point which is everywhere and nowhere, detached from the passions of life, even from the concept of attachment/detachment itself, a concept which inherently implies the existence of separate entities that can attach to or detach from each other. To attach to life in this Third Way is to be a bodhisattva; to detach is to be a buddha.

The context in which I have meant this Third Way of attachment/detachment, as in "Attachment/Detachment, Part 2" (~608~), is the bodhisattva's full participation in the dualistic temporal life of the body-mind while also in possession of the knowledge of eternity – to eat again of the Tree of the Knowledge of Good and Evil having already eaten of the Tree of Eternal Life and gained reentry to the Garden.

My desire to escape the pain of worldly attachments is a defilement in the meaning of the First Way, taking the second poison, as Jesus did with his prayer in Gethsemane. My desire to escape the tension of the Second Way, to detach from worldly duality and attach to the peace of eternity, is itself a selfish attachment in the meaning of the First Way, taking the first poison, as Jesus did in calling out from the cross to the God who seemed to have abandoned him, seeking but not finding eternal peace with him in space-time. I now recognize this multi-layered existential anguish as the essential nature of the bodhisattva.

In the meaning of the Third Way, bodhisattvas are not allowed to turn away from pain, their own or that of others. In fact, they do the opposite; hearing the world's cries, they turn *toward* the pain. Their sacred duty cannot be carried out from the aloof detachment of an arm's-length doctor-patient or lawyer-client kind of relationship; the compassionate bodhisattva must suffer with the world, fully attached and vulnerable. For years I have complained, "It is my curse, that I love too well." This overwhelming love, which has drawn me deeply into seven people so far in my life, is the fully attached, eternal-but-in-space-time compassionate love of the bodhisattva. I must be aware of the inevitable and spiritually symbolic nature of the suffering that this love brings and accept it, joyously attach to it in the meaning of the Third Way.

Once the path of the bodhisattva has been accepted, attachments and detachments are not chosen; they simply arise as the spirits and the karma direct. In remembering my bodhisattva dream (~256~), I see that bodhisattvas may go through cycles of attachment and detachment, occasionally rising above the fray, detaching in their celestial aircraft, then returning to earth and reattaching when the world's cries call them. Perhaps my solitary contemplation since my recent epiphany is one of those celestial trips to recharge my space-time batteries. I will be energized and ready to re-engage with all the joy and suffering of life when I come back down out of the clouds.

Meanwhile, back on earth, I can hear the psychoanalytical mumbo-jumbo going on in Emily's mind. I imagine that she is concerned that what I call love is some kind of fixation, obsession, or transference, substituting a new love to replace the old one. Perhaps she thinks that I have fallen into the trap of sharing emotional intimacy with my therapist and then becoming attracted and attached to her in an unhealthy dependency.

At one level, she would not be wrong. I do feel and exhibit human foibles. But with me there is always more than one level. At another level I love her in a way that is free from all space-time defilements, desires, and dependencies. I manifest my spiritual love completely in the body-mind; all facets are expressed. The fully attached bodhisattva cannot do otherwise. I love her *in every way, in all souls*. When I tell her of my love for her, I am simply relaying from the front of my 5th chakra the spiritual insight that comes in from its back side. My eternal love in space-time reflects the paradox of the *Heart Sutra* – mind/no mind, suffering/no suffering, fixation/no fixation.

~ 611 ~

AT THE BEACH

Waves of karma. Sometimes karma comes in small waves, like the gentle waves that lap up on a sheltered beach. Small causes, small effects. Choices can sometimes be made at this level. Shall I ride the little wave or just swim through it?

Other times karma comes as a towering wall of water, inexorable and unforgiving in its power. Once caught in the curl of this wave, there are no choices to be made. There is nothing to do but surrender to its power and go wherever it takes you. It's God taking you by the scruff of the neck, as Desmond Tutu says.

I have spent most of my life riding a monster wave. Is it about to bring me crashing onto the shore? The far shore, the Pure Land, perhaps?

Allow each moment to stand alone, with its own integrity, not leading to anything, not coming from anything, with meaning only in the moment, the eternal moment.

BY THE STREAM

I want us to live it fully, joyously, in complete surrender, with reckless abandon. Throw off the shackles. Don't be afraid. But maybe the time has not come yet. Like The Unnamed One. I thought it would be easier for Emily than it was for him. Maybe not. Or maybe I just need to let go of this desire.

Emily is a spiritual frame of reference, like a 3-D painting, a portal through which I can see God when I look from a certain angle. She is also a mirror, reflecting back to me my own joy, humor, sorrow, my own God-self. Like the two faces of Janus, through her I look both forward and backward.

I can never get rid of the sorrow; I must experience the pain. Even though I have felt the fusion of space-time opposites in eternity, I cannot reside there. To see and feel the extreme joy of space-time requires feeling the extreme pain as well. That's the bodhisattva contract. I have to give up my desire to be free of pain, to simply accept the pain and be at peace with it.

ON THE PIER

I was sitting on a bench reading a book. A mother carrying her toddler sat on a bench in front of me. The child looked over her mother's shoulder at me and suddenly burst into the most adorable, radiant, glowing smile. I couldn't help but smile back. Our two souls had found instant recognition across an invisible bridge, as if a long-lost ancestor had come back in joyous reunion in the face of this child. Then she looked away, toward a couple of guys playing guitars, and the smile morphed into a curious but more serious expression. Then she looked back at me and the radiant smile instantly returned. This happened several times. The mother was oblivious, intently watching the swimmers in the distance.

I was reminded of my communion with baby Maggie (~426~), another time when I made an intergenerational spiritual connection within inches of oblivious adults.

~ 612 ~

FULL MOON – NEW MOON, Part 3

When I went to the bookstore last month looking for a book for Emily, I casually glanced at the other books nearby on the shelf and noticed a book by Joseph Campbell, *The Inner Reaches of Outer Space*. Remembering that Campbell had guided me well in the past, I bought it.

Yet another case of spectacular timing. Like the Thich Nhat Hanh and Deepak Chopra books, this book came into my possession at the perfect time to help me understand my recent spiritual experiences, and with incredible specificity, in a universal context tying together Hindu, Buddhist, Christian, Greek, Egyptian, and indigenous spiritual concepts. It was as if Campbell had been witness to my own personal experience.

> The next and last two stages of the ascending lotus series are then of the two ways of experiencing what is known as "God," either as "with form" or as "without." The lotus at chakra 6, known as *ajna* ("authority, order, unlimited power, command"), is situated within the head, above, behind and between the eyes. There it is that the radiant image of one's idea of "God" is beheld, while at chakra 7, *sahasrara* (the lotus, "thousand petaled")—which is represented as an inverted corolla covering the crown of the head, "bright with the brightness of ten million suns"—both the beheld image and the beholding mind dissolve together in a blaze that is at once of nonbeing and of being.
>
> In terms of the ascent of the yogic lotus ladder, the ultimate aim of any worshiper of a God with form must be to come to rest forever (as in chakra 6) in an eviternal heaven, "tasting the ambrosial juice" of bliss in the presence of the worshiped form; whereas a fully aspiring mystic will be making every effort to pass through and beyond that moonlike reflecting image to extinction (at chakra 7) in the full light of the sun. "In that state," said Ramakrishna, "reasoning stops altogether and man becomes mute.
>
> A salt doll once went to measure the depths of the ocean. … No sooner did it get into the ocean than it melted. Now who was there to report the ocean's depth?" [28]

I look at Emily and I see God; I behold God with form, "the radiant image of one's idea of God." With her, I experience "bliss in the presence of the worshiped form;" I am seeing her with the third eye of the 6th chakra. I also see that her form, my "moonlike reflecting image" of God, reflects not only the light of a distant sun, but also my own God-self back to me, as all the jewels of Indra's Net reflect all the others.

But there's more. In my epiphany with her last month, being inside her, feeling her pain as my own, I beheld God as formless, "the beheld image and the beholding mind dissolved together." Emily uses the word "light" in place of "love," ushering me to join her at the 7th chakra, where *Light* – "bright with the brightness of ten million suns" – and the overwhelming *Love* that takes me deep into her soul, into the state in which "reasoning stops altogether and man becomes mute," are the same thing. I dissolved into her, and for a moment my joy in loving her and my pain in loving her melded together into pure light. I was the salt doll dipping her toe into the ocean and feeling it melt away.

> There is, however, a third position, typified in the Mahayana Buddhist ideal of the Bodhisattva, whose "being or nature" *(sattva)* is "enlightenment" *(bodhi)*, and who yet with unquenched "compassion" *(karuna)* for his or her fellow creatures has either remained or returned to this suffering world, to teach. Such a one was Ramakrishna himself. Such a one is the Dalai Lama. An equivalent understanding is to be recognized in the figure of **Christ Crucified**, who, as we read in St. Paul to the Philippians, "though he was in the form of God, did not count equality with God a thing to be grasped [or clung to], but emptied himself, taking the form of a servant, being born in the likeness of men. And being found in human form he humbled himself and became obedient unto death, even death on the cross."
>
> For these are threshold forms at the interface of time and eternity. Read in one direction, they symbolize the passage of the light of consciousness from engagement in the field of birth and death (the lunar body, which dies) to identification with an immortal source, "which neither is born, nor does it ever die; not, having once been will it cease to be. Unborn, eternal, perpetual and primeval, it is not slain when the body is slain" (Bhagavad Gita 2:20). Whereas, read in the opposite sense, the figures represent (as in the passage quoted from Paul to the Philippians) the willing participation in the sorrows of space-time of one who, though in the knowledge of himself as of the nature of immortal bliss, yet voluntarily, as an avatar (Sanskrit, *avatara*, from *ava*, "down," plus *tarati*, "he passes across or over") joyfully engages in the fragmentation of life in Time. There is a form of the crucifix known as "**Christ Triumphant**," where the figure of the Savior is shown not broken, bleeding, naked, and with head dropped to the side, but with head erect, eyes open, body clothed, and arms outstretched as though willingly "thus come" *(tathāgata)*, as the very image of a Bodhisattva in whom the agony of time and the rapture of eternity are disclosed as one and the same.[28]

How many times have I described my anguish at "the interface of time and eternity"? How many times have I likened my travails to the life of Christ? In my journey with Emily through the 6th and 7th chakras, I moved from my identification with Christ Crucified to that of Christ Triumphant, seeing that "the agony of time and the rapture of eternity are disclosed as one and the same." I wrote earlier, "I must be aware of the inevitable and spiritually symbolic nature of the suffering that this love brings and accept it, *joyously* attach to it ..." just a couple days before I read Campbell's description of the bodhisattva, who "as an avatar *joyfully* engages in the fragmentation of life in Time."

> In Albrecht Dürer's woodcuts of scenes of the Crucifixion, disks of the sun and moon appear in the upper left and right corners. Likewise, in the upper left and right corners of Tibetan processional banners representing Bodhisattvas, disks of the sun and moon may appear, for the same reason. These are explicit references to that moment ... of the moon rising full on its fifteenth night, confronting with equal radiance the sun setting at that moment on the opposite horizon: the moon not quenched in solar light, but, fully illuminated, self-equaling.[28]

The full moon has always had a strong hold on me. The moon was full on the date of my recent epiphany with Emily.

~ 613 ~

This morning I did not get out of bed at first waking. I lingered for a long while, from about 6:00 a.m. to 8:30 a.m., in that delicious place between the conscious and subconscious, going in and out of sleep. I had several dreams; the only one I can remember was about a large fluffy white mouse who was apparently dead but who came back to life in my hands.

From dreammoods.com:

> **Mouse** – To see a dead mouse in your dream implies that you are not letting minor issues bother you. You are not letting your own fears get in the way of what you want. Alternatively, a dead mouse indicates that there is something that you have ignored or neglected for too long.

> **Resurrection** – To dream that you or someone is resurrected from the dead suggests that you will eventually overcome your current obstacles to achieve your goals. It signals an awakening of your spirituality and renewed energy.

> **Resuscitate** – To dream that you resuscitate someone indicates that you are able offer some insight on a situation. Alternatively, the dream implies that you have resolved some anxiety, fear or tension in your life.

I usually sleep on my side and often wake up with my arms crossed in a kind of self-embrace. This morning at the end of my dream state I put my left hand on my right cheek and said, "Emily, I'm holding you ... and there is no one to report." I began to cry the salty tears of the salt doll. You are me. I am you. We are God inside itself.

This is why I am sad when I am away from Emily. The ocean recedes and the salt doll is left stranded on the beach.

~ 614 ~

"Everything transitory is but a metaphor." But equally, "Everything eternal is but a metaphor." For as already told, long since, in the Kena Upanishad: "That [which is beyond every name and form] is comprehended only by the one with no comprehension of it: anyone comprehending knows it not. Unknown to the knowing, it is to the unknowing known." ... Hence, as the light of the moon is to that of the sun, so my mortal life and the lives of all around me are to that *atman-brahman* which is absolutely beyond name, form, relationship, and definition. – Joseph Campbell[28]

The process of enlightenment is, therefore, not a process of learning, gaining knowledge, but of losing it, releasing God with form to reveal God without form. Like a sculptor taking away chunks of stone or clay to release an image from the block, allowing it to emerge, removing impediments in the way of a clear view of the image inside.

It's not that knowledge is bad; some of it is very useful and can guide us at certain points along our spiritual journey. The obstacle in this case is putting absolute trust in knowledge and expecting that all truth will come to us through the mind. Even the best words, including those of Jesus, the Buddha, prophets, disciples, and yes – even me – are inadequate. Eventually we need to break free from the confines of words and thoughts to access the pure spirit.

We need less limiting, defining, pigeon-holing information, not more, if we are to see what cannot be seen. Fewer thoughts, not more, if we are to get beyond thought. Less knowledge, not more, if we are to know the unknowable and comprehend the incomprehensible. I think this is what Jesus meant when he said, "Let the children come to me, and do not hinder them; for to such belong the kingdom of God. Truly, I say to you, whoever does not receive the kingdom of God like a child shall not enter it."

Last month my ferryman took me almost all the way to the far shore – I could smell the fragrance of lotus blossoms and feel the salt doll dissolving as we approached the end of karma. But I didn't quite make it all the way. My boat turned around and returned to life.

I started comprehending. As the blind poet John Milton gained sight of his beloved wife in a dream and then lost it when he awoke to his blindness in the light of day – "But, oh! as to embrace me she inclined,/I waked, she fled, and day brought back my night" (~607~) – so I lost my beatific vision when consciousness took back control.

Eternity is beyond all categories of thought. This is an important point in all of the great Oriental religions. We want to think about God. God is a thought. God is a name. God is an idea. But its reference is to something that transcends all thinking. The ultimate mystery of being is beyond all categories of thought. As Kant said, the thing in itself is no thing. It transcends thingness, it goes past anything that could be thought.

The best things can't be told because they transcend thought. The second best are misunderstood, because those are the thoughts that are supposed to refer to that which can't be thought about. The third best are what we talk about. And myth is that field of reference to what is absolutely transcendent. – Joseph Campbell[6]

~ 615 ~

It has been almost three weeks since I have been in Emily's presence. All that is left of our once-glorious union at the 7th chakra is a fading memory in broken, splintered fragments, unrecognizable as I saw it whole in my epiphany. I tell myself that she is dead, thinking that will make it easier for me to stop grasping for her. But no. Lou actually being dead did not make it easier for me to let go of him. When the all-too-familiar waves of grief course through my body, I brace and cringe in a defensive reflex that has become almost automatic now, after nearly thirty years of dealing with it.

My image of God has disappeared. I try to conjure it back up, but it seems that my God with form and my God without form are both denied to me. Embrace the pain. Joyfully.

Why does God lead me down roads that turn out to be dead ends? I follow the trail of breadcrumbs that God puts before me, but the roads that seemed so full of promise only take me to frustration. Or am I just a bad bodhisattva? Maybe the roads *are* full of promise, but I turn them into dead ends with my failure of patience. I take the turns too fast and run the car off the road into a ditch.

My love for Emily is not just the pathetic pining of a grieving, grasping, lonely old widow. She has brought me to the edge of nirvana, shown me the face of God, fused with me at the 7th chakra. How could I not want to be with her always? How could I not constantly grieve in her absence, having basked in the light of eternity with her and then been wrenched back into temporal darkness? I am Rudyard Kipling's Kim, filled with joy, eager to follow his holy man and help him find his river. I am also Kim's holy man, filled with sorrow when Kim was taken from him.

I have no life except in the dharma. Most of the time I just go through the motions of daily living. Yet my worldly work, mindless and devoid of conscious concern, nevertheless carries my spiritual message out into the world, gloriously, without any intention on my part. I speak truth from my 5th chakra spontaneously through words, music, laughter, and tears. I don't even know I'm doing it.

~ 616 ~

My words are not reaching Emily. They are failing to take her beyond the metaphors to a true understanding of my revelatory experience. She says that she "gets it" when I talk about my love and spiritual involvement with her, but she doesn't act like it. I knew that Lou got it by his actions. He understood our love intuitively, without talking about it, in that non-comprehending way that Joseph Campbell quoted from the Upanishads. He taught me what divine love is from the core of his being.

I know Emily loves me; I would not have been granted union with her at the 7th chakra had not some part of her at some level recognized our eternal bond and invited me in. I must travel the road that the spirits have lighted for me, the road that took me into her. She is the candle that God has given me to light my path, the ferryman who now guides my journey through and beyond life. I am already living the rest of my life in her.

My wise friends remind me that there is no time but Now. "Abandon all hope for a better past," they say. Let it go, forgive, and move on. Harboring hope for the future is equally pointless; let go of hope and allow life to unfold into something better than anything you might have hoped for. What is all my fretting about? I have seen God and the dancing molecules. I am constantly bathed in the greatest love there is. I live a life of miracles. I have been called to the highest spiritual service there is. Angels and saints hold my tether in the Now.

~ 617 ~

I see and feel all the potential for beauty, pleasure, and happiness in their infinite glory, but I also see everything that could possibly go wrong. I see the domino effect of karma through more layers of cause and effect than most people do. Most people go through life in a state of blissful ignorance of these extremes, free of fear to the extent that they don't know or think about the infinite potentialities or how fragile the fabric of life is.

> Love, you might say, is the burning point of life, and since all life is sorrowful, so is love. And the stronger the love, the more that pain, but love bears all things. Love is itself a pain, but is the pain of being truly alive. – Joseph Campbell[6]

This is why I call my love excruciating, because in this world it is felt not in its eternal oneness, but in the painful separateness of its infinite components. My eternal divine love for Emily contains and transmits the love of all who have ever loved her, going back generations, and takes upon itself, into itself, all her sins, washing them away as if they never were, allowing her to be seen as clean and spotless in the eyes of that love. I see her as God sees her.

This love is absolutely complete, containing all the paradoxical opposites of the *Heart Sutra* – "Form is the void, and the void is form … no ignorance and also no ending of ignorance, … no old age and death; and no ending of old age and death." When this love is experienced in its eternal form, all the opposites unified, as I felt it with Emily at the 7th chakra, it is the most breathtaking white light – complete and yet empty, devoid of color and emotion, pulling all our energies together inside its all-embracing presence.

My first major epiphany on 1/1/09 (~232~) was not about love or any particular person or object. It was a vision of pure eternal emptiness, the melding of space, time, matter, and energy, without passion or compassion. But my second major epiphany on 11/17/13 (~604~) with Emily was intimately tied to love and to a particular person, with the greatest passion and compassion. The first opened a portal to a new mode of extrasensory perception going into the body-mind; the second opened a channel for the expression of spiritual love through emotions and mental formations going out of the body-mind. A connection of both the perceptive and the expressive aspects of my physical being with eternity – a complete physical-spiritual connection – has now been made.

PART 27
Illusions
December 2013 – January 2014

~ 618 ~

FULL MOON – NEW MOON, *Part 4*

Last night was our first meeting outside the office, as real people, friends, no professional formalities. Emily admitted to having fun with me. She asked if I had fun; I said I was ecstatic. She said our dinner was the best part of her day. It was certainly the best part of mine. I sensed her heart beginning to open, the scrim between us beginning to come down.

As we walked through the courtyard toward our cars, bathed in the light of the full moon, she said, "You're looking at me! What do you see?"

"I see God!" I replied, just as we walked past the Catholic church. She reached for my hand. I kissed her hand and said, "I love you, Emily." I saw her facial expression soften and perhaps reveal an awakening of mutual affection on a personal level. I think she caught a glimmer of what I mean when I say I love her. When we met last week, she said I was a gift. Maybe last night she realized that I was a gift *to her.*

~ 619 ~

Emily is spooked when I say that we are the same person, but it is the highest compliment I can pay her. Yes, as she says, we are complementary, compatible, we connect and have much in common, but we are far more than that.

Psychologists would likely dismiss my idea of eternal oneness as a kind of affective empathy gone awry, an extreme self-other overlap, explaining the condition as me conflating myself with someone else, simply responding to chemo-neurological impulses in the anterior cingulate cortex and anterior insula, for instance, that may arise in the brain when someone we are close to is in pain. I do not discount the validity of such scientific explanations, but I give equal or greater credence to metaphysical explanations that recognize the powerful spiritual forces that have been brought to bear in this case.

A Buddhist teacher said, "The bodies of *tathāgatas* are boundless, so the sangha is inexhaustible." In space-time, our material bodies, our force fields, are separate, giving us different identities, physical forms, thoughts, and life experiences. But in our buddha-natures, our eternal *tathāgata* bodies, we are not separate; our energy is boundless, expanding into infinity. We are one, made of the same stuff, emanating from and blending back into it. We are salt dolls born of one and the same ocean.

~ 620 ~

Emily just left for a long trip in a distant land.

Every time I experience beauty or happiness in the sublime extreme, I must also take a dose of its terrifying opposite. This evening, while contemplating Emily's spirit touching mine even though our bodies are thousands of miles apart, my eyes began to tear up with overwhelming love for her. Then the urge to cry was abruptly interrupted, blocked, by a sudden wave of terror over losing her, the awful dissociation in space-time that has become so familiar to me. While in space-time I cannot be allowed to feel the sublimely joyful perfection of our connection without also feeling the sublimely horrible perfection of our disconnection.

I got up and walked around, gasped for breath, and gradually returned to functionality. But later in the evening my heart acted funny. I felt little pings in my chest, not a gripping or aching pain, just twinges. I took my pulse; it was irregular, missing beats. This didn't last too long, just a minute or so, but it reminded me that I need to update my estate documents. I now know what it means, what might be the cause, when someone is said to have died of fright.

~ 621 ~

Some quirk of my anatomy gives my right big toe a greater range of motion than my left big toe. Sometimes I try to move my left toe the way my right one moves, and when I can't, I start to panic. "Why won't it go there?" I ask myself, struggling to get my brain, nerves, and muscles to obey my commands.

My body is not hampered in any way because my left toe won't move as far as my right toe. My foot works just fine. I can stand, walk, run, kick, everything. It is senseless for me to obsess over my toe's minor mobility limitation. Much like the senselessness that invokes my panic over other things. I realize that the things I fear are phantoms, illusions of the mind. But the fear remains.

There is nothing that I need from my body in order to do everything that is really important. Helen Keller was blind and deaf and yet accomplished a miraculous life. Stephen Hawking has figured out how to live totally in his mind, with virtually no physical movement of any kind, not even in the muscles that breathe. And here I am, unable to figure out how to be at peace with my recalcitrant big toe.

~ 622 ~

SEX, Part 20

A native shaman described three gateways to the spirit realm:

1) Tantric sex – sexual ecstasy can approach mystical ecstasy when sex is experienced as a vehicle to the spirit;

2) Meditation – may include facilitation with music, chant, or spirit guides; and

3) Trauma – a body in pain will sometimes expel the spirit, leading to out-of-body experiences. Although the shaman specifically described trauma to the body – physical pain – I think it can also mean mental or emotional trauma, as I suffered with the death of Lou. Just as physical trauma can rattle the spirit, so can psychic trauma.

It seems to me that sex is the spiritual gateway from the pleasure polarity (the nirvana side), and trauma is the gateway from the opposite pole of pain (the samsara side). Meditation is the gateway of equanimity, from a place of balance between the two poles. I have found connections through all three gateways.

Sex can be engaged in merely as a sensory pleasure, like eating a delicious meal, smelling a sweet-scented flower, or seeing a beautiful mountain vista. For many people, sex begins and ends there, as a simple physical pleasure. But for the mystic, it can also reach into places where good food, pleasing aromas, and beautiful sights may not. I have described my sex with Lou in this mystical way, as a sacrament. I also described sex as a way to alleviate grief by recalling the visceral joys of life. Now I see sex in an even deeper light, in its relationship to meditation and trauma as a vehicle for divine connection.

In divine love, sexuality finds expression in all the souls. (~403~/~404~) When the body, mind, and spirit are in full communication, completely open to each other, the particular qualities of each soul radiate through all souls. The pure love of the Spirit radiates from the 4th chakra and harmonizes the *ki* up and down through all the chakras, bringing physical power and health through the lower chakras, and insight and wisdom through the upper chakras. It awakens the sexuality of the body, which then rebounds back to the Spirit and brings Shiva and Shakti to life. The Ego witnesses this boundless flow of loving energy from life to eternity and back again, and rejoices, issuing forth with music, poetry, philosophy, creativity, and discovery.

In each soul, the source of sublime ecstasy is the same – the eternal all-embracing love of God. The characteristics of radiance in each soul – expressed as sacred sex in the Self, as artistic and intellectual creativity in the Ego, and as compassionate love in the Spirit – are also the same:

1) *Emptiness*, no mind, no thinking, no analysis or judgment;

2) *Stillness*, no call to action, no purpose, no past or future, just the moment;

3) *Completeness*, without relation to anything in space-time; nothing is missing, no empty hole is being filled, no explanation is needed; and

4) *Helplessness*, a sense of being taken beyond the body-mind, beyond this world, in the presence and control of forces beyond space-time consciousness.

While in Emily's presence, I am in sublime ecstasy, spellbound by her radiance, basking in eternal light. But this light – visible only in the present moment, fleetingly, at the time-eternity nexus through the precious ephemeral portal which she is – cannot be captured, preserved, or replicated. Separation in space and time dispels it. It has been only a week since I last saw her, but already I cannot see her in my pictures of her. It is as if she were dead, as when I could no longer see Lou in pictures of him after he died. And yet I felt her tugging at me today.

~ 623 ~

In Aristotle's *Poetics*, tragedy is analyzed as a form of dramatic composition in which the leading character is by some passion or limitation brought to a catastrophe. But every life, either knowingly or unknowingly, is in process toward its limitation in death, which limitation is of the nature of life. Moreover, every significant act sets up a counterfield of resistance, in the way of the Buddhist doctrine of "dependent origination, or mutual arising." Opposites arise by mutual consent; so that the stronger the passion of one, the closer the limitation of the other. Dame Prudence advises care to the principle of limitation, tempering one's passion for life to the imminency of King Death. But the heroic life of deeds and fame is of the one whose passion bends Death's margin to the limit. – Joseph Campbell[28]

This rings true to my experience of feeling the pairs of opposites at equal extremes – "opposites arise by mutual consent," pushing each pole "closer to the limitation of the other." Campbell applied the "counterfield of resistance" and "limitation in death" to the heroic life and death of Martin Luther King, Jr.:

> He knew that by persisting in his populist crusade for justice, peace, and righteousness he was challenging not simply opposition, but possible assassination; yet he pressed on.[28]

Looking back on my life, I can see that my truth-telling has given rise several times to a "counterfield of resistance," which has usually led to my symbolic death in the realm of that truth. Opposites arise by mutual consent. I knowingly pressed on, realizing that I was pressing into the limitation in death. This is what happened to my earthly relationship with The Unnamed One; I pressed into its limitation in death.

I must accept my sacrifice as Jesus accepted his, aware that it is the inevitable outcome of bringing truth to power. The harder one presses for good and truth, the more forcefully will evil and ignorance resist.

Conflict arises when pairs of opposites collide. There are two kinds of warfare: aggressive/offensive war, which comes from the first poison of greed – "I want/need what you have. I'll do anything, even kill you, to get it;" and protective/defensive war, which comes from the second poison of fear – "I want/need what I have. I'll do anything, even kill you, to keep it." Defense, a counterfield of resistance, arises to the degree that offense presents itself, in perfect balance as dependent origination would have it.

In this context it can be seen that there is no such thing as a just or righteous war; what appears to be just for one side of duality is unjust for the other. All of the great conflicts in human history have taken the poisons to their respective extremes, to their limitation in death.

Jesus showed us another way to deal with conflict, by lifting it from the lower chakras of survival and power to the higher chakras of compassion and wisdom – turning the other cheek, going the extra mile – not fighting aggression or running from it (taking the third poison), but bearing witness to it, deflecting it, and returning aggression with compassion.

This is not an easy option for most people. It requires being willing to let go of everything, including greed, fear, and ego. This elevated state of being is only achievable at the level of the individual, almost impossible to achieve at the level of nations or societies. However, if a critical mass of individuals are able to reach this moral high ground together, they can turn the ship of state around. This is civil disobedience as practiced by Gandhi and Martin Luther King, Jr.

Philosopher Arthur Schopenhauer said, "All truth passes through three stages. First, it is ridiculed. Second, it is violently opposed. Third, it is accepted as being self-evident." Campbell's "counterfield of resistance" is Schopenhauer's first stage of ridicule. The death of martyrs, Campbell's "limitation in death," is the second stage of violent opposition. In death, the truth transcends the mutually arising opposites and arrives beyond duality and conflict in the self-evident third stage. This is the fruit of the sacrifice of Gandhi, Martin Luther King, and Jesus – "Christ Crucified" becomes "Christ Triumphant."

All life is suffering. We spend our lives trying to end suffering, thinking that happiness will result. But it can't work that way. Happiness must be found in the midst of suffering, in the thick of the battle, in the very struggle that pushes the envelope of truth to its limitation in death. That is what life is.

~ 624 ~

NEW YEAR'S EVE

your picture is blank
you are not there

your ghost, too, has fled
into the Void

anutpattica
dharma shanti

my soul tugs at you
through the ether

no space and no time
can douse the Light

Andrew's organ roars
you are quiet

Amida's chant hums
you are quiet

your window is dark
you are not there

Emily being away from me on her trip, not just away from me in physical space but also out of communication – no phone, text, email, or other correspondence – is, from the vantage point of my moment-to-moment sensory perception, exactly as if she were dead. My body-mind remains intact, patiently waiting in suspended animation, because it sees hope for a future reunion. Can I survive if in fact she is dead and there is no reunion? If she is dead, can I convince myself to continue the suspended animation, to continue to be patient, until our reunion in the hereafter? To live in the now, for now, without her? To be satisfied with emptiness in the illusory void of this life until the emptiness of the Great Void takes over?

Her distance evokes in me a greater awareness of the changing, chameleon-like appearance of spiritual love as it roves around in my body and soul. The existential anguish I feel in her absence and the sublime bliss I feel in her presence are space-time functions of the sensory and emotional body-mind, the physical Self, felt in the extreme because they are expressions of the most extreme spiritual love.

The bliss I feel when I am in her presence is akin to what might be felt on one's deathbed, when the eternal white light beckons from beyond the veil. When I am with her, I say to life, "I want to become one with the light, let me go." When I am away from her as I am now, I say, "I want the darkness to end, let me go." Of course, dying the first way is taking the first poison; dying the second way is taking the second poison. Neither way is the Middle Way.

~ 625 ~

Last night's dream: *I was holding my lower teeth in my hands, examining them. The teeth were gleaming white against a dark background. I noticed that both back molars had inserts, oddly shaped pieces that slipped horizontally into the middle of the body of the tooth that was attached to the bone. They fit loosely in place and could be taken in and out easily. I began to replace one of the inserts, saying to myself, "This might hurt." But it went in and out smoothly without pain.*

From dreammoods.com:

> **Teeth** – Teeth are used to bite, tear, chew and gnaw. In this regard, teeth symbolize power. And the loss of teeth in your dream may be from a sense of powerlessness. Are you lacking power in some current situation? You feel frustrated when your voice is not being heard. This dream may be an indication that you need to be more assertive and believe in the importance of what you have to say. Teeth dreams may occur when you are in a new relationship, when you switch jobs, or during a transitional period in your life.

~ 626 ~

My first karmic love taught me what it is to lose my love object through death.

My second karmic love taught me what it is to lose my love object, still alive in this world, through greed, fear, and delusion.

My third karmic love is teaching me what it is to lose my love object, still alive in this world, simply through the unavoidable separation of space, time, and mind.

That I would find another great love with someone who has difficulty accepting and expressing love has deep karmic purpose. It forces me to sublimate the mind-body expression of my love and live my love beyond the worldly physical and emotional plane. My Soul and Ego get it, but my Self is still hurting.

~ 627 ~

ATTACHMENT/DETACHMENT, Part 4

How do I follow my karmic path in the world of illusion? As long as I have a body-mind, it must remain attached to the world and endure the pain of separation, whatever the cause. For me to die because I am exhausted from suffering would not be a good death. When I find peace within the suffering, when I see both the suffering and the joy as my inevitable and welcomed companions, when the whole of life is fully accepted, I will be ready to die.

Why do people turn to religion? To ease their pain and suffering. That's why I turned to God at the beginning of this journal, to find relief from my overwhelming grief. For many people, religion is indeed Karl Marx's "opium of the people," like Valium for the soul. Comfort is a selfish desire that we use religion to satisfy.

At each juncture of pain and loss in my life I have turned to some kind of religion for solace. When God as I had been taught to know him did not help me, I looked for other ways to know him, and I found some. But I did not find comfort, only a cryptic note inside the scriptures of all religions that says, "Sufferer, heal thyself." And then the mystics of all religions helped me to do that.

But the path cannot be taught, it can only be taken, says the Zen proverb. There are no shortcuts, like simply believing in a savior or chanting his name. Confessing your sins, saying you're sorry, lighting a candle, or making offerings won't work, either, by themselves, although these may be steps along the path if done in the right frame of mind and heart, with a true understanding of the ritual.

We must differentiate between losing the object of attachment vs. losing attachment itself (that is, the desire to attach). Why do we attach? To get something we want. Why do we detach? To avoid something we don't want. There is selfish attachment and selfish detachment. There are also selfless examples of both: A bodhisattva must attach to be of service, and then must detach, painful as it may be, to avoid fulfilling self-serving wishes. The overriding, overarching spiritual love remains constant, however, always with us in space-time and eternity.

~ 628 ~

Eventually wisdom dissolves into silence. For the last couple months, I have struggled to find the words to explain the explosion of thoughts in my head and overflowing love in my soul. In the end there are no words, there are no thoughts. There is only love.

~ 629 ~

I stumbled upon another great inspirational read: a commentary on the Dhammapada[29] by Abbot George Burke (Swami Nirmalananda Giri). Some of his remarks are a bit controversial, but like Joseph Campbell, he finds much commonality in Hindu, Buddhist, and Christian traditions, and what he says rings true.

> The fact that Buddha distinguishes between "bad" and "depraved" bears out my contention that the "bad" are those we never think of as bad, only spiritually out of the picture. The depraved are those who do evil by choice—choice which rapidly escalates into addiction and eventual enslavement. These people can be more easily identified by anyone with good sense, but many of them operate under a veneer of benevolence and even goodness. These are fake, "noble" moralities, requiring no moral strength whatsoever, that are only a cover for their depravity.

Let's see – doing evil by choice, escalating into addiction and enslavement, operating under a veneer of benevolence and goodness that requires no moral strength – as in paying lip service to love and forgiveness, feigning humility, and satisfying his own desires at the expense of others. Who could that be? (But even in his depravity, my compassionate love for The Unnamed One continues unabated.)

> Superior people are those of conscious spiritual evolution who are constantly moving forward to higher and deeper realms of personal consciousness. They are dedicated wholeheartedly to this path of progress. Obviously they are yogis in the truest sense. A superior person not only elevates himself, but elevates those who come in contact with him. Vibrating to truth, he awakens others to truth by his mere presence. Those who cannot be so uplifted are indifferent to him and he is indifferent to them. "He by whom the world is not agitated and who cannot be agitated by the world—he is dear to Me." (Bhagavad Gita 12:15) "I pray not for the world, but for them which thou hast given me." (John 17:9)

The last part struck me – I am not bodhisattva to the world, only to those who have been given to me, who are not indifferent to me, who vibrate to my truth.

> "I say to those who come to me, 'Live in the world; there is no harm in that. But keep your mind on God while living in the world. Know that house, home, family are not yours. All these belong to God. Your home is near God.'" (The Gospel of Sri Ramakrishna, Volume 1, Part 10, Chapter 8) … This is possible only to the yogi. For all others this is mere juggling with the mind.

This is unsupported thought – renouncing all desires, possessions, cravings, whether physical or emotional, living constantly in the dharma. Jesus said something similar: "Truly, I say to you, there is no man who has left house or wife or brothers or parents or children, for the sake of the kingdom of God, who will not receive manifold more in this time, and in the age to come eternal life." (Luke 18:28-30)

> Whether touched by pleasure or pain, the wise show no change of temper. Narada Thera: "Whether affected by happiness or by pain, the wise show neither elation nor depression." Harischandra Kaviratna: "When touched by happiness or sorrow, the wise show no elation or dejection."

> This has a great lesson for us. The idea is current among many yogis that the wise are simply numb to pleasure or pain—that they never experience such things. But Buddha indicates otherwise. He says that they are "touched" by these things, but they do not respond to them with elation or depression. Krishna said: "Water flows continually into the ocean but the ocean is never disturbed: desire flows into the mind of the seer but he is never disturbed." (Bhagavad Gita 2:70)

This is a fact I have recently come to understand. For many years I selfishly sought spiritual elevation in an effort to end my pain and suffering. That is taking the first poison as an antidote to the second. I must stop doing that, and rather accept the touch of pain – the necessarily painful compassionate attachment of the bodhisattva in the world – without being numb to it or disturbed by it.

> Certainly greed and desire for control over others bring about the inner destruction of religion, but an equally pernicious factor is the insistence that the principles of religion be made to accommodate, please, and motivate the crowd, and not the worthy few—the only ones to whom the Masters really speak. That is why Jesus prayed, saying: "I pray for them: I pray not for the world, but for them which thou hast given me; for they are thine." (John 17:9) On one occasion when Jesus had given a particularly thorny discourse: "Many therefore of his disciples, when they had heard this, said, 'This is a hard saying; who can hear it?'... From that time many of his disciples went back, and walked no more with him." (John 6:60...66)
>
> "Few are those among men who have crossed over to the other shore, while the rest of mankind runs along the bank." (Dhammapada 85) ... "Then said one unto him, Lord, are there few that be saved? And he said unto them, 'Strive to enter in at the strait gate: for many, I say unto you, will seek to enter in, and shall not be able.'" (Luke 13:23-24) At any time in history it is indeed comparatively few that cross over.

Beware, Christians and Buddhists who promise easy salvation for the masses – "cheap grace," as Dietrich Bonhoeffer described it. Few can cross over to the other shore or enter at the strait gate.

> Leaving home for the homeless life, let him seek his joy in the solitude which people find so hard to enjoy. (Dhammapada 87, 88) ... What more can be said? This is Buddha's view: monastic life is an absolute sine qua non in seeking true knowledge. That is why the Pali sutras almost always begin with the single word "Bhikkhus," indicating that teaching was for monks.
>
> Someone once complained to Buddha about the fact that he only lived and taught in the forest with the monks and never taught in the towns where the "real" people lived. Buddha made no defense, but asked him to go into the nearby city and ask every single person he met what they most wanted in life. He did so, and it took a very long time. When he returned, Buddha asked: "How many people wanted enlightenment?" "None!" answered the man in disgust. "They wanted all kinds of things—all material and all selfish. No one wanted real knowledge." "Why, then, do you blame me for not forcing on them what they do not want?" was Buddha's response.

Jesus, like Buddha, directed his teaching mostly to his disciples and warned us, "Do not give dogs what is holy; and do not throw your pearls before swine, lest they trample them under foot and turn to attack you." (Matthew 7:6) My love is spread over the whole earth, but I must face the fact that my truth is not for everyone.

> For the bhikkhus were a great multitude externally, but inwardly each one dwelt alone in his consciousness. The word "monk" comes from the Greek *monochos*, which means "one who lives alone." It has been applied for thousands of years to those who physically lived with dozens, hundreds, and even thousands of other monks, because it is a psychological term. By the practice of meditation we are solitary even in the midst of other seekers. And we find joy in that inward solitude which "people" find so tedious and even maddening.

Many years ago I wrote, "My friends are still very dear to me, and they are good for much temporal comfort, but sadly, where my spiritual struggle is concerned, they don't matter. ... even in a sea of loving, caring people I was, and still am, utterly alone." (~5~) Even then, I intuitively understood solitude.

> "Jesus saith unto him, 'The foxes have holes, and the birds of the air have nests; but the Son of man hath not where to lay his head.'" (Matthew 8:20) At first glance this just seems to mean that Jesus had no fixed abode, was a wanderer, but there is a much deeper meaning here. The awakened human being can rest his "head" nowhere upon earth—nor in inner ideas and "contentments." Only in God-realization can he truly find rest. Those of lesser evolution easily and happily dwell in "holes" and "nests," but it is not so with those who have attained true human status—self-awareness and insight into the necessity for continual traversing of the path from relative to Absolute, finite to Infinite.

The holes and nests of the less spiritually evolved are the savior doctrines, building merit, confession and intercession, ritual and ceremony, and the literal interpretation of scripture.

> "Those for whom there is no more acquisition, who are fully aware of the nature of food, whose dwelling place is an empty and imageless release—the way of such people is hard to follow, like the path of birds through the sky." (Dhammapada 92) The liberated pass through this world without leaving a mark. It is the ignorant who build up institutions around their memory and create a "path" and a "teaching" that was supposedly followed or taught by them. In contrast to the free ways of the masters, the "disciples" are hidebound, superstitious, and determinedly narrow-minded. (They call it "focus," "loyalty," and "stability.") ... It is all delusion. As Jesus said: "The wind bloweth where it listeth, and thou hearest the sound thereof, but canst not tell whence it cometh, and whither it goeth: so is every one that is born of the Spirit." (John 3:8)

"The liberated pass through this world without leaving a mark." Neither Jesus nor the Buddha left a mark. Neither of them, nor their disciples, left any direct written accounts of their lives or teachings. The gospels in the Bible and the Buddhist sutras were written generations after the lives of the liberated ones who inspired them, their legacies having been passed on through oral history and storytelling over many years. None of the authors of these scriptures were eyewitnesses to the events they wrote about. These stories were undoubtedly embellished, and unverifiable events of dubious historical accuracy were probably added to bring out the symbolic meaning of the stories. This makes the life of Christ and the life of the Buddha as we have come to know them more powerful and meaningful as mythology than as history.

Shinran and Honen, Joseph Smith, Oral Roberts, Moses, Dogen, Confucius, Martin Luther, Nichiren, Mohammed, Billy Graham, Jiddu Krishnamurti. I'm not convinced that everyone who founds a "path" or "teaching" is necessarily ignorant, superstitious, or narrow-minded, but I concede that the limiting doctrines and dogmas that usually emerge from such schools, often arising from their failure to recognize the allegorical nature of their scripture, pose serious obstacles to truth.

Krishnamurti came to the same conclusion, dissolving his Order of the Star in 1929: "I maintain that truth is a pathless land, and you cannot approach it by any path whatsoever, by any religion, by any sect. Truth, being limitless, unconditioned, unapproachable by any path whatsoever, cannot be organized; nor should any organization be formed to lead or coerce people along a particular path. ... This is no magnificent deed, because I do not want followers, and I mean this. *The moment you follow someone, you cease to follow Truth.* I am not concerned whether you pay attention to what I say or not. I want to do a certain thing in the world and I am going to do it with unwavering concentration. I am concerning myself with only one essential thing: to set man free. I desire to free him from all cages, from all fears, and not to found religions, new sects, nor to establish new theories and new philosophies." [30]

> "He has no need for faith who knows the uncreated." Obviously faith, however positive a force it may be, is not the desired end. Rather, *knowing* supersedes believing—"when faith is lost in sight." But it is not just any kind of knowing that Buddha is speaking about. He means knowledge of "the Uncreated"—knowledge of Brahman which is attained only by the merging of consciousness in Consciousness, the union of the finite with the Infinite. Buddha also referred to this principle of enlightenment as "the Birthless" and "the Deathless."

"Knowing" is revelation – finally seeing that which you previously could only imagine through faith. "Knowing supersedes believing," or as I put it, revelation trumps scripture. My 1/1/09 epiphany was "knowing" the "union of the finite with the Infinite," seeing within the creation "the Uncreated."

> The enlightened act in perfect accordance with their divine nature; they do nothing because it is "good" and avoid nothing because it is "evil." They have no compulsion to either, nor are

they in any way influenced by those concepts. Instead, they see things in terms of Real and Unreal. They look upon themselves as neither good nor evil. They simply ARE.

This helps explain my sense that apology and forgiveness are irrelevant at the highest spiritual elevations, because the concepts of good and evil, right and wrong, are irrelevant. Good or evil aspects of individual acts are washed away along with all karma when one dwells in eternity.

> The psychology of the wise is vastly different from that of the worldly ignorant. As the Gita says: "The recollected mind is awake in the knowledge of the Atman which is dark night to the ignorant: the ignorant are awake in their sense-life which they think is daylight: to the seer it is darkness." (Bhagavad Gita 2:69)

As John Milton awakened to darkness in "On His Deceased Wife." (~607~) As I awaken to the darkness of my sense-life after my nocturnal sojourns in the light of my spirit-life, in dreams, in the collective unconscious, and in looking through the portal of my 6th chakra third eye at Emily, my God with form.

~ 630 ~

I had a discussion with a professor of astronomy at a local university about the illusory nature of matter. I quoted Einstein saying that mass and energy are "but different manifestations of the same thing." My astronomer friend disputed this idea and quoted Boswell, from his *Life of Samuel Johnson*:

> After we came out of the church, we stood talking for some time together of Bishop Berkeley's ingenious sophistry to prove the nonexistence of matter, and that every thing in the universe is merely ideal. I observed that though we are satisfied his doctrine is not true, it is impossible to refute it. I never shall forget the alacrity with which Johnson answered, striking his foot with mighty force against a large stone, till he rebounded from it—"I refute it *thus*."

Then, to demonstrate that our senses can deceive us in both scientific and religious pursuits, I quoted Galileo, forced by the Church to recant his theory that the earth revolves around the sun, allegedly stomping his foot on the earth and saying, "Yet, it moves!"

It would be of no use to tell my astronomer friend that by the grace of God I have actually seen matter dissolve into pure energy, the illusion of solidity stripped away. He still would not believe. As Abbé Dominique Peyramale, the Dean of Lourdes, said at the end of the movie *The*

Song of Bernadette about the miracles at Lourdes, "For those who believe in God, no explanation is necessary; for those who do not believe in God, no explanation is possible."

It could be said that it is audacious, disrespectful, even foolish for me to argue physics with a physicist. The professor will always be able to best me in the scholarly knowledge of physics, but in perceiving the overlap of science, art, religion, and philosophy, in understanding the deeper meaning of physical phenomena, he is far behind me. He exemplifies the unawakened condition described in the Upanishads: "That [which is beyond every name and form] is comprehended only by the one with no comprehension of it: anyone comprehending, knows it not. Unknown to the knowing, it is to the unknowing known."

His knowledge is an impediment to his understanding. He must put aside his comprehending mind and his technical and theoretical knowledge – come to Jesus as a little child – and open himself to another kind of truth that is beyond comprehending. He is a Flatlander who cannot understand when I tell him that, while all he knows about two-dimensional Flatland is true, there is an invisible three-dimensional truth all around him that none of his Flatland-based knowledge can elucidate. As the Thomas Gospel says, "The kingdom of the father is spread upon the earth and men do not see it."

I had hoped that he would at least be intrigued by my thoughts and seek to explore further, but he rejected them. It seems that his curiosity begins and ends at the boundary of space-time. I am not upset by this; on the contrary, I am grateful. This discourse is driving home to me three important things that were brought to my attention by Abbot George Burke:

1) *Many people will not understand my truth, and may even condemn it.*

The Dhammapada says, "Few are those among men who have crossed over to the other shore, while the rest of mankind runs along the bank." The professor is ridiculing my truth (and Einstein's!), appearing to seek truth, asking questions, but not liking the truthful answers he gets. He is, like my niece Kathy and The Unnamed One, still running along the bank.

2) *I must not keep company with people who are not able to engage with me on my spiritual level.*

Again from the Dhammapada, "If on one's way one does not come across one's better or an equal, then one should press on resolutely alone. There is no companionship with a fool." Jesus said, "If the house is worthy, let your peace come upon it; but if it is not worthy, let your peace return to you. And if anyone will not receive you or listen to your words, shake off the dust from your feet as you leave that house or town." (Matthew 10:13-14)

Brené Brown, in *The Gifts of Imperfection: Let Go of Who You Think You're Supposed to Be and Embrace Who You Are*, reinforces this idea: "Choose carefully who you open up to. If you share your story with the wrong person, they can easily become one more piece of flying debris in an already dangerous storm. We want solid connection, something akin to a tree, firmly planted in the ground. You share with people who have earned the right to hear your story. Don't cast your pearls before swine. Who am I in a relationship with who can bear the weight of this story? Someone who will show up and wade through the deep with me."

I don't consider the professor a fool by any means, and I think he is sincere in his desire to understand, but at this point I am wasting my time with him. Searchers like him, well-meaning as they may be, hold me back and drag me down. I only spin my wheels with them.

3) *I cannot pursue my spiritual journey to higher levels and still maintain a life in the world.*

George Burke said, quoting the Dhammapada, "'Leaving home for the homeless life, let him seek his joy in the solitude which people find so hard to enjoy.' What more can be said? This is Buddha's view: monastic life is an absolute *sine qua non* in seeking true knowledge."

Saint Peter said, "Lo, we have left our own homes and followed you." And Jesus said to them, "Truly, I say to you, there is no man who has left house or wife or brothers or parents or children, for the sake of the kingdom of God, who will not receive manifold more in this time, and in the age to come eternal life." (Luke 18:28-30)

As long as I let the professor hold me back and drag me down, I am stuck on a sidetrack of my spiritual journey. But as much as I honor the truth in these three admonitions from Abbot Burke, I realize that a bodhisattva's life in the world must allow exceptions to these directives. The bodhisattva cannot serve without connecting with those she serves, who are likely to be less spiritually elevated and less able to understand the deeper truths. She postpones her chance for complete awakening in order to stay among those who suffer in the world. She renounces her own monastic solitude, her own spiritual nourishment, to multiply her loaves and fishes and feed the hungry multitude here and now.

I must accept the limitations of duality, but eternity is also in me. The trick is to maintain an elevated inner solitude, an abiding awareness of eternal light, even when surrounded by a crowd still in darkness. No one holds me back or drags me down without my permission.

PART 28
Breakdown, Breakthrough
January 2014 – February 2014

~ 631 ~

My phone rang. It was Emily, sobbing. "I didn't tell you before, but I went on my trip last month with my lover Arthur, and we broke up. I'm a very private person, you know, but I can't take it anymore. Come be with me!! Bring a bottle of wine."

I gathered up some wine and scampered to my car, worried sick for her. I arrived around midnight; Emily was waiting outside to meet me. She had already had plenty to drink. There was loud music playing, as if to drown out the painful noise inside her head. She started dancing, grabbed my hands and danced with me. She pulled me close and kissed my cheek.

> *Do you like my house? Isn't it pretty? I never invite anyone over to my house.*

> It's very pretty.

> *What do you want from me? You want to have sex with me, I know it. But we can't have sex.*

> I don't think either of us is a lesbian.

> *So how do we do this?*

> What I want from you tonight is for you to talk to me, let me comfort you.

> *If you were with me, would you look at other women? … Don't ever do that to me.* [She said in a voice not her own]

> Is that what happened? Did he cheat on you? Why did you break up?

> *You came along.*

We moved to the couch. I held her hand and lightly stroked her arm as tears poured out of her.

My heart is broken. Why do men do this? Why does it hurt so much? I've worked so hard all my life. Tried so hard. I can't keep it up … I want to end it all … I think I'm crazy.

I rubbed her back gently. She lifted my arm around her head and nestled her head on my shoulder, crying softly.

This is a side of me that no one else has ever seen.

I'm glad you would let me see it. Are you sleepy? It's time to think about going to bed. (2:25 a.m.)

Are you going home, or staying the night?

I'd like to stay and see you through the night.

Sleep on the couch.

Okay.

Would you rather be on the bed?

What would be more comfortable for you?

Come on. Let's go to bed.

We laid together, fully clothed, not touching, for a few minutes. Then her hand came reaching toward me.

Are you looking for something?

Give me your arm.

She pulled me close and folded my arm tightly into hers. My face was nestled in the nape of her neck.

I'm hungry. I'm going to make a sandwich. Let's go out on the deck and eat …
Is this the most romantic night of your life?

Coming close.

We went back to bed and spooned a little more. I put my hand on her hip, she wrapped her leg around mine.

Let's go to Morocco. But don't make me drink any damn Moroccan beer.

Okay, no damn Moroccan beer! [We both laugh.]

I need to kick you out now. I need my space.

I moved to the couch. Then, around 6:00 a.m., while she was fast asleep, I went back to the bedroom and sat in the corner on the floor. The cat came down from the bed and sat with me. Around 7:00 a.m., Emily awoke.

I read about not associating with people who are not your spiritual equals. That was my mistake, wasn't it? He just didn't get it. Why does this happen?

Because we are sensitive and vulnerable, and we give our hearts easily.

I just want to be loved.

As long as I'm around there will always be someone who loves you.

We hugged as I prepared to return home. With one more kiss on her forehead …

I love you so much, Emily.

I left around 7:30 a.m. Never before had I lived so completely in the moment.

~ 632 ~

I have no doubt the powerful miracles that have been sent to me are necessary to give me the strength to bear up under the weight of the tremendous pain that is being and will be placed upon me. The deep suffering, often expressed in anger, rejection, insult, and abuse, that has been revealed to me in The Unnamed One and Emily is the life burden of the bodhisattva. They heap their pain upon me and I accept it with the forbearance of the 3rd Perfection. And I suffer with them. "Surely he has borne our griefs and carried our sorrows; yet we esteemed him stricken, smitten by God, and afflicted." (Isaiah 53:4) Brené Brown asked, "Who am I in a relationship with who can bear the weight of this story?" I have been prepared to bear the weight.

I don't cry much. I tear up a little from time to time, but unrestrained sobbing is very rare for me. I can remember only three times in my adult life when I have broken down that way: twice after Lou died, once after my father died. Tonight, as I felt the horrific magnitude of Emily's pain, was the fourth time.

~ 633 ~

I don't want to be a surrogate for the men who are no longer in Emily's life, nor a source of mere pleasure or escape. I am the good shepherd watching over her. It is for this purpose I was called to her service; it is the destiny to which all the incredible miracles and serendipitous timing pointed.

She says she wants her space, but she also wants to hold my hand. She can have both. She can have her space while holding my hand. I want her to respond not to me, but to the love that I am. When she holds my hand, she is holding Kuan Yin, the love itself, carried in my physical form.

She said that I saved her that night at her house. She saved me, too. She brought me back to life – for the first time in twenty-eight years, I lay in bed holding my karmic love in tender embrace, in the flesh. We did not have physical sex, but we most certainly had spiritual sex – I was Shiva holding my Shakti, Osiris holding his Isis and being reborn, coming alive again in union with her.

~ 634 ~

Otherworldly events in this world – the Eternal in the Temporal, God made Flesh, Energy made tangible as Matter, Past and Future inside the Present – are very hard to explain in words. How can I convey in words the horrible side of compassionate love, the sacrificial nature of it? The life of a bodhisattva, fully engaged in the world, is one of intense and endless suffering, not of painless peace.

Over and over again my love is poured out, my life is given away, spontaneously, effortlessly, without limit or restraint, to those I am called to serve. And all the while I bear their suffering, staying in the pain, sitting in the fire, immovable. I would have crumbled by now under the weight, my vessel emptied to the last drop, except that my soul is shored up, steeled against the pain, by the powerful miracles that light my path. I must learn how to accept both the beauty and the horror and then let go of both, to find peace and joy in the midst of the inevitable, inexorable suffering.

All this emotional turmoil, Emily's and mine, is illusion – but our night together at her house was *real*. She was saved, and my spirit was returned to life in the flesh. There *is* such a thing as unconditional love, and she has it, right now, through me. But alas, she has closed the portal to that love. I grieve for both of us, but mostly for her, for the grip that her dark side continues to hold on her psyche.

My life has been given over in deep karmic love to three people so far. In no case was it a matter of choice; it was an assignment from God. Lou accepted the assignment, and we had heaven on earth for as long as he lived. The Unnamed One acknowledged the assignment, played at love for a while, but then was overcome with fear. What are you going to do with this assignment, Emily?

~ 635 ~

Once again, a book comes to me at exactly the moment I need it. Rita introduced me to her spiritual counselor, Martha, who led me to Brené Brown, then to Marianne Williamson, who wrote a book titled *Enchanted Love*. It is all about Emily and me:

> We stumble into adulthood as broken beings, many of us, carrying the wounds of childhood on our hearts like invisible scars. Contagion seeps from the broken psychic flesh of our battered places, expressed less as vulnerable tears than as angry shrieks, until we have done our inner work. Until then, others do not feel our pain, so much as the pain we inflict on *them* because of it.

> But there's something altogether different that happens when the one you love stands before you and says, "I will descend into the fire with you, and come out on the other side. I see it all and I can take it all. I love it all. Let's hunker down and do the work together."

> There comes a point where we have done as much of the inner work as we can do by ourselves. For a long time, many of us felt the need to forgo intimate relationships while we did our inner work, from which those dramas distracted us. But the emotional *zeitgeist* has shifted now; at this point, we need intimate relationships *in order to go further* with our inner work.[31]

Our relationship is as intimate as it can be. We both need each other to go further with our inner work. But Emily is not accepting my gift of enchanted love and we are stalled on the threshold of liberation.

~ 636 ~

It has now been two weeks since I have seen Emily, touched her, held her. I am in agony over the distance between us. I know that my spiritual depth takes her into dark places where she does not want to go, but I had thought that her spiritual elevation was sufficient to enable her to jump that hurdle. I guess not.

I heeded the signs that sent me to her. I followed God's trail of bread crumbs that led me to her office and into her heart and then to her home and into the heart of her pain. But now the trail has gone cold. I am stranded out in space, again untethered, asking why God has forsaken me. Is this another dead end, another failure in my bodhisattva quest to bring eternal love to bear on worldly suffering? I am grieving for her now as if she were dead. I need her as much as she needs me to go further with our inner work. If she is dead, so am I.

~ 637 ~

MADNESS UNMASKED

We spent a day and a half together, at her house and then overnight at a luxury hotel. Emily gave me a frightening view into her troubled psyche. She demanded that I book the most expensive suite in the hotel, and then spent most of the evening dancing and striking up conversations with strangers at the bar. The next morning, she demanded that I buy her a massage at the spa, and then she spent the rest of the morning coming on to other women in the hotel lobby. I could only look on in amazement, occasionally running for cover. By noon I wanted to go home, but she wouldn't leave. I began to feel as if I were imprisoned in the hotel. By late afternoon she was finally ready to go home. We went back to her house.

Then her worst demons came out. She alternately praised, caressed, and gratified me, then manipulated, abused, and humiliated me. A voice came out of her that was not hers – vicious, vengeful, vile. She played psychological mind games with me to tear down my self-esteem and invoke fear. I indulged her; I let her rant, make demands, insult, belittle, berate me, and hold me hostage to her mania. I endured it all, with the equanimity and imperturbability of the eighth bhūmi, to see how far it would go. It went to the farthest extreme and over the edge. When I agreed to give her money, her abusive rage suddenly stopped and she was friends with me again. Psychological extortion.

I did not defend myself, I did not challenge or argue with her, I did not respond in kind, with anger or vengeance. Even though her attacks were extremely personal, I did not take them personally. I forgave all sins before they happened, knowing that everything happens as it is supposed to.

I am stunned and emotionally bruised from her battering, but I feel only compassion, suffering with her, feeling her pain, despairing that I cannot help her, that she is not able to open herself to love and accept its healing, cleansing fire. I understand that her healing cannot happen anytime soon. What I witnessed was not just a brat throwing a temper tantrum; it was a severe dissociative episode that reflects a deep psychosis.

I continued to practice the Perfections, mindfully centered, even while under heavy attack. Although at the emotional level her hateful words and actions hurt me, at a higher level I understand that they come from a deep, dark place where her suffering is incredibly severe, the place I visited with her spirit at the 6th chakra but where her conscious mind cannot yet go.

Is showing me the horror of her dark side a cry for help? Although she appears to be driving me away, I think she knows that she needs me standing by. I am here, her good shepherd ready to return when she is ready to unlock her prison door.

~ 638 ~

Why is it that I am brought into lives of such deep suffering? Why is it that I come to them in innocence, offering them everything I have, seeking to use the power of eternal love to heal their afflictions, and then I am met not with gratitude and joy, but with their deepest darkness? Isn't this what happened to Jesus, coming into the world on a mission of love and salvation, only to evoke the wrath of those he came to save?

~ 639 ~

The Buddhists tell us that life is a blessing, and to be born into the human realm is an honor. Why is that? Only now do I know the answer to that question.

An unawakened human life, mired in mundane concerns and the darkness of fear and greed, is indeed sacred, but only to the extent that all life, human and non-human, is sacred. For such people, life's spiritual potential is still only latent. But at higher levels of awareness, potentiality becomes kinetic. It is then possible in human life to experience the glorious world of duality in all its separateness, each of us in our splendid and unique individuality manifesting in space-time as illusions of matter, sensation, emotion, and thought, while *at the same time* perceiving our oneness in the Dao. Only as alive, enlightened human beings is it possible to experience this multiple consciousness, straddling the cusp connecting all worlds.

There's a wonderful formula that the Buddhists have for the Bodhisattva. The Bodhisattva, the one whose being, *satva*, is illumination, *bodhi*, who realizes his identity with eternity, and at the same time his participation in time. And the attitude is not to withdraw from the world when you realize how horrible it is, but to realize that this horror is simply the foreground of a wonder, and come back and participate in it. "All life is sorrowful," is the first Buddhist saying, and it is. It wouldn't be life if there were not temporality involved, which is sorrow, loss, loss, loss. – Joseph Campbell[6]

Seeing Emily's pain with my third eye at the 6th chakra, and then seeing the resolution of that pain in oneness with her at the 7th chakra, was the awakening that brought me back to life, to the understanding of the wonder that life is.

~ 640 ~

VALENTINE'S DAY

> Sometimes we can use meditation as a way of hiding from ourselves and from life, like a rabbit going back to his hole. Doing this, we may be able to avoid some problems for a while, but when we leave our "hole" we will have to confront them again. – Thich Nhat Hanh, *Peace Is Every Step*[25]

It was great to see Emily, however briefly. I was again, for a moment, in heaven. But as we parted, my sorrow returned in full force with the realization that she is steadfast in her denial of her serious mental disorder, content to meditate around the problem rather than through it, skirt it rather than face it. She doesn't want my help or anyone else's. She said that all she needed was some time alone to meditate, refocus, re-center. But she only crawled back into her rabbit hole. She took no steps to heal her wounded child within. All she did was return that child, bound and gagged, to her cage. Her happy façade is firmly pasted back on. She has found superficial peace in her psychological rationalizations.

As she is returned to a semblance of normalcy, I am thrown back into existential anguish, facing the fact that my divine love is not recognized or returned. She expresses superficial affection for me, but does not seek my company or my counsel, only my money. I understand that in her present state she is incapable of giving or receiving love; her repressed pain is a mighty obstacle. I do not hold anything against her; I know the horrible torment that blocks her buddha-nature and the even greater torment that she would suffer if she tried to remove the blockage – like lifting a bloody scab that is the only thing holding back a fatal hemorrhage.

I know that I am here to serve her, to help her tend the wounded child inside, to staunch the bleeding from her emotional and spiritual hemorrhage. But she is not ready.

My soul is one with hers in eternity, with her always, everywhere. But while our body-minds are in temporal-spatial separation I am with her never, nowhere. Living in both worlds feels like being stretched on the rack. The phenomenon I see in eternity refuses to arise in this world. Wait, wait, wait. *Anutpattica dharma shanti* – forbearance in unarisen phenomena – the 3rd Perfection. Stay in the fire. For as long as it takes. Find peace there.

My love pours out in service to my beloved, but there is no echo coming back. No one to receive my love, no one to return it. No one to whom I am the beloved. No one to hold me in tender embrace, no one to ease my sorrow. No one to love me as Lou did. I hear the world's cries, but no one hears mine. Yet my love and my life continue to flow unabated from the empty vessel. Solitude crushes me like a bug.

~ 641 ~

Emily is pushing me away again. Her demons have closed the door on me. By doing nothing – except love her – I did too much.

I unearthed among my old tapes an album of classic Christian hymns by gospel singer Sandi Patti. Like the Bach cantatas that facilitated my great epiphanies, this music reaches into my soul. The sacred sounds of the Christian tradition, like that of the great Jewish, Buddhist, Hindu, and native traditions, resonate deeply in me. The saints and prophets of all places and ages speak to me. The message is always the same – deep, pervasive, unquestioning, unconditional love, a love embedded in the ancient chants and songs. The sound rolls over me like a mighty wave.

~ 642 ~

I have been returning to my favorite Richard Strauss tone poem, *Also Sprach Zarathustra*. I discovered this introduction to the work, taken from Friedrich Nietzsche's book of the same title:

> When Zarathustra was thirty years old, he left his home and the lake of his home, and went into the mountains. There he enjoyed his spirit and his solitude, and for ten years did not weary of it. But at last his heart changed, and, rising one morning with the rosy dawn, he went before the sun, and spake thus unto it: "Thou great star! What would be thy happiness if thou hadst not those for whom thou shinest! For ten years hast thou climbed hither unto my cave: thou wouldst have wearied of thy light and of the journey, had it not been for me, mine eagle and

my serpent. But we awaited thee every morning, took from thee thine overflow, and blessed thee for it. Lo! I am weary of my wisdom, like the bee that hath gathered too much honey; I need hands outstretched to take it. I would fain bestow and distribute, until the wise have once more become joyous in their folly, and the poor happy in their riches. Therefore must I descend into the deep: as thou doest in the evenings, when thou goest behind the sea, and givest light also to the nether-world, thou exuberant star! Like thee must I go down, as men say, to whom I descend. Bless me, then, thou tranquil eye, that canst behold the greatest happiness without envy! Bless the cup that is about to overflow, that the water may flow golden out of it, and carry everywhere the reflection of thy bliss! Lo! This cup is again going to empty itself, and Zarathustra is again going to be a man." – Thus began Zarathustra's descent.

This is a story of the descent of the bodhisattva from eternity to space-time, bestowing his wise honey, the golden water from the overflowing cup that carries everywhere the reflection of the sun's bliss, to the hands outstretched to take it. Zarathustra's cup, my cup, again empties itself.

PART 29
Kundalini Love
February 2014 – April 2014

~ 643 ~

I spent almost five hours today at my sacred place in the park, reading and reflecting on another Joseph Campbell book: *Transformations of Myth Through Time*. Once again I am given new insights into my experience, again with incredible specificity to my particular situation.

My understanding broadens and deepens with each new perspective that comes to my attention. As with the Chopra book, this one had been sitting on my bookshelf for decades; my eyes just happened to casually catch sight of it last week. Synchronicity again – I am brought to the needed message at exactly the moment I need it, the book slumbering on my shelf until awakened at the spirit-appointed time.

The arising of my great love caused the arising of Emily's equally great demons – fear and anger – love's counterfield of resistance. Opposites arise by mutual consent, to the limitation in death. But is death always inevitable? Might she be able to break through the limitation in death, vanquish her demons, and rise out of the vicious darkness of fear into the virtuous light of love? If she could join me in the light, her demons would no longer have any power over her.

Campbell describes the five orders of love in yoga, from the lowest to the highest: between servant and master, friend and friend, parent and child, spouse and spouse, and finally,

> The highest order of love is where there is nothing but love—mad, engaged, illicit, careless of the rules of the world, a breakthrough into the transcendent. This is the comparable experience to that of saving somebody at the risk of your own life. Passion, impulse has taken over to such extent that the world has dropped off. This is the idea of courtly love … which was by definition adulterous love … "rule-breaking erotics." [2]

This explains why I was absolutely sure that my apparently adulterous love with Lou was righteous; why loving the married Unnamed One was no sin, his wife also being blessed by our love and embraced in its net of infinite compassion; and why my same-sex love with Emily is absolutely perfect in the transcendence of "rule-breaking erotics."

And then Campbell explains why there is always sexual attraction in this highest form of love:

> The ideal, from the point of view of someone interested in life, is to come back to the heart where the two are together, to Chakra 4, where we realize that the energy of Chakra 3 has functioned at 5, the energy of 2 at 6, and the energy of 1 at 7. Thus we know how to translate our earthly experience into the spiritual exercise.[2]

"The energy of 2 at 6" – now I get it! This is why, at the highest order of love where my spirit operates, I feel sexual union with a man who is impotent, with a woman, with bodies that are old, diseased, or disfigured (not the alluring qualities we normally associate with sexual attraction) but which nevertheless are treasured temples of beautiful spirits. At Chakra 6 my third eye sees these perishable and imperfect bodies as the perfect image of God, and the Chakra 2 energy of my physical self rises to Chakra 6 to make compassionate love with them. (I have been in a near-constant state of sexual arousal since my love with Emily was awakened at the 6th chakra.) I do not see gender, age, functionality, beauty, or ugliness. I see God – God with form.

The Buddha functions from the heart center. The energy comes right from the heart center. When the Buddha says "No" to the tempter, his hand is in the earth-touching posture. But when he has experienced what is to be experienced, his hand turns around and bestows boons. And so the Buddha returns to bestow boons, returns from his austerities to teach.[2]

The idea of the Buddha's energy coming from the heart center – the 4th chakra – is a revelation. I had thought that the Awakened One would arrive through the 7th chakra, from the place of unity, the oneness of the Dao. Or maybe through the 5th chakra, where spiritual communication takes place. But I see now that the 4th chakra – where love arises, the place I have so often described where time and eternity meet, where awareness of a realm beyond space-time duality awakens, where the tension between the polar opposites is most keenly felt, where the lower physical chakras connect to the higher spiritual ones, where the eternal Buddha touches the earth – *is where I am*. I am the loving bodhisattva in communion with the forces of both earth and sky, time and eternity, touching the earth, suffering with the world, teaching, and bestowing boons.

Following the logic of Campbell's Chakra 3-to-5 and 2-to-6 connections, I posit that the stillness of Chakra 1 in the womb of life becomes the stillness of eternity at Chakra 7.

I am not just a loving person, I am love *itself*. God is love. I am God. I straddle time and eternity. I am the Buddha touching the earth at the 4th chakra. By saying this I am not elevating myself to buddhahood, but rather removing my "self" altogether. My body-mind is an illusion. It is but a vehicle, a path – the Way – for eternal love to reach into the world of time and space.

Revelations pile up faster than I can digest them. I feel like the computer playing tic-tac-toe with itself at the end of the movie *WarGames*. I am approaching the speed of light. The spiritual messages have been coming so fast over the last few weeks that I can barely keep up, in the books that have been brought to my attention; the people who cross my path; the music I hear; the tingling at the back of my 5th chakra; even my spirit guide, the turtle who poked his head out of the water and winked at me last evening as I sat on the wall by the ocean. I am being prepared, set up, for something.

~ 644 ~

At the end of Ignacio's theology discussion today, my friend Judy came up to me and said, "You speak my language. I like what you had to say about the chakras. I like just being in the same room with you."

~ 645 ~

It was good to see Emily today. She talked and talked and talked. I was her therapist, listening to her story. The message I got was clear – she doesn't want to go there, to the place where her pain is. She has mastered the art of covering it up, pasting a forced smile over it, and finding a tenuous peace inside her prison, her demons fiercely guarding the prison door.

I am getting an idea of why she does not use the L-word. Sometime in her life, probably in childhood, the word "love" was used when pain was inflicted. Deepak Chopra explains:

> Social workers are well aware that abused children have a strange desire to defend their parents. The need for a protector is too strong—one could say that love and cruelty are so interwoven that the psyche can't separate them. If you try to remove the child from the abusive environment, he is deeply afraid that you are snatching away his source of love. This confusion doesn't end with adulthood. The old brain has an overriding need for security, which is why

so many abused wives defend their husbands and return to them. Good and evil become hopelessly confused.[26]

In one of our early conversations, Emily told me she never knew a love that was not clouded by hurt. I said that love is not supposed to hurt. "If it hurts, it's not love." Her only experience of "love" has been with this hurtful imposter of love, which reminded me of The Unnamed One saying that he had never experienced a love that didn't exact a price. (~362~) With me he had a chance to experience priceless love, but in his fear he chose instead to exact an unpayable price from me. What will Emily do with my priceless love? In every case, hurt comes not from love offered from the outside, but from fear arising on the inside.

Psychologists describe six defensive responses to trauma – fight, flight, freeze, attachment, submission, and appeasement. Love as Emily knows it is a defensive response manifesting all six of these behaviors (especially the last three, which relate to ongoing abusive relationships) in an effort to prevent or mitigate further abuse.

Love as I know it is not a defense. It is the ultimate vulnerability, exhibiting none of the six defensive responses, rising above all emotionality, staying in the fire, turning the other cheek, understanding with compassion the cause of negative behaviors and joyfully participating in the sorrows of the world. It is the one and only cure for love that hurts.

~ 646 ~

When a deity like Yahweh in the Old Testament says, "I'm final," he is no longer transparent to transcendence. He is not, as the deities of the older cultures, a personification of an energy which antedates his personification. He says, "I'm it." And when the deity closes himself like that, we too are closed like that, so we're not open to transcendence either. And you have a religion of worship; whereas when the deity opens, you have a religion of identification with the divine. And that was what Christ mentioned when he said, "I and the father are one," and he was crucified for it. Read mystically, all of these traditions are telling us this great, great story of our identity with the eternal power and our loss of that sense of identity when we get involved in the ego-bound world of fear and desire.

People living on the levels of Chakras 1, 2, or 3 are living on animal levels. Animals, too, cling to life. Animals, too, beget their future. Animals, too, fight to win. So people on these levels have to be controlled by social law, dharma. Just think of what our popular religions are concerned with—prayers for health, wealth, progeny, and victory. That is asking the gods to serve your animal nature. This is popular religion. It doesn't matter what the god's name is. The job of the priests, those in charge of the historical temple, is to get the name of their god linked up with this thing, and the money pours in like crazy. – Joseph Campbell[2]

The Yahweh of the Old Testament (who also appears occasionally in the New) is the anthropomorphic god of the lower three chakras, of the "ego-bound world of fear and desire." This is the god that organized religions usually identify with, God created in the image of man, with human attributes like vengeance and mercy. This god addresses the baser needs of humanity and thus "the money pours in like crazy." Paleontologist Tim Flannery describes this phenomenon in terms of human social evolution: "The deity is the alpha male, controlling all manner of profound mysteries, beginning with life and death. The group's creation story is the sacred text. Question it, and you are marked down for punishment, for to question the alpha male is to challenge the integrity of the group." [32]

Jesus introduced us in the New Testament to the power that antedates Yahweh, the eternal Source (who also appears occasionally in the Old Testament and, as Campbell says, in other cultures), and introduced us to the "religion of identification with the divine." Jesus brought a new kind of godly love – nonjudgmental, unconditional, not dependent on good works, not earned – the kind of love that is first awakened in human beings at the 4th chakra and developed to enlightenment through the 5th, 6th, and 7th chakras.

This depiction of two different gods in the Bible may also help address Ignacio's puzzlement about Jesus as the Son of God vs. the Son of Man. Jesus is the Christ, the Son of God – of the pre-anthropomorphic eternal power of the Great Void; and also a human being, the Son of Man – of Yahweh, the anthropomorphic god of the "ego-bound world of fear and desire."

Deepak Chopra also had some interesting things to say about the nature of God:

> One bald fact stands at the beginning of any search for God. He leaves no footprints in the material world. From the very beginning of religion in the West, it was obvious that God had some kind of presence, known in Hebrew as *Shekhinah*. Sometimes this word is simply translated as "light" or radiance. *Shekhinah* formed the halos around angels and the luminous joy in the face of a saint.

> The power of creation—whatever it turns out to be—lies even beyond energy ... pre-quantum level ... When you go beyond energy, there is nothing, a void ... all properties vanish. Light no longer shines, space covers no distance, time is eternal. This is the womb of creation, infinitely dynamic and alive. The virtual domain is so inconceivable that only religious language seems to touch it at all.

> A fully awakened brain is the secret to knowing God. In the end, however, the seventh stage is the goal, the one where pure being allows us to revel in the infinite creation of God. Here the mystic Jews searching for the *Shekhinah* (divine light) meet the Buddhists in their search for *satori*, and when they arrive, the ancient Vedic seers will be waiting in the presence of Shiva, along with Christ and his Father. This is the place which is both the beginning and the end of a process that is God. [26]

"Pre-quantum level" – Chopra describes Campbell's energetic god that antedates Yahweh. *Shekhinah* conveys the same meaning. So we see that the Jews with *Shekhinah*, like the Christians with Jesus, recognize the pre-quantum transcendent radiance as well as the anthropomorphic god of worldly worship. (And of course I am thrilled that Chopra, Campbell, and also Thich Nhat Hanh [~582~] join me in relating Einstein's relativity to the metaphorical "light" that is God!)

~ 647 ~

Emily said that having a difficult childhood might have been valuable in bringing her to therapeutic work and making her good at it. Her own experience of pain and suffering could help her empathize with her clients. True, but to really be able to hear the cries of others and help heal their wounds, she must heal her own first. As Thich Nhat Hanh says:

> Psychotherapists are also human beings. There are those who can listen deeply to us and those who, because they themselves have suffered so much, do not have the capacity. Psychotherapists have to train themselves in the art of listening with calm and compassion. How can someone who has so much suffering within himself or herself, so much anger, irritation, fear, and despair, listen deeply to us?[33]

Emily is right, but so is Thich. Emily claims to have responded to my cries for help, but her responses held no compassion for me; they quickly turned into venting that was all about her. She did not listen with an ear for my pain, but rather for resonance with her own.

Emily is attached to her pain. It is her security; a life of pain is all she has known, and she is afraid to lose it. I sense that she has never known real love, only a shallow kind of conditional love, seeped in dependency and clouded by abuse. Is it any wonder that she cannot understand my unconditional love and find joy in it?

Letting go of pain and taking hold of love is necessary for her to find freedom from her demons. She thinks she can find this freedom by moving to a new house or with a change of scenery in the monasteries of Asia. If freedom is to be found, it will be found inside herself, and can be found anywhere. It is not a matter of geography.

It is a matter of love, the love that God has brought to her through me. I want her to know this love, so great that every moment of my life, every dollar in my bank account, every drop of my blood, every ounce of my emotional energy, is enlisted for her benefit. She doesn't have to love me back. (I know that in her present condition she is incapable of it.) All that salvation requires is that she accept this love, open to it, and allow it to transform her. It's a frightening prospect, to let go of safety, let down defenses, and let in unknown forces. A shudder goes through me thinking about the psychic upheaval that she would have to face to do this. It's no wonder she resists.

~ 648 ~

This morning, while driving in my car, I started chanting. As often happens when I chant, I began to enter a trance-like state, momentarily losing track of where I was and what I was doing, and I unintentionally closed my eyes. BANG! I hit the car in front of me. Just a minor bump, no damage, no injuries. My victims were wonderful people, more concerned about me than about themselves or their car. We exchanged information, hugged, apologized, and gave thanks that all was well. It was Sunday morning, and we were all on our way to church.

This is the first time I ever hit anything with my car. Yesterday I marveled at the wonder of my car, how it takes me easily and miraculously from place to place and turns willingly at my command. I reveled in the magic of life in space and time. Well, today I got the flip side. I learned the danger of taking the miracle of the car for granted, of mindlessly abdicating control, of mishandling the magic.

> So the devil says, "Oh, you are so, so subtle. Let's go up on the top of Herod's temple. Now cast yourself down, God will bear you up." And Jesus said, "No. I am still alive. I am still a body." – Joseph Campbell[2]

Lesson learned today: I am still a body. I can't jump off Herod's temple – or drive a car with my eyes closed – and expect God to save me. The words of my chant say "Grant Us Wisdom." I got some.

Oh yeah – one more lesson learned: DON'T CHANT WHILE DRIVING!

~ 649 ~

Yesterday I finished reading *Living Buddha, Living Christ* by Thich Nhat Hanh. Cecilia gave the book to me a couple weeks ago, having mindfully rescued it from the library's throwaway pile. Yet another marvelous serendipity. Just after I had sent her my essay quoting Campbell on the subject of "Son of God" vs. "Son of Man" (~646~), I read Thich Nhat Hanh in this book saying almost the same thing on the same subject:

According to Buddhism, there are two types of causality: causation within the historical dimension and causation between the historical dimension and the ultimate dimension. When we say, "I was born from my parents, and I was raised and nourished by my family and society," we are speaking about causation within the historical dimension. When we say, "Waves are born from water," we are speaking about causation as relationship between the historical dimension and the ultimate dimension. When Jesus called Himself the Son of Man, He was speaking of causation in terms of the historical dimension. When He referred to Himself as the Son of God, He was speaking of the relationship between the historical and the ultimate. We cannot speak of the ultimate in terms of the historical. We cannot treat the noumena,[vii] the ontological ground, as a detail or aspect of the phenomena. The Father-Son relationship is not the father-son relationship. God does not make the world in the way a baker makes bread. Samsara and nirvana are two dimensions of the same reality. There is a relationship, but it is a phenomena-noumena relationship, not a phenomena-phenomena one. Buddhists are aware of that. That is why they speak of "the separate investigation of noumena (*svabhava*) and phenomena (*laksana*)." [33]

The way this book found its way to me, the person through whom it came, and the timing of it are part of my karma, magical manifestations of the Holy Spirit at work. Ignacio and Cecilia are clearly angels sent to help me through this stage of my awakening.

~ 650 ~

MY LOVE LETTER TO EMILY

Your dark side is very close to the surface with me. Something inside you knows that I am supposed to see your demons, and so you show them to me. It's all right. Let them come out. This is as it was meant to be.

Your demons don't like me because they know that my love is the one force in your life capable of exorcizing them. It is getting harder and harder for you to hold them down. This makes it difficult for you to be with me. It's okay. I understand.

Some afflictions cannot be cured with drugs or psychotherapy or meditation. Only with love. And only with the highest form of love there is, the kind I have. The kind that forgives all, seeks nothing in return, and remains immovable in the fire. The kind that takes all the sorrow and abuse you can dish out and comes back for more.

I want you to know this love – a love that nurtures and comforts, that does not use or abuse you; to know a relationship of complete safety, a sheltering haven where thoughts

---

[vii] *noumenon* – as related to *thing-in-itself* in the philosophy of Kant – a thing as it is in itself, not perceived or interpreted, incapable of being known, but only inferred from the nature of experience (*phenomenon*).

and emotions will not be trampled or betrayed; to know physical intimacy of infinite tenderness, that treats your body as the sacred temple of your soul, not as an object used for another's pleasure; to hear words that soothe and support, not chide, threaten, or demand; to hear the word "love" and know that there is no hurt associated with it.

But even if you never discover this fabulous love, even if your pain cannot be healed in this life, I can still be your safety net. I can see to it that you have the basic necessities – physical, emotional, spiritual. I am the one person with whom you can totally be yourself, demons and all, and not be judged or criticized or rejected. I will sit with you in your dark nights of despair, hold you in my arms when fear overwhelms you, care for you when disease and infirmity gain the upper hand – even as your demons tell me how horrible I am. It's okay.

It is of course possible that you could find this liberating love with someone else. If you did, I would rejoice, as long as that love was indeed of the highest order and not just another imposter dooming you to another tragic disappointment. But of this you may be sure: You have never and will never experience in your life any love greater than what I have for you. There is no love greater.

I have tried to give you a clear idea of what my love means, but still I have only scratched the surface. I have tried to convey my love to you through grossly inadequate thoughts and words. In the end, our relationship – our eternal spiritual love – can best be expressed in silence. In a state of being that is much richer and more powerful than any thoughts or words. Love speaks most powerfully without words. Please try to hear me speaking from that silence.

~ 651 ~

Lou's love opened me to eternity. I became receptive to spiritual messages and accepted their direction. I have said that God took me by the scruff of the neck and compelled me to go where he led me. Other people say that I chose to take the paths I have taken and to love the people I have loved. I wonder if these aren't the same thing. Who is the "I" who made the choices?

Love is the most painful thing there is. The greater the love, the greater the pain. The pain is caused by the separation between lovers, whose bodies are apart in space and mortal in time, but whose souls are one and immortal in eternity. Love is the portal through which space-time and eternity connect. Love is the pull of the Source drawing all its separate pieces back into itself.

Disconnection between us can be so painful. The struggle most lovers live through, on some level, is the harmonizing between our soul purpose, i.e., our desire to connect, and our earth purpose, i.e., our need to individuate. Finding a way to integrate the two is the basic challenge of a spiritually mature love. – Marianne Williamson[31]

Emily says she doesn't want to see me before I leave on my trip. She tells me this already, even though my departure is more than a week off. As disappointing as this is, I take it as a sign. The pressure is mounting.

~ 652 ~

SPIRITUAL ROAD TRIP

Today was the first session of the Hay House Writer's Workshop. Doreen Virtue was the main speaker. Her focus is angels. Although her approach to spiritual matters is more simplistic and populist than mine, and I am usually suspicious of such approaches, she pays homage to the same gurus that I do, and her words ring true.

At one point in her presentation she wanted to gauge how much time she had left and asked what time it was. "4:40," said the host. Doreen seemed pleased by that number, saying that the number 4 represents angels. My house number at home is 440. My hotel room number right now is 1440. Here is what Doreen's book *Angel Numbers 101* says about the number 440: "God and the angels love you very much, and are helping you through this situation."[34]

Zero, a closed circle with no beginning and no end, is the numerical representation of God. Four represents angels. Indeed, it is the divine love of God and the angels that is helping me through this difficult situation with Emily.

In Japanese, the spoken word for "four" and "death" is the same – "shi." For this reason, most Japanese hotels and especially hospitals have no 4th floor, as many public buildings in the West have no 13th floor, bowing to a similar superstition. Note that the integers of 13 – 1 and 3 – add up to 4. 1 + 3 = 4 = shi = death = angel. Amazing. (Also amazing – the miracles I experienced at my sacred places in 2009 all took place at 4:00 p.m.)

Later Doreen brought up the increasing social acceptance of spirituality in the world. She said that everyone in the room was an earth angel, and that we have all been progressing up the spiritual ladder with each ensuing incarnation. She pointed out that a century or two ago spiritual people were called heretics or blasphemers and were burned at the stake. Then she said, "Part of us remembers this. If you feel a tingling in your body now as I recall that time of persecution, that means you probably experienced it in a past life." The back of my 5th chakra was tingling, which then spread through my entire upper body. "But now," she continued, "we get publishing contracts and appearances on TV talk shows!"

~ 653 ~

On the second day of the Workshop we watched a video of an interview with Louise Hay. She said, "When I entered the spiritual path, life took care of me. Life leads me here … there." I know that feeling.

At a point during the video I drifted off into a daydream, into my subconscious: *I saw myself sitting on the edge of a stairwell, like the well in the center of a spiral staircase. I looked down into the darkness at the bottom of the well. I thought, "It's okay to fall into the abyss."* I awoke before I fell.

From dreammoods.com:

> **Staircase** – To see a staircase in your dream symbolizes change and transformation. To see spiral or winding stairs signifies growth and/or rebirth.

Then we did some writing exercises. The instructions were to write a sequence of thoughts beginning with "I remember …" I produced this poem:

> I remember my mother's love.
> I remember my mother's pain.
> I remember my mother's hugs.
> I remember my mother's scolding.
> I remember my mother's reassuring late-night chats.
> I remember my mother's disease.
> I remember my mother's laughter.
> I do not remember my mother's death.
> I died first.

When a new revelation comes to me, it is not pride of accomplishment that fills me, but a wave of peace, one more shackle being removed from my soul. I realized that my book is already written. I just haven't lived all of it yet.

~ 654 ~

My next stop was a workshop with the Joseph Campbell Foundation. More powerful synchronicities. The mythological and metaphysical words of Campbell came alive in the flesh.

On the last day of the workshop, I described the bodhisattva's unconditional sacrificial love to the group. Few, if any, of the people truly understood what I meant, or believed me when I said that I don't want or need anything from my relationships, that in the highest spiritual love the self dissolves and all is for the other. Such divinely inspired compassion is not chosen or deliberately committed to, but is put before you by God. You don't find this love – it finds you – and you don't say no to it.

~ 655 ~

I brought two bags with me on this trip that have cloth webbing shoulder straps. Both straps broke, one early in my trip and the other at the airport on the way home. They both tore at weak spots in the fabric when the strain on them was too great. I repaired the first break, and the strap appeared to be good as new, but then it broke again at a different spot, as if to tell me that it was meant to break and stay that way. What does this mean?

When something like this happens in a dream, I turn to my trusty dream interpretation guide, dreammoods.com. I could not find anything specifically about torn straps there, but this might be relevant:

> **Bag** – To see a bag in your dream represents the responsibilities that you carry. If the bag is ripped or torn, then it indicates that you are carrying a lot of burden.
>
> **Baggage** – To see or carry baggage in your dream refers to the problems and things that you are carrying on your shoulders and weighing you down. You feel that you are being held back by past emotions or problems. Alternatively, baggage symbolizes your identity.
>
> **Break** – To dream that you break something indicates that changes are ahead for you.

When the strap broke on my canvas shoulder bag at the airport, it dropped heavily to the ground. While I was concerned about the condition of my computer after the fall (it was fine), I did feel a pleasant relief from the weight of the bag. Does losing my attachment to these heavy burdens, whether of responsibility or emotion, mean that I am now released from them? Or am I losing the baggage of my old identity? Perhaps my ritual death and rebirth at the Joseph

Campbell workshop was more than just symbolic. I have often found myself actually living the experiences that rituals symbolize; perhaps this is another case.

I am intrigued by the possibility that my dreams have now burst through the barrier between my subconscious and conscious minds, and have even broken into the illusion of physical life that we call reality. The symbols in my dreams now join the myriad other miracles of the spirit realm that are visited upon me in space-time.

~ 656 ~

I don't see Emily as intentionally mean or cruel when her demons abuse me. I see her as a person in extreme pain, responding to that pain the only way she knows how – the way her abusers taught her, as they were taught by the abuse that was inflicted on them.

I have seen at least four facets of Emily:

1) *The Wounded Child* – the persona who sobbed uncontrollably when she broke up with Arthur, deeply hurt, just wanting to be loved and protected.

2) *The Flatterer* – the too-nice, saccharin-sweet persona who builds up my self-esteem with flattery and says what she thinks I want to hear to get something out of me, like money, under the guise of love and friendship.

3) *The Haranguer* – the vicious, critical, insulting, belittling persona who tears down my self-esteem (as hers must have been many years ago) to get something out of me, like money, under threat of punishment.

4) *The Therapist* – the public persona most people see most of the time; the calm, affable, clinical analyst who practices healing therapies and meditation, trying to reconcile herself and find peace.

The Flatterer and The Haranguer are the two faces of her demons. Together they cajole, coerce, intimidate, browbeat, and manipulate everyone in her inner circle. The sophistication of her abusive skills is awesome. She has techniques to produce both short-term and long-term domination and subjugation. She can call up either of these two false faces instantly when needed, turning on a dime, even in mid-sentence. All of the major players in her life – her business partner and all her lovers, as well as the hidden aspects of her true self – are firmly under demonic control. The Wounded Child and The Therapist are no match for these powerful demons.

When I came along with my divine love, the demons faced their first real adversary. I am not dependent on Emily; I do not need or want anything from her. The demons cannot hurt me. There is no leverage they can use on me, as long as I walk the Middle Way and do not let my own longing color my compassion, or let my practice of the Six Perfections – my armor in this fight – flag or go to excess.

I don't think Emily consciously knows just how dark her dark side is. She warned me that she has a problem with anger, and now I have seen it – visible in brief flashes and also on three occasions in prodigious, frightening extreme. I may not be the only person who has seen her dark side, but I may be the only person who has *really* seen it, really understood it. Because of this understanding I may be capable of helping her dispel her darkness, expel her demons and release her pain. I don't know how I will do that, but I trust that divine love will guide me.

I must eventually push back against her abuse. She is hurting herself more than me when she is abusive. I mustn't enable or encourage that behavior with my tolerance. Some venting, relieving of pressure, is useful to a point, but ultimately it is necessary to get to the root cause and heal the pain, so that the hurtful behavior naturally ends.

As The Therapist, Emily playacts at being loving and caring, but her act is not convincing. Her ego believes, and keeps reminding her, that she is the flawed, pathetic creature she accuses me of being – stingy, selfish, manipulative, judgmental, immature, insensitive. "All minds are joined. Whatever thoughts we hold toward others we are holding about ourselves as well," said Marianne Williamson.

None of these façades is the real Emily. I have never met the real Emily, except as I was psychically melded with her at the 7th chakra in my November epiphany. I know there is a beautiful spirit locked up inside her, but the demons are jealously guarding the prison door. The total banishment of her shining spirit from her life, its inability to find expression in this world, is the source of my overwhelming sorrow.

I will never be able to talk with her about this in psychological terms; she is a professional, and my analyzing her would just unleash her anger. I leave it to her and her therapist to duke it out over the psychological technicalities. There is one area, however, in which I am a post-doctoral authority: *Love*. If she awakens to our love, it can set her free.

There is also a fifth aspect to Emily – her deeply buried buddha-nature/God-self. I don't want to be with her because I enjoy her company. She is *not* easy to be with; her company is not always enjoyable. I want to be with her because by the grace of God I was given a vision of her divine essence; my love was directed by God to nurture that essence. Yes, I crave being with her because, even in her darkness, she is my blissful portal to eternity. But I don't want her to be with me just because I want to be with her. I want us to be together *because we can't not be* – because we have *both* discovered the love that eternally binds us to each other.

~ 657 ~

THE SEVEN HERMETIC PRINCIPLES

I stumbled upon (another way of saying "was divinely led to") a video and ancient writings on the Seven Hermetic Principles. Here is my summary:

1) **Mentalism** – The universe is a creation of the infinite mind of "The All." It was created mentally, in the mind of God, as we create mentally, in our imagination. Such mental creations do not require any fragmentation of or subtraction from their source, yet the creation is imbued with the essence of its creator.

2) **Correspondence** – There are three planes – physical, mental, and spiritual. The same energy runs through all planes, and they are in harmony with each other. Transmutation – mental and spiritual energy can be used in the physical plane to change the material world. *[As happened in my breaking shoulder straps (~655~) and the physiological changes in my body in response to mental and spiritual forces]*

3) **Vibration** – The physical plane vibrates at the lowest frequencies, and thus appears as solid matter and audible sound. Every thought and mental formation also has a vibration. When people lock into the same vibration, they can read minds – telepathy. The highest frequencies are on the spiritual plane. *[Kathy's $12,000 dream (~564~)]*

4) **Polarity –** If something exists, its opposite also exists. *[interdependent co-arising.]* Both poles are available to you. What you think, what you create in your mind, is what you attract.

5) **Rhythm** – Everything moves like a pendulum between opposite poles. By moving to the higher energy planes and staying there, the master refuses to participate in the pendulum's backward swing to lower levels or escapes its influence over him. Be like the wise sailor who stands clear of the boom mast as it swings. Bad doesn't always have to follow good. *[Reminds me of Lao-tzu: "Because the sage always confronts difficulties, he never experiences them."]*

6) **Cause and Effect** – Everything has a cause. Events that appear to be by chance simply have causes that are not known. You can't change or stop principles and laws, but you can use higher will over lower will. Keeping polar levers at the high positive pole doesn't escape causation at the higher plane, but allows higher laws to overrule lower laws; *serve* on higher plane, *rule* on material plane.

7) **Gender** – Not about sexuality on the physical plane, but rather that all things on all three planes, animate and inanimate, even atoms, have both masculine and feminine energy. The two combine to create manifestations; the word "gender" comes from the Latin root meaning "to generate." [35]

These seven principles, derived from the ancient art and science of alchemy, lead to the same conclusion as my transposition of $E=mc^2$ to $E/m = c^2$. (~545~) As we move from lower to higher energy planes, we move from the denominator (m) to the numerator (E) of the fraction. As we are en"light"ened, we leave the fraction entirely and move to the right side of the equation (c^2). We become one with the Light.

~ 658 ~

Another book jumped off my bookshelf at me, *Transcending Madness*, which had been sitting there, source unknown, for decades. A collection of lectures by Tibetan Buddhist Chögyam Trungpa, it is about *bardo* – the no-man's-land between time and eternity, between the extremes of the six lower realms, and between sanity and insanity. It is giving me exactly what I need to understand and possibly help my beloved psychotic Emily.

My new friend from the Joseph Campbell workshop, a psychotherapist, helped me diagnose Emily: Borderline Personality Disorder (BPD). A serious condition. Prognosis not good. Chögyam Rinpoche, in his description of the realm of *asuras*, the jealous gods, seems to confirm this diagnosis and prognosis:

> STUDENT: Rinpoche, socially how does one deal with or how does one communicate with this type of person?
>
> TRUNGPA RINPOCHE: It seems to be very difficult to communicate with an *asura*. It is kind of an isolated situation of its own. You see, the trouble is, if you try to communicate with an *asura* person, *asura* being, each communication could reinforce their trip. Communication could be interpreted as trying to destroy them.
>
> STUDENT: It sounds rather hopeless, that there is no chance of communication.

TRUNGPA RINPOCHE: It depends on how you find the means to communicate to them. It is very intricate, and you have to do it accurately at once. That communication comes from your style and the style of the other person. It is feasible that you may be able to help, but quite likely it is impossible.[36]

Jesus was tempted by Satan, and the Buddha by Mara. In both cases, evil appeared in delightful forms meant to arouse desire and in terrible forms meant to arouse fear. I feel myself being aroused by Emily's incredible physical and spiritual beauty, but also being terrorized in fear of her, and for her, by her horrific mental, emotional, and psychological dysfunction. I must walk the Middle Way and not give in to either my desire or my fear.

~ 659 ~

Although I enjoy the organ music and singing in the Christian church, and the chanting and drumming at the Buddhist temple, I resist singing hymns in church or using vocal sounds like "om" or mantras in meditation. For me, adding words, tones, or pitches reinforces temporality, engages the mind, and breaks the expanse of stillness by which eternity expresses itself to me.

I have come to terms with my tinnitus, sort of. I think of it as the sound of the 4th chakra, *anāhata*, "no hit," the sound that is not made by one object striking another. It is the voice of God ringing in my ears.

~ 660 ~

I finished reading *Transcending Madness* today. At the end of the book, Trungpa Rinpoche gave me hope that Emily's madness can be cured:

> You could say the present situation is based on the past in some sense, but at the same time, you are free from the past. The present is free from the past; therefore, it could be present. Otherwise it would continue to be past all the time. And the future is an independent situation. So there is a sense of freedom happening constantly. For instance, we could say that we arrived and we entered into this hall and now we are here. That doesn't mean that we cannot get out of it. It is purely up to us. So the case history is that you are already here. Whether you walked here or you came here by car does not make any difference.[36]

Our love is here, now, in the present, eternal, and free from the past. Love is the element of the present that liberates us from our past. We can walk out of the hall of past fear, anger, and pain anytime. It doesn't matter how we got there. Our transcendent love empowers us to break free from the past, whether it is the past of last week or the childhood trauma of a half-century ago.

Our love also frees us from the future. Just as no past deeds can tarnish it, nothing that may happen in the future can destroy or diminish it. It is independent of all karma, past and future, good and bad. This is true liberation.

~ 661 ~

My friend Rita casually mentioned that she knew Joseph Campbell and his wife very well. Had dinner at their place in Greenwich many times. ... Who knew??

I also discovered that she had worked with The Unnamed One and his mother briefly many years ago. ... Who knew??

I have known from the beginning that Rita and I have a strong spiritual connection, but now I find that she shares these two very deep personal connections with me. ... Who knew??

~ 662 ~

Yesterday I went looking for a new strap to replace the one that broke on my travel bag. I pulled open a drawer that I knew contained some extra shoulder straps. Found a couple straps that would do nicely for the bag. I tried to close the drawer, but met resistance. On closer inspection I found that the plastic mechanism that held up the drawer had broken. The drawer fell helplessly from its moorings. My old life is literally collapsing around me.

~ 663 ~

I am not allowed to have friends. Not the kind of friends who warm the cockles of my heart, who can comfort and support me in my existential anguish and abide with me through the fire. I must look to God and the angels, not my fellow humans, for that kind of succor.

I know the great depth of the Buddhist concept of "unsupported thought" – no support, no dependency in this world, not material or emotional or spiritual. As with everything else about my divinely guided life, unsupported thought is not a matter of choice for me. I do not choose to live without support; there is literally no support possible, no one alive who is capable of providing the kind and degree of support that would sustain me through my ultimate trial. I have friends as Jesus had disciples, who sort of get who I am, but yet slumber as I face my sacrificial life alone.

> And they went to a place which was called Gethsemane; and he said to his disciples, "Sit here, while I pray." And he took with him Peter and James and John, and began to be greatly distressed and troubled. And he said to them, "My soul is very sorrowful, even to death; remain here, and watch." And going a little farther, he fell on the ground and prayed that, if it were possible, the hour might pass from him. And he said, "Abba, Father, all things are possible to thee; remove this cup from me; yet not what I will, but what thou wilt." And he came and found them sleeping, and he said to Peter, "Simon, are you asleep? Could you not watch one hour? Watch and pray that you may not enter into temptation; the spirit indeed is willing, but the flesh is weak." And again he went away and prayed, saying the same words. And again he came and found them sleeping, for their eyes were very heavy; and they did not know what to answer him. And he came the third time, and said to them, "Are you still sleeping and taking your rest? It is enough; the hour has come; the Son of man is betrayed into the hands of sinners. Rise, let us be going; see, my betrayer is at hand." (Mark 14:32-42 RSV)

~ 664 ~

Last night there was a moment when we musicians found that golden place where everything aligns perfectly – tone, balance, rhythm, intonation, everything. It was like the whole universe was resonating. Musicians go for years waiting for a moment like that. I have experienced several such moments in my forty-year career, each one special and worth the wait.

~ 665 ~

My heart is breaking over my failure to reach my loved ones, or inspire them to reach out to me. The Unnamed One and Emily are both distant, still wrapped up in ego and denial, unwilling or unable to accept my healing love. If the soil that my love falls on is infertile, why am I drawn there? Why am I sent to people who are not ready? Or are they sent to me, not me to them, for my benefit, not theirs? Or am I just botching the job? Is my approach wrong? Wrong motivation? Wrong intention? Am I really just acting out of selfish desire, seeking their response to my love for my own gratification, not for their healing?

Perhaps Emily will awaken to spiritual love through my graphic demonstration of it. If she will let me in. Or perhaps not. It doesn't matter. My devotion is the same either way.

~ 666 ~

MY MYSTIC JOURNEY WITH KATHY, Part 3
On Judgment and Sex Trafficking

Upon watching a man procure the sexual services of a young woman at a bar, Kathy writes:

> *Don't you see how blinded you are, tainted child of God? This isn't what you're looking for. These sweet, precious women are not who you are actually looking for.*

Whose sin is worse, the man's, who merely purchased a product that was offered for sale, or the scared young girl's, who made the choice to sell her body, enabling the subsequent sins of others? Or the pimp's, who coerced, probably threatened, the girl into sin?

Why is he blinded? What is he blind to? Are you also blind, and not seeing how blinded you are? Is this perhaps what Jesus meant when he said, "He who is without sin, cast the first stone," "Judge not, lest ye be judged," and "You hypocrite, first take the plank out of your own eye, and then you will see clearly to remove the speck from your brother's eye"?

Can a "child of God" truly be tainted? Who is he actually looking for? Is he in that bar looking for God? Maybe, without realizing it, he is.

I wrote to Kathy:

> Judgment is always dangerous because sin is complicated. Good and evil, right and wrong, benevolence and malevolence, can sometimes be hard to tell apart, and often coexist in the same act. The people and situations that make us most uncomfortable are our best teachers, and require our greatest compassion.

~ 667 ~

Dialectical Behavior Therapy (DBT) is a method for treating Borderline Personality Disorder, developed by psychologist Marsha Linehan, herself a sufferer of the disease. It emphasizes the development of four skill sets:

> *Mindfulness*, to help you learn to live in the moment and fully experience your emotions and senses. *Interpersonal effectiveness*, which can help you increase your assertiveness and relationship skills. *Emotion regulation*, to help you listen more closely to your emotions and learn to better manage them. *Distress tolerance*, which can help you find better ways to control impulsive behaviors.[37]

I think Emily is trying to practice these. I have noticed in particular her exhibiting these techniques used by Linehan:

> She [Linehan] added elements, like *opposite action*, in which patients act opposite to the way they feel when an emotion is inappropriate; and *mindfulness meditation*, a Zen technique in which people focus on their breath and observe their emotions come and go without acting on them.[37]

Another useful therapy is Cognitive Behavioral Therapy (CBT). It is characterized by getting the sufferer to recognize her aberrant behavior and the problematic beliefs that lead to it, and then alter her thought processes to change her emotional reactions and behavior:

> "The goal of cognitive behavior therapy is to teach patients that while they cannot control every aspect of the world around them, they can take control of how they interpret and deal with things in their environment. The client begins to learn and practice new skills that can then be put into use in real-world situations. For example, a person suffering from drug addiction might start practicing new coping skills and rehearsing ways to avoid or deal with social situations that could potentially trigger a relapse."[38]

My insight into Emily poses an uncomfortable social situation that triggers her relapse. The sign of true healing, however, is the ability to be in triggering situations and *not* relapse. That I might turn from being a trigger for darkness into a trigger for light is my dream.

Both DBT and CBT are methods for putting a bandage over the wound, relieving the symptoms, changing the outward behavior, but not necessarily healing the underlying disease. To truly heal, Emily needs love, not just therapy — love as deep as her pain, as bright as her disease is dark.

~ 668 ~

HUMAN IMPERFECTION

So often we are told that humans are flawed, imperfect, incomplete. Yet, in eternity, we are perfect, complete. C.S. Lewis explains how this can be, in much the same way as each cell's DNA contains all the genes necessary to replicate the entire organism, but some genes are expressed and others are not, giving each cell its specialized, differentiated, but limited, nature:

> I know that there are some who like to think of Our Lord Himself as a poet and cite the parables to support their view. I admit freely that to believe in the Incarnation at all is to believe that

every mode of human excellence is implicit in His historical human character; poethood, of course, included. But if all had been developed, the limitation in a single human life would have been transcended and He would not have been a man; therefore all excellences save the spiritual remained in varying degrees implicit. – C.S. Lewis, *Christian Reflections*[39]

Not just for Jesus, but for all of us, "every mode of human excellence" is implicit in our "historical human character." May we, as did Jesus, reveal our spiritual excellence in everything we make explicit. We are not imperfect or incomplete; we are simply human.

The End of Volume Two

to be continued ...

First in the Series:

Volume One
The First Awakenings

Next in the Series:

Volume Three
Love Is God Is Love

Volume Four
The Mystic Milieu

Volume Five
Plumbing the Depths Above the Clouds

Cast of Characters

Each of the five volumes of *Love and Loss* can stand alone, but for those who read later volumes without having read the earlier volumes, it may be helpful to know the roles played by the recurring characters introduced early on:

Lou – my husband and first karmic love

The Unnamed One – my second karmic love

Emily – my third karmic love

Jean & Joan – the twins who reawakened my ability to love

Archie – a brief but meaningful love object

James – my rude office colleague who taught me to see through bad behavior

Ignacio & Cecilia – my Christian angels

Kathy – my niece who hears me in her dreams but is afraid to listen

John – Lou's favorite brother

Elaine – John's wife and my Buddhist angel

Natalie – John's and Elaine's daughter

Joe – a business associate and my atheist angel

June & Marilyn – a lovely gay couple who understood my pain

Vincent, Arthur, & Danny – Emily's on-again, off-again lovers

Martha & Rita – my intuitive angels

Hugh & Josie – my shamanic angels

Patrick – my best friend in the band

Acknowledgments

One of the great virtues I have discovered in my life's journey is gratitude. I am grateful for all the joy and all the sorrow, and especially for all those who helped me learn and grow through the joys and sorrows. There are so many over the decades who gave me encouragement, comfort, understanding, and support, whose tender care kept me from falling off a cliff of despair. Some of these people go back thousands of years, others are alive and with me now. I cannot thank my contemporaries by name or the anonymity of this book would be destroyed. But you know who you are! Thank you all so much. A few of these angels are characters in the book; you do not know their true names, but you know their true souls.

Of course, at the top of the gratitude list are the heroes of this book, my karmic loves, to whom I literally owe my life in the spirit. Fanning out from them, I also thank their families, ancestors, and descendants to and from whom our eternal love will always flow. Speaking of ancestors and descendants, I humbly thank my parents, who raised me well, kept every door of opportunity open, and prepared my heart and mind to welcome the wisdom of every place and every age. And I thank my siblings and their children, who had the temerity to challenge my beliefs and make me think about the difference between what is true and what I *think* is true, testing the mettle of my ideas in the fire of their skepticism.

This story includes many different religious and philosophical perspectives. I pay homage to the many branches of the Judeo-Christian tradition, as well as the Eastern traditions of Buddhism, Hinduism, and Daoism; the Greco-Roman gods and goddesses; several ancient indigenous religions; and various world philosophies with little or no religious basis. My spiritual growth would not have been possible without major input from luminaries in all the arts and sciences. I am therefore especially indebted to the writers of the Bible, the Hindu, Daoist, and Buddhist scriptures, and the work of, among many others: William Shakespeare, Albert Einstein, Dave Brubeck, Pang-yun, John Wesley, Deepak Chopra, Joseph Campbell, John Milton, Jacobo Timerman, Felix Mendelssohn, Robert Olson, Martin Luther King, Jr., Carol Burnett (and her fabulous comedic cast), Kahlil Gibran, Anthony de Mello, Plato, Henrietta Lacks, St. Francis of Assisi, Sandi Patti, Martin Heidegger, Dietrich Bonhoeffer, Marianne Williamson, T. S. Eliot, Lao-tzu, David Oistrakh, C. S. Lewis, Socrates, Wayne Dyer, Thomas Hardy, the Dalai Lama, Jorge Luis Borges, Brené Brown, Vince Gill, Carl Jung, St. Augustine, Thich Nhat Hanh, Alan Watts, J. S. Bach, Doreen Virtue, Alexander Pope … and on and on and on … and the myriad artists, scientists, authors, philosophers, and other great souls of every age who influenced them.

I must give a special nod to the filmmakers. Like most people of my generation, I came of age watching movies, and I marched faithfully in step with my contemporaries as the movies moved from theaters to television to videocassette to DVD to the Internet. A great film is a work of art, like great literature, stage plays, and opera, with which they often share common themes and subject matter. I owe the screenwriters, actors, directors, producers, designers, cinematographers, composers, musicians, and all the creative people who make movies a debt of gratitude for putting deep spiritual messages into sounds and pictures – dramas, musicals, and documentaries – that can reach into the hearts of the masses. I will name the movies that I can remember contributing to my spiritual growth, but I know there are many more that escape my recollection: *Song of Bernadette, Star Wars (all episodes), It's A Wonderful Life, Gandhi, Guess Who's Coming To Dinner, Flight, The Buddha, Sophie's Choice, The Last Samurai, Mary and Tim, Einstein's Universe, The Heart Is A Lonely Hunter, Judgment At Nuremberg, Avatar, Romeo and Juliet, West Side Story (R&J modernized and musicalized), Invasion of the Body Snatchers, Julia, The Shawshank Redemption, Titanic, WarGames, Inherit The Wind,* and the Jesus flicks: *Greatest Story Ever Told, Jesus of Nazareth, Jesus Christ Superstar, King of Kings, Ben-Hur.*

Everyone who has passed through my life, in person or through writings, art, music, or historic legacy, has added a piece to my spiritual puzzle. Some pieces are larger than others, but each piece is essential to completing the puzzle. The final piece I must add myself.

Virtually all of my thoughts and opinions in this book were developed with inspiration from the great work of others, as reflected in the references below. I do not claim to be a Bible scholar, Zen master, psychologist, or an expert in history, literature, art, science, or humanities. I am a layperson relating what inspiring works of art, science, religion and philosophy say to me, amplified by my own experience and revelation. No religious or scholarly authority has formally endorsed my interpretations. However, like the infinitely connected jewels in Indra's Net, all ideas are connected to all others. I claim no originality in any of the thoughts herein; as Goethe said, "Everything has been thought of before; the task is to think of it again."

As is the case with most diaries, in this journal I am talking to myself. In that private environment of my own heart and mind, there were no holds barred, no subjects off limits, no level of intimacy too deep. Under normal circumstances the deeply personal thoughts, feelings, ideas, analyses, and speculations herein would only be shared with the most intimate confidants, if at all. I am sharing this journal now because the miraculously abnormal circumstances of my life demand it. So my final acknowledgment goes to the Source, however you know it, and to you, the readers of this book, who have all become my most intimate confidants and who are yourselves miraculous manifestations of the Source.

A Word About Sex

I thought long and hard about how much sexually explicit material to include in this book. I knew I had to include some; the evolution of my sexuality, as concerns the crossing from spirit to flesh and back again, is central to my story. In such stories, the sexual questions are the ones usually left unanswered, in deference to modesty, privacy, and propriety, yet are the ones on everyone's mind:

What is the role of sex in divine love? When does "having sex" become "making love"? How does a widow for whom joy in sex has ended find satisfaction with a man whom she has never even seen naked? And with a woman thousands of miles away? How does the eternal creative union of Shiva and Shakti play out in real life – and in real-life body chemistry? How do the urges of the body, the thoughts of the mind, and the wisdom of the spirit each play a role in the act of sex, and in the larger sense, of creation? What is tantric love? How does love in the spirit feel in the body?

I knew I had to answer these questions, so I left most of the sexy stuff in, taking a chance that more readers would be grateful and enlightened than offended or titillated.

A Word About Money

The proceeds I receive from the sale of this book after the cost of its production will be donated to nonprofit organizations doing work that is consonant with my spiritual direction. I offer my personal life experiences seeking to enrich the lives of others, not to enrich my own. I have enough money.

Betty Hibod
2020

References & Citations

1. Paulo Coelho, *Manuscript Found in Accra*, trans. Margaret Jull Costa. (Vintage Books/Random House, New York 2013).

2. Joseph Campbell, *Transformations of Myth Through Time*. (Harper & Row, New York 1990).

3. C.S. Lewis, *A Grief Observed*. © 1961 by C.S. Lewis Pte. Ltd. (Bantam/Seabury Press, New York 1963).

4. St. Augustine, *Confessions*, trans. R.S. Pine-Coffin. (Penguin Books, Harmondsworth, England 1961).

5. Jacobo Timerman, *Prisoner without a Name, Cell without a Number*, trans. Toby Talbot. (University of Wisconsin Press, Madison 1930).

6. Joseph Campbell, *The Power of Myth*, transcript of the PBS documentary hosted by Bill Moyers. (Apostrophe S Productions, Inc., New York 1988). Used by permission.

7. Alan Watts, *The Way Of Zen*. Excerpt(s) from WAY OF ZEN by Alan Watts, copyright © 1957 by Penguin Random House LLC, copyright renewed 1985 by Mary Jane Watts. Used by permission of Pantheon Books, an imprint of the Knopf Doubleday Publishing Group, a division of Penguin Random House LLC. All rights reserved.

8. *www.dreammoods.com*. © 2000-2014 Dream Moods, Inc. All rights reserved.

9. Robert Olson, *An Introduction To Existentialism*. (Dover Publications, Inc., New York 1962).

10. Kahlil Gibran, *The Prophet*. (Alfred A Knopf, New York 1923).

11. *wikipedia.com*. Descriptions of the ten bhūmi used in this book are from the Avatamsaka Sutra, as illuminated in commentaries at wikipedia.org: http://en.wikipedia.org/wiki/Ten_bhūmis.

12. Abhaya, http://www.freebuddhistaudio.com/search.php?q=kshanti&r=10&o=ya&b=p&l= en&at =audio&lang=en.

13. C.S. Lewis, *On Stories: And Other Essays on Literature*. © 1982, 1966 by C.S. Lewis Pte. Ltd. All rights reserved.

14. Anita Moorjani, *Dying To Be Me.* (Hay House, Carlsbad CA 2012).

15. C.S. Lewis, *God in the Dock.* © 1970 by C.S. Lewis Pte. Ltd. All rights reserved.

16. Paraphrased from *Traveling the Path of Compassion: A Commentary on the Thirty-Seven Practices of a Bodhisattva* by His Holiness the Seventeenth Karmapa (KTD 2009), translated by Ringu Tulku Rinpoche and Michele Martin. (*from the January 2010 issue of Shambhala Sun*).

17. The Enneagram Institute, www.enneagraminstitute.com. Copyright 2014, The Enneagram Institute. All Rights Reserved. Used with permission.

18. Martin Heidegger, *An Introduction to Metaphysics*, trans. Ralph Manheim. (Yale University Press, New Haven 1959).

19. Cyndi Dale, *The Complete Book of Chakra Healing.* (Llewellyn Publications, Woodbury MN 1996, 2009).

20. Rebecca Skloot, *The Immortal Life of Henrietta Lacks.* (Crown Books 2010).

21. Hsuan Hua, *The Chan Handbook.* (http://psychology.wikia.com/wiki/Dhy%C4%81na_in_Buddhism)

22. http://www.africa.upenn.edu/Articles_Gen/Letter_Birmingham.html.

23. Neale Donald Walsch, *The Complete Conversations with God.* (Putnam/Penguin Group, New York 2005).

24. Viktor Frankl, *Man's Search for Meaning*, Part One, "Experiences in a Concentration Camp." (Pocket Books, pp. 56–57. via *Wikipedia*).

25. Thich Nhat Hanh, *The Thich Nhat Hanh Collection* ("Peace Is Every Step," "Teachings On Love," "The Stone Boy" and other stories), trans. Mobi Warren and Annabel Laity. (One Spirit, New York 2004).

26. Deepak Chopra, *How To Know God.* (Harmony Books/Random House, New York 2000).

27. C.S. Lewis, *Miracles: A Preliminary Study.* © 1947, 1960, 1996 by C.S. Lewis Pte. Ltd. All rights reserved.

28. Joseph Campbell, *The Inner Reaches of Outer Space.* (Novato, CA; New World Library 2002, pp.

39,41,43,86-87, 92, 93-94, 101-102, 103). Quotations from *The Inner Reaches of Outer Space* by Joseph Campbell, copyright © 2002; reprinted by permission of Joseph Campbell Foundation (www.jcf.org).

29. Abbot George Burke, *Dharma for Awakening* (http://www.ocoy.org/dharma-for-christians). Used by permission.

30. https://en.wikipedia.org/wiki/Jiddu_Krishnamurti.

31. Marianne Williamson, *Enchanted Love.* (Touchstone/Simon & Schuster, New York 1999).

32. Tim Flannery, "Only Human: The Evolution of a flawed species." (*Harper's Magazine*, December 2014).

33. Thich Nhat Hanh, *Living Buddha, Living Christ.* (Riverhead Books, New York 1995).

34. Doreen Virtue, *Angel Numbers 101.* (Hay House, Carlsbad CA 2008).

35. Doreen Virtue, "Hermetic Philosophy and the Seven Hermetic Principles." (https://www.youtube.com/watch?v=8t3AkVvFuqk); and *The Kybalion.* (The Yogi Publication Society, Chicago 1912, 1940).

36. Chögyam Trungpa, *Transcending Madness.* (Shambhala Publications, Boston 1992).

37. Marsha Linehan, http://www.nytimes.com/2011/06/23/health/23lives.html?sq=linehan&st=cse&scp=1&pagewanted=all.

38. Cognitive Behavior Therapy: http://psychology.about.com/od/psychotherapy/a/cbt.htm.

39. C.S. Lewis, *Christian Reflections.* © 1967, 1980 by C.S. Lewis Pte. Ltd. All rights reserved.

The Holy Bible, Revised Standard Version. Biblical quotes are from www.biblegateway.com, © 1995-2010, The Zondervan Corporation. Revised Standard Version of the Bible, © 1946, 1952, and 1971 by the Division of Christian Education of the National Council of the Churches of Christ in the United States of America. Used by permission. All rights reserved.

Most of the isolated quotes from Buddhist and Hindu scriptures and by various ancient and modern religious masters came from the Internet, from websites such as wikipedia.org, dharmanet.org, freebuddhistaudio.com, buddhanet.net, and others I cannot even begin to remember. In cases where I was able to identify the authors or translators of the quotes, I sought and obtained their permission to use their material. In some cases, however, I could not find the original source.

Unless otherwise attributed, all poems (and prose) contained herein were composed by Betty Hibod.